MRS MOREAU'S WARBLER

How Birds Got their Names

_____

STEPHEN MOSS

First published by Guardian Faber in 2018

Guardian Faber is an imprint of Faber & Faber Ltd,
Bloomsbury House, 74–77 Great Russell Street
London WC1B 3DA

Guardian is a registered trade mark of
Guardian News & Media Ltd,
Kings Place, 90 York Way, London N1 9GU

This paperback edition first published in 2019

Typeset by Faber & Faber Limited
Printed and bound by CPI Group (UK) Ltd, Croydon, CR0 4YY

Illustrations by Alexander Fussell and John Thompson, originally produced
for William Yarrell's *A History of British Birds* (1843)

A CIP record for this book
is available from the British Library

ISBN 978–1–78335–091–9

2 4 6 8 10 9 7 5 3 1

MRS MOREAU'S WARBLER

Stephen M͟ ͟s is a naturalist, broadcaster, television producer and author. In ͟ ͟listinguished career at the BBC Natural History Unit his credits ͟cluded *Springwatch*, *Bird Britannia* and *The Nature of Britain*. H͟ books include *The Robin: A Biography*, *A Bird in the Bush*, *Th͟ ͟umper Book of Nature*, *Wild Hares and Hummingbirds* and *Wild ͟ngdom*. He is also Senior Lecturer in Nature and Travel Writing ͟ ͟ath Spa University. Originally from London, he lives with his ͟nily on the Somerset Levels, and is President of the Somerse͟ ͟ildlife Trust.

Further ͟ ise for *Mrs. Moreau's Warbler*:

'Stephe͟ ͟ss has told his story well, combining a relaxed style of writing ͟th an impressive amount of scholarship, conveying once again hi͟ ͟scination with the cultural relationship we have with our birds.' ͟ e Everett, *British Birds*

Selected titles by Stephen Moss

For Suzanne: after whom, one day,
I hope to name a new species of warbler.

CONTENTS

CHAPTER 7: TOMORROW NEVER KNOWS
The Future of Bird Names

ILLUSTRATIONS

INTRODUCTION

> And out of the ground the Lord God formed every beast of the field, and every fowl of the air; and brought them unto Adam to see what he would call them: and whatsoever Adam called every living creature, that was the name thereof. And Adam gave names to all cattle, and to the fowl of the air . . .
>
> Genesis, 2:19-20

Swallow and starling, puffin and peregrine, blue tit and blackcap. We use these names so often that few of us ever pause to wonder about their origins. What do they mean? Where did they come from? And – Old Testament mythology aside – who originally created them?

Sometimes it's easy to assume that we know what a bird's name means, and often that assumption is quite correct. Treecreepers creep around trees, whitethroats have a white throat, and cuckoos do indeed call out their name.

The origin of other names can seem obvious, but may not be quite as straightforward as first appears. Even the simplest of English bird names, 'blackbird', turns out to be more complicated than you might imagine. There is also a whole range of folk names, from 'scribble lark' to 'sea swallow' and 'flop wing' to 'furze wren', each of which has its own tale to tell about our language, history and culture.*

---

* Referring to yellowhammer, common tern, lapwing and Dartford warbler respectively.

Ornithologists have often been rather dismissive of 'folk names', as though they are somehow inferior to the official, authorised ones. Yet, as the French scholar Michel Desfayes points out in his monumental two-volume work on the origins of European bird names, it is purely a matter of chance that, while some folk names remained localised, others were adopted as the name we still use today.[1]

Another pressing question is, *when* were birds given their names? Broadly speaking, it is reasonable to assume that most common and familiar birds were named a long time ago, by ordinary people – hence the term 'folk' names – while scarce and unfamiliar birds were named much more recently, by professional ornithologists.

Another general rule is that most early names were based on some obvious feature of the bird itself: its sound, colour or pattern, shape or size, habits or behaviour. Some of our longest-standing names reflect this, such as cuckoo and chiffchaff, blackcap and whitethroat, woodpecker and great tit.

Once the professionals got involved, from the seventeenth century onwards, names began to be based on more arcane aspects of birds' lives, such as where they live or the locality where they were found. These include habitat-based names such as reed, sedge and willow warblers, along with place-based names such as Dartford warbler and Manx shearwater. Many compound names, such as black-tailed and bar-tailed godwits, and pink-footed and white-fronted goose, also arose during this period, to help tell similar species apart.

The final category of bird names – most of which also originated fairly recently, during the eighteenth and nineteenth centuries – is in many ways the most beguiling. These are the species called after people, such as Montagu's harrier, Bewick's swan, Cetti's warbler and Leach's petrel.

The stories behind these birds, and the people after whom they were named, are told in Chapters 4 and 5. They include the country parson Gilbert White, author of *The Natural History of Selborne*; James Clark Ross, a young midshipman who shot his eponymous gull on a failed expedition to reach the fabled North-West Passage; and the disgraced military officer George Montagu who, following a midlife crisis, fled to Devon with his mistress, where he pursued the study of birds for the rest of his days.

According to the opening book of the Old Testament, once Adam had been created, almost the very first thing he did was to give names to the birds. As one commentator has shrewdly pointed out, this means that – more dubious claimants aside – taxonomists can justifiably claim to be the world's oldest profession.[2]

Since then, names have always fascinated us, yet they can also frustrate us. In *Romeo and Juliet*, Shakespeare's lovelorn heroine laments,

> What's in a name? That which we call a rose
> By any other name would smell as sweet.

Superficially at least, the Bard makes a valid point. As philosophers have long argued, the name we give to a person, place or object often has little or no connection with its sense and meaning: if we called a rose something completely different, it would still be the same flower.

But is that always the case? After all, names are not always random or meaningless labels, unconnected with the object to which they are attached. More than any other words, names carry with them the baggage of their etymological history: a history that, once we begin to investigate more deeply, reveals unexpected origins, and often yields a profound association between the name and the object that bears it. That's certainly true of onomatopoeic names, which derive from the sound the bird makes, and also of many names based on a bird's colour, pattern, habits and habitat.

At other times, though, a bird's name can cause confusion and misunderstanding. Some lead us down a blind alley, as in hedge sparrow – long used for the dunnock – which is not a sparrow at all, but an accentor. Other misleading names include stone curlew, a bird only distantly related to the true curlews; and bearded tit, which is neither bearded (it sports magnificent 'moustaches'), nor a tit.

In an ideal world, the names we give to birds would all make perfect sense. But in the real – and far more fascinating – world, they do not. This is for one simple reason: they were not handed down to mankind since time immemorial, as depicted in the Book of Genesis. Instead, they were coined by a whole range of different people, over many thousands of years, from the prehistoric era to the present day.

For this pressing urge to name the things we see around us dates back to our earliest ancestors. Initially, at the dawn of human civilisation, it would have been for purely practical reasons. Our hunter-gatherer ancestors would have soon realised that they needed to give names to the various wild creatures they came across, so they could easily distinguish between those that might be good to eat, and those that might kill and eat them.

As the evolutionary biologist Carol Kaesuk Yoon has pointed out, the ability to name things – and then recall what they were named at a later date – would have been essential for survival: 'Anyone living in the wild who could not reliably order, name, communicate about, and remember which organisms were which – who could not do good caveman taxonomy* – would most likely have led a considerably tougher and possibly shorter existence.'

From roughly ten thousand years ago, the coming of agriculture brought a new dimension to the naming of living things. Those first farmers needed to know when a particular wild flower would come into bloom, or at what time of year a migratory bird would depart and return. Understanding the timing of these events allowed them to chart the changing of the seasons, and know when to plant and harvest their precious crops.

As a result of these primordial needs, human beings evolved to notice the plants and animals around them, perceive their similarities and differences, and give them names based on those characteristics. Indeed, had our ancestors not learned to read the natural world, and shape that world around their needs, it is

---

* Carol Kaesuk Yoon, *Naming Nature* (New York and London, 2009). 'Good caveman taxonomy' applied to plants, too. Knowing which plant was good to eat, and which might be poisonous, would also have been vital. Later, this working knowledge of plant names, and their various therapeutic uses, would develop into the earliest form of medicine.

unlikely that human society and culture would have made such rapid and spectacular progress.

So although in the modern world we no longer need to learn names to know which creatures are good to eat – and which might in turn eat us – there can be no doubt that we live with the legacy of that early impulse. Having evolved as a hunter-gatherer, we continue to use many of those skills and techniques, even today. For what is birding, if not a sublimated form of hunting?

Names – and in particular the names of the other living things around us – help us make sense of the world. But do they do more than that? Do they also affect the way we perceive the very objects to which we give those names? And if, as we can probably agree, they do, then is this a positive or negative thing?

A strong case can be made for the idea that when we know the names of living creatures, it helps us appreciate the diversity of the natural world, and treat other species better. The Indian entrepreneur Aishwarya Shiva Pareek goes a step further, making an explicit connection between naming and being human: 'This is the main objective of human life . . . to give unique identity to unknown things in our native languages and to categorize them. . . Without us these things are nameless. . .'[3]

But this anthropocentric world-view has its dangers. It raises the valid concern that by naming living creatures, and bringing them under our own sphere of control, we may somehow diminish them. As the author Joanne Harris perceptively notes, 'A named thing is a tamed thing.'[4] When we give a wild creature a name, are we not perhaps extending mankind's sovereignty over other species, in an act that goes right back to Adam's naming of 'every fowl of the air' in the first book of the Bible?

So on the one hand, it is clear that names enable us to better know, understand and appreciate the natural world. Yet on the other hand, they can create an artificial barrier between the rest of nature and humankind. 'Names are masks', argues the American novelist Matthew Woodring Stover, 'they get in the way':[5] naming can reinforce the growing gulf between humanity and other living things.

The author John Fowles had no doubt on which side of the argument he belonged: 'Even the simplest knowledge of the names and habits of flowers or trees . . . removes us a step from total reality towards anthropocentrism; that is, it acts mentally as an equivalent of the camera viewfinder. Already it destroys or curtails certain possibilities of seeing, apprehending and experiencing.'[6]

Fowles's belief that by naming other species we create a distance between them and us, as when we look at the world through the lens of a camera, is a potentially seductive idea.* Indeed, this creative tension – whether names bring us closer to the natural world or distance us from it – reverberates through this book. But although I can sympathise with Fowles's point, I must come down firmly on the side of the namers.

I believe that by giving linguistic labels to the multifarious

---

* In his Introduction to a short work, *Animal. Vegetable. Mineral.* (London, 2016), the nature writer Tim Dee has expanded on this theme: 'Go to your window in the morning, open your curtains and think how not one blackbird you might see knows that it is a blackbird; not one tree cares that it is an oak, an ash, or a lime. Not one; and yet the blackbird lives as a blackbird not as a blackcap; the ash is an ash and not an alder. We are right to tell the difference because difference tells.'

wonders of life around us – by watching, seeing, focusing on and separating one organism from another, closely related species – we are then better able to understand and appreciate the natural world in all its glorious variety and confusion.

Sometimes, of course, the origin of a bird's name is simply lost. We can only guess at the meaning of the names we call many of our commonest and most familiar birds: swan, goose, sparrow and starling. As the man who spent more time studying the origins of bird names than virtually anyone, the late Professor W. B. Lockwood, pointed out, 'There is good reason to believe that in a number of cases answers may for ever elude us.'[7]

What we *do* know is that the process of naming birds was, like so many other aspects of our language, strongly influenced by major events in our own history. This began with the initial shift from a nomadic, hunter-gathering existence to the beginnings of settled agriculture on the fertile river plains of present-day Iraq, more than ten thousand years ago. It continued via the emergence of the ancestral language of so many modern tongues, Proto-Indo-European, on the steppes of central Eurasia, about three thousand years before the birth of Christ. And it developed and changed as a result of the successive invasions and conquests of our own islands, and our later expansion and empire-building, both of which helped define the nature of the English language spoken not just by 65 million Britons, but also as a *lingua franca* around the rest of the world.

The story of how birds got their names takes us on a journey through the major events in our language, history and culture. We shall discover how a small band of Anglo-Saxon invaders began the process of giving English names to birds; how the Norman Conquest led to a linguistic and cultural divide between lords and servants, still reflected in many modern bird names; and how writers like Chaucer and Shakespeare made their own important contributions to our knowledge and understanding of what our birds were called.

Yet, as we'll also find, despite radical changes in our language a surprising number of names dating back well before 1066 are still in use today, including yellowhammer, redstart and wheatear, all of whose real meanings are very different from their apparent ones. The persistence of these ancient names (all at least a thousand years old, and probably far older) reflects the extraordinary tenacity of names of any kind – whether of birds, people or places – to persist in the language long after other words from that time have been lost.

Some of our bird names are even older than the Anglo-Saxon era. These include gull (from Cornish), auk (Old Norse), ptarmigan and capercaillie (Scottish Gaelic), rook, crow and raven (West Germanic) and goose. The last is possibly the oldest of all the names we still use today, and may go all the way back to the language spoken on the steppes of eastern Europe and western Asia more than five thousand years ago.

As already noted, though, not all bird names are quite so ancient. From the seventeenth century onwards, as more and more species were discovered, a cohort of professional ornithologists – men such as William Turner and John Ray, Thomas Pennant and William MacGillivray – devised new names and attempted to codify and standardise those already in use. Some new names were created from scratch, while others were based on ones already long in existence, with many folk names ultimately gaining formal status as the 'official name' for the species.*

Meanwhile, the Ages of Exploration and Empire saw a vast increase in the number of species discovered around the world, many of which were given their new name by intrepid Britons as they explored the far reaches of the globe. From the yellow-bellied sapsucker of North America to the locust finch of Africa, and the many-coloured rush-tyrant of Patagonia to the short-billed leaf-tosser of the Amazonian rainforest, the world's ten thousand and more different species of bird now sport a mind-boggling variety of common names.

Back home in Britain, by the start of the twentieth century the vast majority of birds had been given the names we use today. Even so, there have been a number of changes during living memory, such as the switch from 'redbreast' to robin, and 'hedge sparrow' to dunnock.

But throughout this period, the wishes of tidy-minded scientists have often been trumped by what Lockwood calls 'ordinary users of the language . . . [who] do not necessarily feel bound by the prescriptions of the ornithologists, indeed . . . will generally not even be aware of them.'[8] So however much the bird books insist on the official name dunnock, many people still choose to call the little

---

* It's important to note that, as Lockwood points out, only when an ornithologist has specifically coined a name can we date its creation precisely. In other cases, even though we may be able to discover the first recorded mention of the name in print (for example, by looking it up in the *Oxford English Dictionary*), we have no idea how far back the usage of the name may go.

bird foraging unobtrusively around the base of their shrubbery a hedge sparrow.

So what of the future? As we shall see in the final chapter of this book, a radical change in the way scientists classify species is already leading to an explosion in new names, even as the birds themselves are threatened with extinction. Yet despite the pressures of globalisation, and the resulting homogenisation of the English language, most bird names are still proving remarkably resistant to change.

So next time you hear the croaking call of the raven, remember that the name we use for this huge and fearsome corvid is not all that different from what our prehistoric ancestors might have called it, as they stared up into a cold, grey sky and watched these huge black birds passing overhead. For me, that revelation is, in equal measure, both astonishing and comforting.

How did I come to write this book? It began with the influence of my late mother, Kay Moss, who in spite of her rather limited formal education passed on to me her deep and abiding love of the English language, and also encouraged me in my lifelong passion for birds. Together, these have made me endlessly curious about the origin of bird names.

I can still recall sitting in my grammar-school playground some time during the mid-1970s with my friend Daniel,* testing each other on the scientific names of British birds. In those days I certainly knew my *Anthus pratensis* from my *Prunella modularis*, and my *Crex crex* from my *Coccothraustes coccothraustes*, even if I

---

* Now Professor Daniel Osorio of Sussex University, one of the world experts on the way birds and other organisms perceive colour, and still a dear friend.

struggle to remember some of them now.*

In the early 1980s, when I was studying English at Cambridge, I made a special study of the bird poetry of John Clare (see Chapter 4). Later on, as I pursued a career as a writer and TV producer, I began to take a closer interest in the cultural side of our relationship with birds. This culminated in the BBC 4 television series and accompanying book *Birds Britannia*.[9] Subtitled 'How the British Fell in Love with Birds', this examined the profound and longstanding connection between the British and our birdlife, expressed through both popular and high culture.

While making that series I interviewed my friend and fellow birder David Lindo (aka 'The Urban Birder'). Like me, David acquired his fascination with birds at a very early age, and in a similar suburban setting (he in Wembley, me in Shepperton), during the late 1960s and early 1970s.

Like most young birders in those days, David knew no one else who shared his interest, and so resorted to making up his own names for the species he saw. Sparrows were 'baby birds', starlings 'mummy birds' and blackbirds 'daddy birds'. We may smile, but that early desire to name and categorise shows that we have an instinct to give names to the living things we see around us, even in early childhood.

When it comes to naming birds there is also – and I may be touching on a controversial subject here – some difference between the sexes. Broadly speaking, most male birders have an urge to put a name to every bird they see or hear, often interrupting ordinary day-to-day conversations to do so (in what the TV presenter and

---

* Meadow pipit, dunnock, corncrake and hawfinch respectively.

keen birder Mike Dilger calls 'birding Tourette's'). This can result in a perhaps unhealthy obsession with keeping lists: of birds seen in your garden, on your local patch, in your home city or county, in the UK and ultimately around the world.*

Women, on the other hand, often take a more holistic (and perhaps less stressful) approach – preferring to take a deeper interest in what the bird is doing, and why, rather than always needing to label it. Of course, not all men are obsessive listers and not all women are fascinated by bird behaviour, but there is more than a grain of truth in this distinction.

I hope that *Mrs Moreau's Warbler* will appeal to both groups equally. Anyone interested in detail can find out how many of our birds got their names; while those who prefer the big-picture view can better understand the sweep of history and how it shaped the names we call our birds today.

And if you still prefer to give your own names to the birds, then may I refer you to the performance-poet A. F. Harrold,[10] whose splendid verse 'Among The Ornithologists' mixes wonder, imagination and confusion in equal measure to produce a cornucopia of evocative names. These beguile and inspire us – as all good bird names should:

> Like the Fool at Court I can see the truth, speak a true name:
> This one I'll call the *Fifth Day of Christmas Bird* for its eye's
>   gold ring,
> Here's the *Nervous Bugger* who's always a step ahead, twittering,

---

* In case you're wondering, I keep all of those lists, which currently (spring 2017) stand at 84, 97, 214, 374 and 2,627 species respectively.

I'll call this one the *Golden Glimpse* as I miss it sitting still again,

But here's the *Puffed-Up Lover Bird*, strutting grey and wooing.
A stately *Snaked-neck Bird* makes its slow way along the stream.
A *Single Drop of Blood in the Darkest Night Bird* paddles out of
    a dream
And under the river bank, and as I wonder what it's doing

I see the *Surprising Single Snowfall In The Night Bird*, twig in beak,
build an unruly, unshapely, unhandsome home of a nest
and think it's doing fine. And look! *A Blue Sphere With A
    Yellow Vest*
cocks a momentary eye at me, but then declines to speak.

For all I know it's just named me inside its tiny brain
Or left me unlabelled, unpinned down, free to be anything I
    claim.*

Most of all, this book is a tribute to the pioneering and far-sighted
men and women who named our birds. Many of these people are
anonymous: our distant ancestors, whose curiosity about the natural world led them to try to create order by giving names to the
creatures they saw. Others are long dead, but not forgotten: their
names live on in the plethora of eponymous bird names, mostly
coined during the eighteenth and nineteenth centuries, but some –
such as Mrs Moreau's warbler – devised more recently.

* I guess that the birds are, respectively, blackbird, pied wagtail, goldcrest, wood pigeon,
mute swan, moorhen, coot and blue tit – but you may prefer your own versions!

It is these heroes and heroines who are the centre of this book; they, and the myriad variety of more than ten thousand different kinds of birds, in every corner of the globe, which bear the names they bestowed on them.

Stephen Moss
Mark, Somerset
May 2017

PROLOGUE

Mrs Moreau's Warbler

Winifred's warbler (*Scepomycter winifredae*), also known as Mrs
Moreau's warbler, is a species of bird in the Cisticolidae family . . .
endemic to montane forest in the Uluguru Mountains in Tanzania.
It is threatened by habitat loss.

WIKIPEDIA ENTRY: 'Mrs Moreau's Warbler'

When I think back to the year 1970, lists of names often come to
mind. John, Paul, George and Ringo, whose band, the Beatles, broke
up in April of that year. Lovell, Haise and Swigert, who in that same
month, against all the odds, guided their stricken spacecraft Apollo 13
back to Earth. Jairzinho, Tostão, Rivellino and the incomparable Pelé,
Brazil's formidable forward line, who thrashed Italy 4-1 to win the
World Cup, thus forever defining football as 'the beautiful game'.

All these people – and their incredible achievements – made a
lasting impression on me. But there was one other name that would
shape my life even more profoundly: that belonging to the wife of a
now long-forgotten ornithologist.

I was ten years old, and had been obsessed with birds for as long
as I could remember. To encourage my interest, for four shillings
a week (the pre-decimal equivalent of 20p), my mother subscribed
to a weekly 'partwork' of magazines, with the beguiling title *Birds
of the World*.

Every Saturday morning, I would wait eagerly for the paperboy to drop the latest issue through our letterbox, and then spend the rest of the day absorbed in its contents – the full-colour photographs, the text packed with fascinating facts about the world's birds and their extraordinary lifestyles.

Even in nine large-format volumes, *Birds of the World* could only cover a fraction of the 8,600 or so different kinds of bird known to exist at that time. But in a concession to completeness, its editor John Gooders had decided to include a full list of every single species. So it was that, some time in late 1970, on page 2,110 of Volume VII, part 3, I came across the name of the bird that gave this book its title: Mrs Moreau's warbler.

Something about the strangeness of the name struck me, even then. I already knew – or could guess – that birds could be called after their colour or their size, their habits or their habitat, the sound they made, or the place where they came from. Some, I also realised, were named after people: even at this early stage in my ornithological education I had heard of Leach's petrel, Montagu's harrier and Bewick's swan.

But '*Mrs* Moreau's warbler'? How on earth had this species acquired such an unusual name? A clue lay in the words in italics beneath: *Scepomycter winifredae*. Even at this early age, I was able to deduce that the bird had been named after a woman called Winifred Moreau.

Nowadays, of course, I can simply Google the name and click on the brief but informative Wikipedia entry. But no such easy shortcuts to knowledge were available back in the dark ages of my childhood. And my mum was calling me downstairs for tea. So I put down the magazine and, for the moment at least, forgot all about Mrs Moreau's warbler.

Yet as the years went by, and my interest in bird names grew, my thoughts kept returning to this obscure little bird, the woman after whom it was named, and her husband, one of the greatest ornithologists of the twentieth century.

Reginald Ernest Moreau – known to his friends and colleagues simply as 'Reg' – was born in 1897. The Moreaus* were a typically respectable, middle-class family, living an unremarkable existence in the Surrey town of Kingston-upon-Thames.

Then one day, when Reg was about ten years old, their quiet, comfortable lives were shattered. Returning home from work, his stockbroker father was struck by the open door of a passing train. Although Mr Moreau senior survived the accident, he became a manic-depressive and was never able to work again. As a result of their straitened circumstances, the family moved out of town to a more modest property in rural Surrey. There, during long bicycle trips around the local countryside, Reg developed his lifelong interest in birds.

In 1914, the year the First World War broke out, the seventeen-year-old Reg left school and took an exam to enter the Civil Service. He just managed to scrape through, in ninety-ninth place out of a hundred, and ended up in the Army Audit Office in Aldershot. Then, however, he fell ill with rheumatoid arthritis. The family doctor prescribed a complete change, and Reg applied for a posting abroad, to Egypt's capital Cairo.

He took to colonial life immediately, as his son David recalled many years later:

* The rather exotic family name came from a French ancestor who had moved to London to sell books.

Once in Egypt, he began to behave like the Indiana Jones character that he had clearly always wanted to be. Adopting a bush hat, khaki shirts and shorts . . . he began making long journeys by ancient car, rail and on foot into the surrounding desert. He took to flies, protesting camels, leather water bottles and Bedouin as if Kingston-on-Thames [*sic*] had never existed.[1]

Reg Moreau spent much of the next thirty years or so living and working in Africa. He became an expert in the study of bird migration: the epic, twice-yearly journeys made by hundreds of millions of birds, as they travel between the northern latitudes of Eurasia and the vast continent of Africa.

In his final years, by then living in the quiet Oxfordshire village of Berrick Salome, he brought together his lifetime's work into a book, *The Palearctic-African Bird Migration Systems*. This was published in 1972, but sadly Reg did not live to see it in print, having died, aged seventy-three, on 30 May 1970.

Despite the less-than-snappy title, the book was a masterpiece, distilling decades of hard-won knowledge and experience into clear, precise prose. Even now, almost fifty years after it was published, it is full of insights into the incredible journeys made by migrating birds.

As Reg Moreau lay on his deathbed, in the spring of 1970, he had time to write a short page of acknowledgements, which began with heartfelt thanks to his wife Winifred: 'This book would never have been written but for the devotion of my darling diminutive wife, known to generations of ornithologists as Winnie.'

A touching tribute, certainly. Yet Winnie Moreau contributed far more to their relationship than simple devotion. She was also a leading ornithologist in her own right, and an equal partner with Reg in their field trips and discussions; so much so that perhaps, in a less chauvinistic era, she might have been given a joint credit for the book.

Winnie and Reg first met on a fine spring day in the early 1920s, in a chance encounter that would radically shape the course of their lives. At the time, she was picking wild flowers and he was watching migrant birds. But this meeting did not take place on some wind-swept English headland, but under clear blue skies near the port city of Alexandria, where Winnie – a vicar's daughter from Cumberland – was working as a nanny.

More than forty years later, in 1966, Reg recalled that first meeting:

> Here one March afternoon, where the steppe was still bright with flowers and was twinkling with short-toed larks and wheatears, I came across a small person picking scarlet ranunculuses. . . She was knowledgeable in birds. Improbably we met twice more, for an hour or two, before she returned to England. We were married in Cumberland in June 1924.

After the wedding, they returned to Egypt. Four years later, they moved to Amani, a hill station in the scenically beautiful and biologically fascinating Usambara Mountains of north-east Tanganyika (now Tanzania), where Reg had taken up a new post in the accounts department of a biological research station.

But while auditing may have been his profession, his main

passion – shared by his wife – was ornithology. Fired up by their new and exotic surroundings, Reg and Winnie embarked on a long-term study of the birds around their new home. As well as the long-distance migrants that would form the subject of his book, they also focused on the sedentary 'Eastern Arc endemics': a unique group of very localised species, found nowhere else in the world but here.

In 1938, a year before the outbreak of the Second World War, Reg and Winnie embarked on an expedition to the Uluguru mountain range, several days' journey south of the Usambaras. There, high in the montane forest, they discovered an obscure and endangered songbird which, in a perhaps surprising act of marital devotion, he named *Scepomycter winifredae* – Mrs Moreau's warbler.

I say surprising, because in the few rather grainy, black-and-white photographs of him that survive, the short, stout, bald and bespectacled Reg bears more than a passing resemblance to Captain Mainwaring from *Dad's Army*. But beneath that stern-looking exterior he was a sociable and fun-loving man. And he clearly had a romantic streak, as the naming of this obscure little bird after his wife proves.

When Reg Moreau died in 1970 his obituaries were uniformly warm and positive. He was remembered as 'a squat, square figure [with] . . . a rugged face, a heavy square jaw, thick glasses, and just a fringe of curly hair which he brushed upwards'. His rather unusual dress sense was also mentioned: '[He was] adorned frequently in the summer with a transparent green eyeshade, and more often than not, if the weather was warm, with huge knees and strong shoes protruding from a pair of shorts.'

But most of all, Reg Moreau was regarded a key influence on

both professional and amateur ornithologists. As my friend and mentor James Ferguson-Lees recalled just before his death, he was always keen to share his vast knowledge and experience, yet also prepared to listen to other people's thoughts and opinions. 'Reg was a remarkable man – a great enthusiast about birds and bird migration – like a God to us youngsters!'*

Winnie, though, remained tantalisingly vague, the dutiful wife hovering in the background. Although six years older than Reg, she survived for another eleven years, dying in 1981, in her ninetieth year.

Now, almost forty years later, she is finally being recognised as an equal partner in Reg's life and work, not simply his willing and devoted assistant.[2] The American academic Nancy J. Jacobs has discovered that in his writings on new birds discovered in the Usambaras, Reg always used the first person plural, to highlight that these had been jointly found and named by him and Winnie.†

As Reg himself wrote: 'The frequent use of the pronoun "we" . . . is a natural result of our close collaboration.'[3]

Amidst their busy lives, Reg and Winnie also found time to raise two children: a daughter, Prinia – named after a family of African songbirds – and a son, David, who later made a career for himself

---

* James Ferguson-Lees was one of the most influential birdwatchers and ornithologists of the second half of the twentieth century. He was a successful author, editor, conservationist and dedicated field birder, who influenced his own and subsequent generations. It was a privilege and a pleasure to get to know him in his later years, until his death, just after his eighty-eighth birthday, in January 2017.

† The only other female ornithologist to rival Winifred Moreau is Maria Koepcke. Born Maria von Mikulicz-Radecki in Leipzig, Germany, in 1924, she and her husband Hans pioneered ornithology in Peru, before her untimely death in an air crash on Christmas Eve, 1971. She has two species of bird named after her: Koepcke's hermit (a type of hummingbird) and Koepcke's screech-owl.

as an author of rather racy novels, mostly set in expatriate circles in Tanzania.*

David Moreau – who narrowly escaped being christened 'Buphagus' after the scientific name for the oxpeckers – depicted his parents as a loving but rather unpredictable couple. He claimed that Reg once warned Prinia to 'cover your ears. There's going to be a loud bang', just before he shot and wounded a leopard hiding beneath her bed.

Reg delighted in reciting saucy limericks to his dinner guests, while Winnie frequently cared for abandoned baby birds, tucking them into a sock, which she then placed inside her bra. Indeed, she once did so while entertaining the visiting provincial governor. Such recollections suggest that Reg and Winnie Moreau's long and happy marriage and family life were enlivened by a great sense of fun.†

The only photograph I can find of Reg and Winnie together comes from late in his life, long after they had returned to England. They stand side-by-side in front of a brick fireplace: he wearing a jacket, tie and jumper, she looking rather smarter, in a neat two-piece outfit. Both are smiling, as well they might, given their many achievements: not least the discovery of the warbler that bears Winifred's name.

*

---

* I later discovered that Reg himself had also written a collection of short stories under the barely concealed pseudonym 'E. R. Morrough' – because, working for the Civil Service, he was not permitted to publish under his own name.

† *More Wrestling than Dancing*, the memoir by Reg's son David, contains many more wonderful anecdotes and descriptions of family life with the Moreaus.

In January 2017, almost half a century after I first read about Mrs Moreau's warbler, I finally travelled to the Uluguru Mountains in eastern Tanzania, on a quest to see this bird for myself. For the story of that journey – and whether or not I succeeded – you will have to wait until the end of this book. . .

SOUND AND ECHOES

The Origins of Bird Names

Names turned over by time, like the plough turning the soil. Bringing up the new while the old were buried in the mud.

Joe Abercrombie, *The Heroes*

1: *The Cuckoo's Calling*

The sound, as it percolates into my consciousness with the full force of an early-morning espresso, is quite unmistakable. Two notes float across the fresh spring landscape, hanging momentarily in the warm, still air, before fading away. Way out of sight, in the far distance, a second bird echoes with another round of notes, followed by a third, this time almost beyond the horizon.

'Cuck-ooo, Cuck-ooo, Cuck-ooo. . .'

The spring call of the male cuckoo.* The very name encapsulates its sound, and is so familiar that, even if you have never caught a glimpse of the bird itself, you are instantly aware of its identity. Despite the cuckoo's recent decline, it remains the classic harbinger of spring; even today, a letter to *The Times* newspaper traditionally marks the first sighting of the bird each year.

In the West Yorkshire village of Marsden, local people still celebrate the cuckoo's annual return towards the end of April with the 'Cuckoo Day Festival'. There is a craft fair, a village procession and that staple ritual of English village life: a maypole around which Morris dancers, complete with white handkerchiefs, perform their terpsichorean displays.

Along with other 'cuckoo fairs' that used to take place up and

* Throughout this chapter, I have used the word 'call' to describe the spring sound of birds such as the cuckoo, hoopoe and crows, which are not usually thought of as 'songbirds'. However, as the wildlife sound recordist Geoff Sample has pointed out (*in litt.*), these 'calls' have exactly the same function as song: to defend a territory against rival males, while at the same time attracting females.

down the country, the Marsden festival was once a key event in the rural calendar. It marked the shift from winter into spring, with all the hope the new season brings. Traditionally, villagers also took part in the ritual of 'penning the cuckoo': building a wall in order to capture the returning bird, and so supposedly prolong the summer. In rural Shropshire, as soon as the first cuckoo was heard each year, farm labourers would down tools and drink beer for the rest of the day.

So why, of all our spring migrants, was the cuckoo's return so widely marked and celebrated? After all, it is not a showy bird: even where cuckoos are common, in the far north of Scotland, they are still more often heard than seen. The reason for the cuckoo's fame is, of course, its distinctive and inimitable sound. As the Victorian clergyman-naturalist, the Revd C. A. Johns, pointed out, the cuckoo's call is closer to the human voice than that of any other bird. This, surely, explains why it has been so important to rural communities, for whom it was the unmistakable signal that winter was finally over, and spring was here to stay.

The cuckoo's sound appears in the very first entry of the *Oxford Book of English Verse*. It is the subject of a poem created by an anonymous scribe some time during the mid-thirteenth century, and widely regarded as the earliest verse written in something clearly recognisable as English:

> Sumer is icumen in,
> Lhude sing cuccu!*

---

* Summer is coming in
The cuckoo sings loudly!

Surprisingly, perhaps, this is the very first recorded use of the word 'cuckoo' in written English. That's because its origins lie across the Channel: it came into our language from the Old French word *cucu*, which derives from the Latin *cuculus*, still used in the cuckoo's scientific name. Both of these are, of course, also onomatopoeic.

Before this time, people would have used a very different name: 'yek', which came from the Old English 'geac'. This is similar to the names for the cuckoo in today's Scandinavian languages (such as the Swedish *gök*), indicating its ancient Germanic lineage.

The old name remained remarkably resistant to the more obvious charms of the new one. Cuckoo did not gain the upper hand until quite late on, as can be seen in the writings of Randle Holme, who in 1688 stated: 'The Cuckow is in some parts of England called a Gouke.' Incredibly, in some parts of northern England and Scotland the word has survived right up to the present day: the wildlife sound recordist Geoff Sample remembers growing up in Northumberland during the 1960s and hearing people being called 'a daft old gowk'.*

The cuckoo – or rather the geac – first appears in written Old English in the earliest dictionary of our language, the *Corpus Glossary*, which dates back to AD 725. It can also be found in a contemporary poetic tribute to the monk Guthlac of Crowland (later canonised as Saint Guthlac), who lived from 673 to 714.

For much of his life, Guthlac lived as a hermit on a small island in the Lincolnshire Fens. When he first arrived in this watery

---

* As he points out, this is tautological, as 'gowk' is also a dialect word meaning a foolish person.

31

wonderland at the start of spring, it's hardly surprising that one of the first birds he encountered was the cuckoo:

> Bright was the glorious plain and his new home;
> sweet the birds' song; earth blossomed forth;
> Cuckoos heralded the year. [1]

This early reference to the species – which in the original is referred to by its Anglo-Saxon name 'geac' – is unusual: according to the great ornithologist and broadcaster James Fisher the cuckoo is one of just sixteen species of bird recorded in Anglo-Saxon literature.[*]

Yet it's only by pure chance that these particular names lived on to the present day, while others did not. As Fisher points out, the entire surviving corpus of Old English writings totals less than a quarter of a million words. So doubtless many other birds were named in written works that sadly perished from fires, flood or simple neglect.

But we do have one vitally important manuscript from this period. Dating from the final decades of the first millennium – somewhere between AD 960 and 990 – the *Exeter Book* is the largest collection of extant Old English writings, and one of the oldest surviving books of poetry in the world.[†]

---

[*] In *The Shell Bird Book* (1966), in my view the most readable yet scholarly history of Britain's birds ever written. The other 15 species are: robin, crane, (white-tailed) sea eagle, crow, wood pigeon, nightingale, swallow, chaffinch, raven, whooper swan, gannet, whimbrel, kittiwake, tern and quail. All would have been named by the year AD 700.
[†] Donated to Exeter Cathedral some time during the mid-eleventh century by its first bishop, Leofric, it remains there to this day, protected by his ominous warning: 'If any-one should take it away from thence, let him lie under eternal malediction'.

On a fine spring afternoon, I was briefly tempted to join the sun-seekers lounging on the grass on Exeter's Cathedral Green. But instead I headed indoors, to the red sandstone library and archive, tucked out of sight around the corner of the cathedral. As I entered, a charm of goldfinches flew overhead, delivering their light, tinkling songs – a good omen, I hoped.

I had come, along with a handful of other curious visitors, on the one day each month when the *Exeter Book* is on display to the public. We were shown round by Stuart, one of those people whose deep historical knowledge is matched by an engaging ability to deliver fascinating facts.

As Stuart pointed out, this stout volume has had its ups and downs in the millennium or more since it first arrived here. It was, at some stage, used as a chopping board for cutting manuscripts (and still shows the stains from glue pots on some of its pages), and probably lay on a dusty bookshelf for most of its long lifetime. Indeed, the *Exeter Book* was only truly appreciated when, some time during the seventeenth or eighteenth centuries, these ancient manuscripts began to be valued once again.

The reason the book was overlooked was simple: hardly anyone could read or understand its contents. That was because less than a couple of centuries after it had been produced, the English language had changed out of all recognition.

Soon after the Norman Conquest, Anglo-Saxon began to be neglected as a written language. Even a few decades after they were transcribed, therefore, the poems contained in the *Exeter Book* would have been incomprehensible to any but the most determined scholar. So in many ways it is incredible that it has survived at all.

Stuart beckoned us forward, so we could examine the volume more closely. To my surprise, the first impression was not of poetry, but of densely written, evenly spaced prose. As he explained, that is because sheepskin parchment was so expensive that the scribe could not afford to waste space by writing in short lines, so he filled each page all the way up to the margins. The yellowish sheets are etched with words written in dark-brown ink, made from a mixture of oak galls, gum to make it sticky, and either vinegar or urine as a preservative. This unpromising recipe worked: after more than a millennium the book still looks clean and fresh, and the script has hardly faded at all.

The *Exeter Book* contains roughly forty poems – and almost a hundred verse riddles – composed many centuries earlier, and handed down through the generations by word-of-mouth. Amongst the riddles is a verse devoted to a very familiar bird:

> In former days my mother and father
> forsook me for dead, for the fullness of life
> was not yet within me. But a kinswomen
> graciously fitted me out in soft garments,
> as kind to me as to her own children,
> tended and took me under her wing;
> until under shelter, unlike her kin,
> I matured as a mighty bird (as was my fate).
> My guardian then fed me until I could fly
> and wander more widely on my
> excursions; she had the less of her own
> sons and daughters by what she did thus.[2]

This is, of course, the cuckoo. Whoever wrote this riddle was clearly aware of this bird's unusual habit of laying its eggs in the nests of other species, and fooling them into raising its young, at the expense of their own offspring.

Fascinating though this and the other riddles are, they were not what I had come to see. I wanted to read (or, given my lack of fluency in Anglo-Saxon, gaze at) a much longer work: the 124-line autobiographical verse known as *The Seafarer*.

Written by an anonymous mariner, some time towards the end of the seventh century, this haunting and evocative poem wonderfully captures the hardship of life on the high seas. More importantly, for anyone searching for the origins of English bird names, *The Seafarer* is an ornithological goldmine:

> There I heard nothing but the roar of the sea,
> of the ice-cold wave, and sometimes the song of the wild
> swan;
> I had for my amusement the cry of the gannet
> and the sound of the whale instead of the laughter of
> men,
> the sea-mew singing instead of the drinking of mead.
> Storms beat on the rocky cliffs, where the tern, ice on its
> wings, gave answer;
> Very often the dewy-winged eagle screamed. . .[3]

In an earlier translation, James Fisher chose different identities for some of the wild creatures in the poem, suggesting that the 'whale' could have been a flock of whimbrels (a smaller cousin of the curlew), and that the 'sea-mew' (a kind of gull) was the kitti-wake. His translation runs as follows:

> There heard I naught but seething sea,
> Ice-cold wave, awhile a song of swan.
> There came to charm me gannet's pother
> And whimbrels' trills for the laughter of men,
> Kittiwake singing instead of mead.
> Storms there the stacks thrashed, there answered them
> the tern
> With icy feathers; full oft the erne wailed round
> Spray-feathered. . .[4]

Fisher speculated that *The Seafarer* would have been written around the year AD 685, at Bass Rock, a vast and noisy seabird colony just off the east coast of Scotland. He suggested that the (whooper) swans would have been heading north, back to their breeding grounds in Iceland; while the whimbrels would have just arrived back from Africa, en route to Shetland or Scandinavia. As Fisher pointed out, this could only have occurred during a brief window at the height of spring migration – in his view, the week from 20 to 27 April.

The language in which *The Seafarer* was written is not easy for the modern reader to comprehend, but even in the original West Saxon (a dialect of Old English) we can recognise some species, including 'ganot' (the gannet, our largest seabird), and 'stearn' (the tern, one of our smallest).

Both 'earn' (erne, or white-tailed eagle) and 'mæw' (mew, a kind of gull) are of very ancient origin, almost certainly predating Old English. They were ultimately supplanted by 'eagle', from Norman French, and 'gull' – which, perhaps uniquely amongst modern English bird names, comes from one of the south Celtic languages, probably Cornish.* Yet they have endured as folk names right up to the present day.†

Variations on the word 'mew' – including 'maw', 'maa' and 'ma' – are still heard to describe common or herring gulls in the Lowland Scots dialect. The word also survives in the North American name for the common gull ('mew gull'), and in a more ancient form in the name fulmar, from the Old Norse, which means 'foul gull', because of the bird's habit of spitting smelly, sticky oil on any intruders that come too near its nest.

The continued existence of ancient names such as gowk, mew and erne, along with many other names from the same period, is not merely a quaint historical footnote in our story. Instead, it goes to the very heart of the way we use language.

We live in an age of globalisation; as a result, our language is being pulled in two different and conflicting directions. One trend sees English becoming simpler, as different dialects merge and disappear under the onslaught of the mass media and the Internet. Yet at the same time, it is becoming more rich and varied, through its longstanding habit of borrowing words from other tongues. In the linguist David Crystal's memorable phrase, English is still 'a

---

* Earlier versions in these languages include the Welsh 'gŵylan', Cornish 'guilan' and Breton 'goelann'. 'Puffin' may also be of Cornish origin.
† Although it is no longer in general use, 'erne' regularly features as a crossword clue – the answer usually being 'sea eagle', but occasionally just 'eagle' or 'seabird'.

vacuum-cleaner of a language, sucking in words from any other language that its speakers come into contact with. . .'[5]

Yet one key area of language – the names we use for birds – goes against both these trends, by staying more or less the same. Some, indeed perhaps the majority, of the names we use every day have remained virtually unchanged over centuries, and in some cases for millennia. This is all the more surprising, given the extraordinary shifts that have occurred in the English language during the past 1,500 years.

If we try to read poems such as *The Seafarer* and *Beowulf* in their original Old English, they appear utterly impenetrable. Even the Middle English used by Chaucer and the *Gawain* poet can at first be hard to understand, though on a closer look (or better still, when read out loud) it does become more or less comprehensible.

For most of us, the first easily recognisable works, written in what we now call Early Modern English, appeared during the late sixteenth and early seventeenth centuries. The poetry of Edmund Spenser and John Donne, the poems and plays of William Shakespeare, and the majestic King James Bible, are often regarded as the zenith of our literary achievement, and are also the earliest still readable examples of the global language now spoken by millions of people around the world.

Given these dramatic changes, it is little short of astonishing that so many bird names with Anglo-Saxon origins have lasted to the present day – albeit often in a rather different form from the original. This is one of the most intriguing aspects of the story of our bird names, and one to which I shall return many times, for it tells us much about the crucial importance of the natural world in our society, history and culture.

But before I do, we need to go even further back in time. For although many of the names we use for birds today have changed, or been lost and forgotten along the way, a handful go back well before the beginnings of English: to the very dawn of human civilisation, roughly 3,000 years before the birth of Christ.

Their origins lie very far from here: with a small group of early farmers living thousands of miles to the east of Britain, on the vast open grasslands of central Eurasia – the place we now know as the Russian steppes.

2: *Trade Routes and Translations*

Try to imagine, if you can, the day-to-day existence of those first farmers on the steppes of central Eurasia, so distant from us in space and time. In the words of the seventeenth-century philosopher Thomas Hobbes, we can surely guess that their lives would have been 'solitary, poor, nasty, brutish, and short'.

We can picture them spending long, hard days cultivating the steppe grasslands, planting and harvesting their meagre crops, and caring for their precious livestock. They would also have needed to cope with the vagaries of weather and climate, which could so easily mean the difference between success and failure and, ultimately, survival and death.

For these early farmers, life had changed little for several millennia, ever since their own ancestors had first renounced the nomadic, hunter-gatherer lifestyle in favour of agriculture, which required a permanent, settled home. Life in one place may have been easier, in some ways, yet it would still have been very tough and unrelenting.

But then, roughly 5,000 years ago, the world began to change. Two developments – one cultural, the other technological – dramatically improved the lives of these ancient people.

The first was the domestication of the horse, arguably the most important wild creature ever to be subjugated for human use. The second, which followed soon afterwards, was the invention of the spoked wheel. For the first time in human history, this simple breakthrough allowed people to build fast, light and manoeuvrable vehicles. These could in turn be pulled over longer and longer distances by the newly tamed horse. The eventual dominance of vehicular transport over our lives had begun.

The newly developed wagons and carts, pulled by horses, made life much easier, allowing heavy items such as firewood and crops to be carried on short journeys from woods and fields to villages and homes. But more importantly for our story, they also opened up the possibility of moving goods and people over far longer distances.

Thanks to these long-forgotten people, the greatest change in human history was set in motion: the beginning of trade between different groups, communities and, ultimately, nations. At first, they would have simply bartered their produce with their immediate neighbours, perhaps exchanging a bushel of wheat for a couple of chickens. But over time, the bleak, hostile and treeless steppe where they lived turned into a thriving trade corridor, which would eventually stretch for thousands of miles, to and from Europe in the west and Asia in the east.

Opening up this transcontinental route had another, even more profound, effect on later civilisations. As these ancient steppe-dwellers gradually migrated westwards and eastwards, their language – originally spoken by only a handful of people in this remote and landlocked location – began to spread across a vast swathe of Europe and Asia. In the process, it changed and developed into a huge range of new tongues, including Latin, Welsh, French, German, Hindi, Swedish, Spanish, Greek and English.

At first sight, these languages do not appear to have all that much in common. They do of course share some common terms, borrowed from one another relatively recently: English in particular has proved adept at appropriating words as varied as chutney and bungalow (from Hindi), schadenfreude and kitsch (from German) and coracle and corgi (from Welsh). But we are far more aware of the differences in vocabulary, word and sentence structure between one language and another, than any similarities.

Yet as linguists first discovered back in the eighteenth century, many of these differences are in fact superficial, and even apparently dissimilar languages may be related. And just as the similarities in facial appearance between two people are often because they share a common ancestor, languages too have a 'family tree'.

So, while it may come as a surprise to anyone who has struggled with a phrasebook while attempting to make themselves understood abroad, all these languages, and many more, are ultimately descended from a single tongue. Known by linguists as 'Proto-Indo-European' or PIE, this was first spoken on those windswept central Eurasian grasslands, roughly three thousand years before the birth of Christ. Extraordinary though it may seem, the languages that descend from it are still spoken by roughly half the world's population – almost four billion people. And as David Anthony points out in his book, *The Horse, the Wheel and Language*,[6] this means that the languages we speak today are almost entirely the result of those two developments that give his book its intriguing title.

We have no written records of the actual words those people used to speak to one another as they went about their day-to-day lives. Yet by comparing words still used in one modern language with their equivalents in another, linguists have been able to painstakingly reconstruct some of their lost vocabulary.

Amongst those words, there are a tiny number that, amazingly, have lasted – albeit in different forms in various modern languages – all the way down to the present day. These include the name of a species of bird that would have been very familiar indeed to our distant ancestors: the goose – or, as linguists now believe it would have been originally called, *ghans*.

Long before the domestication of the horse, the invention of the wheel, or even the earliest agriculture, prehistoric peoples right across Europe and Asia would have been aware of the twice-yearly migration of geese.

Looking up each autumn, they would have seen straggling, V-shaped skeins of birds arriving from the north, silhouettes etched against the grey skies as the land echoed with their distinctive, honking calls. They also would have noted the date when the flocks headed back north towards their breeding grounds in spring.[*]

* In many cultures, the date of the autumn arrival of geese would be used to predict the weather for the season to come – the belief was that an early arrival date meant a hard

During the winter months, when vast flocks of geese fed on grasslands and wetlands, they would no doubt have used whatever primitive weapons they had – rocks, stones and perhaps flint spears – to try to kill the plump, tasty birds, so they could supplement their meagre diet.

It would only have been a matter of time before it occurred to more intelligent individuals that, rather than spending time and effort trying to hunt and kill geese, there might be an easier way to ensure a regular, reliable and year-round supply of eggs, flesh and feathers. So it was that, almost 5,000 years ago, the greylag goose became only the third (or possibly fourth) species of bird – after the chicken, duck and perhaps the pigeon – to be domesticated.

The central importance of geese to our ancestors' lives meant that these birds would have been given a vernacular name far earlier than more obscure, less useful species. That is no surprise. But what is truly extraordinary is that this name has lasted – in different forms in different languages – all the way down to the present – especially given the ways languages have evolved, and vocabulary has changed, over thousands of years.

Take a look at the modern name for goose in both German and Dutch: *gans*. At first sight this does not appear very similar to the word we use in English; but think of the name we give to a male goose, 'gander', and the connection becomes clearer. Likewise, the Spanish name, *ánsar*, may not appear to have much in common with 'goose'. But it is remarkably similar to the scientific name of the

winter, and a late arrival a mild one. In reality the arrival date of migratory wildfowl has no link with the weather in the coming winter, and is purely a result of immediate weather conditions at the time of travel.

greylag goose, *Anser anser* and, via *gans*, to goose. So even if bird names in different languages may not appear to be related, a closer look reveals that they often are.

The point of this exercise in linguistic archaeology is this: because these European languages began to diverge from one another roughly 5,000 years ago, we can show that the precursor of these related words for goose in use today must have already been in existence at that time. And that means it must go all the way back to the Proto-Indo-European spoken by those early traders, on the Central Asian steppes.

Thus, of all our bird names, 'goose' can justifiably claim to be the oldest.

Other names we still use today go almost as far back in time; again, we can demonstrate this by looking at another crucial period: the Early Iron Age. Lasting from roughly 1000 to 500 BC, this period saw the first widespread use of iron and steel, smelted from iron ore, to make tools and weapons.

This major technological breakthrough coincided with – and also triggered – a series of important social and cultural changes. These included more advanced agriculture, the first major religious written texts (including the early books of the Old Testament) and, most importantly for our story, the development of the earliest written languages, through the invention of abstract alphabetic characters.

The first alphabets arose in the Middle East, later spreading westwards into Europe, where the Greeks developed the form that would become the ancestor of all European alphabets. In north-west

Europe, another ancestral tongue had not yet been written down, but was spoken across a wide geographical area. Proto-Germanic, as it was later called, eventually split into two forms. One branch, to the north, evolved into the various Scandinavian languages such as Danish, Swedish and Norwegian, while the other developed into modern German and Dutch and – following successive invasions into Britain from continental Europe – English.

Although English has since diverged markedly from these continental tongues, we can still identify many words that share a common origin, and therefore must date back to this distant time. Prominent amongst these are some of our best-known bird names, including swallow and swan.

The swallow and the swan are two birds that, like the goose, would have been very familiar to our ancestors right across northern Europe.

Like the cuckoo, the swallow is one of the classic signs of the coming of spring. A long-distance migrant, it spends about half the year raising a family in our rural barns and outbuildings, before returning south to Africa each autumn to spend the winter there, hunting for insects amongst the vast gatherings of game animals on the grassy savannah.

'Swan' could refer to one of three closely related species: the resident mute swan, with its black-and-orange bill, or the black-and-yellow-billed Bewick's and whooper swans. These are both winter visitors to Britain and north-west Europe, and like the geese they fly south and west in autumn and head back north and east in spring.

The English word swan is linguistically almost identical to

the German *schwan* and the Dutch *ʒwaan*, the differences simply being the result of the standard shifts in pronunciation and spelling between the three languages. Likewise, swallow is *Schwalbe* in German and *ʒwaluw* in Dutch. That these birds have virtually the same name in all three modern European tongues is clear evidence that they share a common origin in the language known as West Germanic, which was spoken around the time of Christ's birth.

But that's not the whole story. For the names of both species can also be found in Old Norse, as *svanr* and *svala*.* Because, like West Germanic, Old Norse is also derived from Proto-Germanic, we know these names must go back even further, to at least 500 BC.†

Simply knowing that these names have a common origin in the ancestral language of northern Europe still leaves one crucial thing unexplained: how did they end up being used here in Britain? As with so many aspects of our culture, they did so via a series of dramatic events: a series of invasions that brought people – and their languages – from mainland Europe to our island home.

---

* Their equivalents in modern Scandinavian languages are *svan/svane* and *svala/svale* – again, clearly related to our modern English names.

† As to the actual meaning of these ancient names, Lockwood suggests that swallow derives from a word meaning 'cleft stick'– a reference to the bird's long, forked tail; while 'swan' may come from a word meaning 'noise', which he speculates may refer to the sound made by the mute swan's wings as they fly overhead. I must say I am not entirely convinced.

3: Invasions and Conquests

The first great historical invasion of our isles is, as every schoolchild knows, the conquest of the Ancient Britons – led by Queen Boadicea (also known as Boudicca) – by the Roman Empire. Yet despite ruling much of Britain for close to half a millennium, following Julius Caesar's arrival in 55 BC, the Romans never quite managed to fully subsume this outlying land and its recalcitrant people into their mighty empire. This was never more apparent than in the stubborn resistance amongst ordinary folk to speaking the language of their conquerors.

Although Latin was widely spoken amongst the Romans, and continued to be used as the language of scholarship long after they left, the Ancient Britons managed to keep hold of their own languages for the whole of the Roman occupation. This was very different from the situation in Gaul (modern-day France), where Latin rapidly replaced the indigenous language, driving it to outlying lands such as Brittany. This explains why the modern French language is so closely related to Latin.

Ironically, it was only when the Romans finally departed – more than four centuries after their initial invasion – that the various native tongues finally began to decline. The cause was the arrival of a new group of invaders, this time from the near continent.

They were a motley bunch: variously known as the Angles, Saxons and Jutes, and hailing from Denmark, southern Sweden, the Low Countries and north-west Germany. They succeeded by taking advantage of the social chaos left by the decline of the Roman

Empire, and the continued warring between the various groups of Britons left behind.

Having crossed the North Sea to land on the east coast, they eventually extended their influence throughout much of the area we now call England. Here, the existing Romano-British population intermingled and interbred with the newcomers. In the outlying parts of the British Isles – present-day Ireland, Wales and Scotland, the Isle of Man and Cornwall – which the invaders did not manage to reach, those peoples, often erroneously lumped together as Celts,* retained their separate identity. They also continued to speak their own languages, the precursors of modern Irish and Scottish Gaelic, and Welsh.

But the conquest of these isles by those invaders from the east was not as brutal, or as sudden, as we might imagine. It took place over several hundred years, from the middle of the fifth century to the end of the seventh. So most historians, rather than seeing this as a single, momentous event, now regard it as a more gradual, measured process: not so much an invasion as a migration.

Of all the many lasting influences these newcomers had on their new home, by far the most important and enduring was their language. Known as Anglo-Saxon or Old English, this ancient tongue marked the birth of what is now spoken as a first or second language by more than two billion people, all over the world.

This eventful period in our history also saw the first appearance of a significant number of English bird names, many of which

* The idea that these people were a single, homogenous group known as 'Celts' is an eighteenth-century invention; in reality they were a motley group of different tribes with little in common with one another.

– including rook and raven, sparrow and wheatear, gannet and crow – we still use today. And even though some species have since been given a more modern name, other old names still managed to cling on until relatively recently. These include 'erne', meaning sea eagle, and 'ruddock', for robin.

It is important to remember that all these names would have been part of an almost exclusively *spoken* language, rather than a written one. Centuries before the invention of the printing press, written works were rare indeed, and the vast majority of the population was functionally illiterate. As a result, the oral tradition thrived, with stories and poems – such as *Beowulf* – passed down the ages from one generation to another with remarkable fidelity. So it is not surprising that the names given to birds also arose in a purely oral setting, being coined by ordinary people to describe the creatures they saw every day as they toiled in the fields and forests.

Many of these early names are onomatopoeic: they imitate or echo the sounds made by the birds themselves. There are two good reasons for this: one cultural and one practical.

From a cultural point of view, there is growing evidence that we possess a 'music instinct': the ability to make sense of what we hear in the world around us, and the urge to imitate it ourselves.* What could be more natural than a human being, having heard a bird sing, trying to mimic it? Surely one reason why so many ancient bird names are based on sound could be that our distant ancestors

* See, for example, Philip Ball, *The Music Instinct* (2010), and also the relatively new science of 'Biomusicology', a term coined by the veteran Swedish musicologist Nils L. Wallin in 1991, which looks at the connections between the sounds made by birds and other wild creatures and the music made by humans.

learned to sing by listening to birds. If so, that would make song the earliest art form – well before the emergence of cave paintings.

Another reason is more pragmatic. In an age long before the invention of optical aids such as binoculars and telescopes, which allow us to see feather-by-feather detail, visual features were far less important in identifying birds. By far the easiest way to tell one species apart from another, similar-looking one would have been by listening to the sound it made. If our ancestors then wanted to remember what a bird was called – perhaps because it was particularly good to eat or, like the cuckoo, marked the changing of the seasons – then the logical next step would be to turn this sound into the bird's name.

But this process wasn't as straightforward as simply repeating the sound; first this had to be transliterated into human speech. And as we shall now discover, this is not quite as simple as it might appear.

4: The Nature of Birdsong

At this stage in our story, we need to make a brief digression. Let's start with the reason birds make sounds in the first place.

The primary way birds communicate with one another can be divided into songs and calls. The purpose of song is to defend a territory and attract a mate, while the various calls perform specific functions such as warning against predators, begging for food, or simply keeping in touch with other birds in the same flock.

Sound is not the only way birds communicate, of course. Many species use their brightly coloured plumage and visual displays to do so. These include the extraordinary courtship dances of the multi-coloured birds of paradise, the strutting parade of the male pea-cock and, closer to home, the display of the black grouse – these are just three of the best known examples among many in the bird world.

But communicating by sound has three major advantages over vision. First, it is more consistent, working in poor light or even total darkness, or when the bird is hidden in a woodland, hedge-row or dense reed bed. Sound also carries further than vision: the bittern's low, booming call can be heard several kilometres away. And sound has another major advantage: when a bird is calling or singing it does not always need to show itself, meaning that it can hide from predators, whereas during a visual performance it makes itself vulnerable to attack.

During the breeding season, male birds – and in the northern hemisphere these are usually the only ones that sing – need to defend a territory against their rivals. At the same time, they must attract and keep a female, otherwise all their efforts will have been in vain. That is why on a fine spring day, from long before dawn until after dusk, a songbird will sing his heart out, at a time when he could be doing all kinds of other essential tasks, such as building a nest or finding food.

Few other kinds of behaviour in nature are quite so persistent; and none perform two such critically important functions. The per-formance-poet A. F. Harrold summed up this dual purpose with admirable clarity and brevity in his verse, 'Dawn Chorus':

> From hedgerow, telephone wire,
> aerial and tree
> sings out a double-edged request
> *fuck off or fuck me*.[7]

But it's not just *why* birds sing that is important; we also need to understand *how* they do so. The way they form sounds is fundamentally different to the way we do, because of their very different anatomy.

Human beings make sounds by using our lungs to pump air through our larynx and vocal cords, which fine-tune pitch and tone. We then use our lips and tongue to articulate these sounds to make specific words and phrases.

When a bird sings or calls, it uses an organ called a syrinx.* This is the avian equivalent of our larynx, but with one crucial difference. The human larynx is situated at the top of the trachea (or windpipe), but a bird's syrinx is much lower down, at the junction of the two bronchi, the passages that carry air in and out of the lungs. This means that the bird can mix two sources of sound, simultaneously producing two different songs at the same time – in what the ornithologist C. H. Greenewalt dubbed the 'two-voice' phenomenon.†

That is perhaps why we feel so inadequate when we hear a master songster like the nightingale or song thrush. We admire birds partly because we find them so difficult to imitate – with the possible exception of a handful of species that make far simpler sounds, such as the cuckoo. And when we try to represent their sounds in our own language, for example to form the names of birds, we struggle

---

* The syrinx has recently been found to have evolved far earlier than we thought: evidence of its existence has been found in the fossilised skeleton of a duck-like bird, *Vegavis iaai*, that lived more than 66 million years ago, in the age of the non-avian dinosaurs.

† The wildlife sound recordist Chris Watson once allowed me to listen through headphones to a blackbird singing. Using a parabolic reflector to magnify the sound enabled me to hear a whole series of normally inaudible high-pitched notes, uttered simultaneously with the deeper ones that we usually hear.

to do so, with different people hearing each sound – and then trying to vocalise it – in their own individual manner.

There is also variation in the way people speak any language over time, as we have seen, and so the way we use bird sounds to form names has also varied considerably. Today, when we hear a wood pigeon make its monotonous yet strangely soothing sound, we represent it with the word 'coo'. But according to the linguist W. B. Lockwood our ancestors heard exactly the same sound quite differently, representing it as 'doove', from which we get the modern name 'dove'.* Although it may not be immediately obvious, this is just one example of how the call of a bird can end up as its name, through the power of onomatopoeia.†

There are many others. Take the crow family. Globally there are about 120 different species of crow, only eight of which live in Britain. Four of these are mainly black – the carrion crow, jackdaw, rook and raven – while the other four are more striking and varied in appearance: the chough, with its bright red bill and feet, the grey-and-black hooded crow, the black-and-white magpie and the multi-coloured jay.

At first sight – or perhaps I should say first hearing – the only onomatopoeic name appears to be jackdaw, whose name mimics the 'chack, chack' sound the birds make as flocks fly overhead to roost at dusk on a cold winter's day, looking like scraps of black

---

* The *OED* suggests a different etymology, linking 'dove' with a now lost Old English word meaning 'to dive' or 'to dip'; I have to say I side with Lockwood here.
† Incidentally, the name 'turtle dove' comes from the bird's soft, repetitive call, usually written as 'tur-tur-tur'.

bin-bags caught by the wind.* Yet the other three mainly black species, the raven, rook and carrion crow, are also named after their distinctive sounds.

Each name reflects a version of their harsh cries: just try saying them out loud in the tone of the bird and that becomes far clearer. Given the familiarity of these species, which thrived alongside the early settlers as they ploughed the earth to grow crops, and their superficially similar, mainly black plumage, it is not surprising that they were called after their sound rather than their appearance.

The names raven, rook and crow can all be found in Old English,† which in turn, as we have seen, derived from earlier Germanic languages, the ancestors of modern-day German, Dutch and Scandinavian tongues as well as English. So we might reasonably expect the names we use today for these members of the crow family to be found in other northern European tongues – and we'd be absolutely right. A quick glance at the Scandinavian and Dutch languages soon confirms the links between these birds' names, and their common origin in the sounds made by each species. Rook is *råka* in Swedish, *råge* in Danish and *roek* in Dutch, while the crow is *kråka*, *krage* and *kraai*, and the raven is *korp*, *ravn* and *raaf*. And

---

* The use of the prefix 'Jack' may of course simply be a nickname, as in Robin redbreast or Jenny wren. 'Jack' often signifies male birds, but given that, according to the *OED*, this is particularly used for birds of prey, in which the males are significantly smaller than the females, it may also imply smallness (as in 'jack curlew' for whimbrel, or jack snipe). In the case of the jackdaw, it could be all three at once: signifying a nickname, the bird's smaller size and its onomatopoeic call!

† As *hraefn*, *hroc* and *crawe* respectively. The modern Icelandic word for the raven, *hrafn* (which is also used as a Christian name) is almost identical to the one our Anglo-Saxon ancestors would have used. Incidentally, in both Old English and Old Norse the 'f' sound would have been pronounced as a 'v', making *hraefn* sound even more similar to the modern 'raven'.

we know that because they are so similar in all these languages, they must be very ancient indeed – going back for thousands of years.

Imagine those early hunters, clad in animal skins and carrying primitive spears, glancing up as a raven passed overhead. They would have heard that deep, penetrating cry: a sound so resonant you can feel it passing into the core of your body. Is it too fanciful to assume that one man, inspired by this extraordinary sound, was tempted to imitate the calling bird, and was then copied in turn by his companions? From there it is but a short step to the bird's call becoming its name, and then persisting – with minor changes – to this very day.

But what of the chough, another member of the crow family? Unlike the other 'black' crows, choughs are easy to distinguish, with their glossy blue-black plumage, comically red legs and a long, crimson, de-curved bill, which they poke into the short turf on clifftops to find their invertebrate food.

Take a walk along a Welsh coastal headland, and you may hear the chough's cries being swept away by the fierce wind: a strong, resonant 'chow, chow' sound. How 'chow' became 'chough' is due to one of the English language's most troublesome suffixes. In the English language the suffix 'ough' can be pronounced in at least ten, and arguably twelve, different ways: as in the words cough, rough, plough, through, though, thought, thorough, hough (an alternative spelling of 'hock'), slough (pronounced 'slew' in American English, and meaning a marshy lake), lough (a word used in Ireland, also for a lake, or loch),* hiccough and Middlesbrough.

---

* Surprisingly there is no link to the Gaelic word 'loch' – 'lough' in fact comes from Middle English.

Given this profusion of different ways of pronouncing those four letters, which so confuses the poor learner of English (whether a native child or foreign adult), it is reasonable to surmise that the name of the chough was originally pronounced 'chow' (to rhyme with plough). Some time later, it must have changed to 'chuff' (to rhyme with rough), the pronunciation we still use today.*

5: The Sound Approach

Neither the cuckoo nor those various kinds of crow could be said to have a tuneful voice. Indeed, paradoxically, it is the very simplicity of their sounds that explains why they were originally adopted as the bird's name. Birds with complex, varied songs, such as the blackbird, robin and nightingale, are rarely given onomatopoeic names; those that have simple, repetitive and above all memorable songs, like the cuckoo and chiffchaff, are.

But for many other groups and species of bird, the link between the sound and the name is not so clear. Who would have thought, for instance, that the names rail, crake, kite, smew, bittern and knot all have an onomatopoeic origin? In each case the link between name and sound has become corrupted and changed over time, so that the original connection is not always evident.

With other names, that link with the bird's sound is still there, but may take a little delving to uncover it. Nightjar is, like many English bird names, an amalgamation of two words: the first being

---

* The linguist David Crystal (*in litt*) confirms this, pointing out that such transitions between the 'ow' and 'uff' sounds are reasonably frequent in English.

obvious, as these curious birds are indeed nocturnal, the second less so. 'Jar' is in fact a corruption of the word 'churr', representing the bird's weird rattling call, which echoes across moors and heaths at dusk on spring and summer evenings, and which to the untrained ear sounds more mechanical than avian in origin.

Before so many of our heaths and commons were destroyed by the onset of modern agriculture, the nightjar would have been a far more familiar bird than it is today. Hence it has a plethora of now obsolete folk names, many of which confuse the bird (deliberately, perhaps, because of its nocturnal habits) with another creature of the night, such as 'churn owl', 'goat owl' and, my favourite, 'fern owl'.*

Another name for the nightjar, which was still included in the very first bird book I ever owned, *The Observer's Book of Birds*, is 'goatsucker'. This curious name derives from the notion that night-jars were supposed to feed under the cover of darkness on the milk of goats. Like so many other old wives' tales, there is not a shred of evidence for this; however, given that these mysterious birds may have been attracted to paddocks containing domestic livestock because of the concentration of insects found there at dusk, it is perhaps just about understandable.†

Getting back to onomatopoeic names, I can't resist including a name that my two younger sons still find hilarious, even in their teenage years: hoopoe. The hoopoe – pronounced 'hoo-poo', which explains my boys' amusement – is one of Europe's most striking and unmistakable birds: a boldly patterned black, white and

---

* The nineteenth-century poet John Clare wrote one of his most evocative sonnets, entitled 'The Fern Owl's Nest', on the nightjar – see Chapter 4.
† A much better diet-based name, invented by the ornithologist and sometime poet Mike Toms, is 'moth-gobbler'.

pinkish-orange bird with a prominent crest and appallingly insanitary nesting habits. My friend Marek Borkowski, who lives in the middle of the Biebrza Marshes in Poland, has hoopoes nesting in his garden, and tells me that on hot summer days the stench from their nest inside a tree-hole is almost unbearable.

In fact, though, the name 'hoopoe' derives from the bird's call, a pair of echoing, staccato notes, which carries over a surprisingly long distance. It's not a sound we hear very often in Britain, where the species is a scarce visitor and very occasional breeder, but if you visit a patch of rough farmland in southern or eastern Europe during the spring or early summer you have a good chance of hearing it.

The sound-based origin of the hoopoe's name becomes clearer when we discover that its scientific name is *Upupa epops*, which is doubly onomatopoeic. Richard Holme, writing in the late seventeenth century, referred to 'A Upupa . . . [which] is in our country speech called a Whoophoo, or Whopee, or Hoopoe, and Howpe'.*

The birds that make the most complex sounds are, as you might expect, songbirds: the various species and families that make up roughly half of the world's 10,700 or so bird species. But because their songs are so elaborate, they do not often lend themselves to onomatopoeic names.

The exceptions are those whose songs or calls are suitably simple and memorable, such as the metronomic, constantly repeated

---

* The Dutch have an even greater liking for coining names based on bird sounds than we do. Their name for the hoopoe – *hop* – is commendably succinct, as is *oehoe* for the eagle owl, an incongruously short name for such a huge and impressive bird. The Germans go one better in the brevity stakes: their name for the eagle owl is simply *uhu*, while the French prefer the non-onomatopoeic (and rather pretentious) *grand-duc d'Europe*.

two-note song of the chiffchaff. Heard on a fine spring day, the chiffchaff is far easier to recognise and remember than the more complex song of its cousin the willow warbler, which pours out a silvery series of notes descending the scale with a rather wistful, plaintive tone.

But how we translate even simple birdsongs into names varies across different languages. And just as French cockerels say 'coco-rico', Dutch ones go 'kukeleku' and Chinese say 'goh-geh-goh-goh' (whereas as we British know, they are actually saying 'cock-a-doodle-doo'), so other nations disagree about exactly what sound the chiffchaff* is making. Germans call the species *Zilpʒalp*, the Dutch *tjiftjaf*, while the Finns (whose Finno-Ugric language bears no resemblance to other major European tongues, apart from Hungarian and Estonian) prefer the rather splendid *tiltaltti*.

Other bird names based on sound include, appropriately, 'chat', as in those two charismatic little birds of moor and heath, the stonechat and whinchat. Listening to a stonechat's call, which sounds like two pebbles being knocked together, we might understandably conclude that this is the origin of its name. But as is so often the case with bird names, things are not quite so straightforward.

In fact, the name 'stone chack' was originally given to the wheatear, the stonechat's larger cousin, because of that bird's habit of perching on prominent stones in its moorland breeding territory, while uttering a lip-smacking call. Only as recently as

---

* Oddly, despite the ubiquity of the chiffchaff's song, some languages have chosen names entirely unrelated to its sound. The Scandinavian languages all use the habitat-based name *gransanger*, which translates as 'spruce warbler'; the French choose a motion-based name, *pouillot véloce*, or 'speedy warbler'; and the Spanish plump for the species' ubiquity, *mosquitero común*.

the late eighteenth century was it applied to the stonechat – first as 'stone chatterer', then 'stone chatt', and finally as the name we use today.

This may appear rather messy and confusing, but that is the nature of bird names. Most were not decided by an elite group of experts, but emerged organically when ordinary folk, living in different parts of the country, chose their own names for the birds they came across. And thank goodness they did, for otherwise we might have to rely on professional ornithologists to name our birds, which would no doubt have produced far less varied and imaginative results.*

To discover other names based on the calls of songbirds takes a little more digging, as over time the original sound has often been obscured by shifts in spelling and pronunciation.

It may not be immediately obvious, but the name 'finch' is another example of onomatopoeia. It comes from the commonest member of the family in Britain – our third most numerous breeding species after the wren and robin – the chaffinch.

Looking at a male chaffinch, with his splendid pink breast, dove-grey head and white flashes on his wings, you might assume that such a bird would have been named after its colourful and striking appearance. Yet the word 'finch' actually derives from the Old English 'finc', from the bird's rather monotonous call, usually represented today as 'pink'. Perhaps because the chaffinch is so ubiquitous, this name was later applied to other species such as the goldfinch and greenfinch, and thus to the family as a whole. While

* The exceptions to this are those species named after people (see Chapter 5).

the goldfinch and greenfinch clearly took the prefix of their names from their appearance, the 'chaff' part of the chaffinch's name comes from its preference for feeding on grain amongst the chaff produced by the threshing process.

The original sound made by the chaffinch has now been largely lost in the English version of the name. But it is far more apparent in the modern Dutch *vink*, the German *fink* and the various Scandinavian languages (*fink* or *finke*), suggesting that the original name is even older than we might think, going back well before the birth of Christ. And we can still detect it in several English folk names for the species, all of which are more obviously based on its sound, such as 'pink', 'chink', 'twink', 'tink' and 'spink'.[*]

One characteristic of the chaffinch is that different birds in different parts of the country have distinct local accents. Thus whereas those around my home in Somerset end their song with a fairly standard flourish, on a visit to the Scottish city of Dundee I discovered, to my amusement, that they finish with what sounds remarkably like 'ginger-beer' – leading local children to dub the chaffinch the 'ginger-beer bird'.

The chaffinch's propensity to vary its song from region to region is not a new discovery. Writing in 1600, in his translation of an older French text, 'practitioner in physicke' Richard Surflet observed: 'The spinke is a very beautifull and melodious birde, but all spinkes haue not one and the same tunes.'

---

[*] This last name is still widely used in Scandinavia, and would have been brought here by the Viking invaders, over one thousand years ago. In Britain, Spink is a locally common surname, especially in Yorkshire and Norfolk, where the Vikings would have first landed, and is thought to have originated as a nickname for someone who chattered like a finch.

Not all birds called after the sound they make have onomatopoeic names. Warblers do not all warble, but the name is apt enough to have been used for two totally unrelated families, one in the Old World (Sylviidae), and one in the New World (Parulidae).*

Given the importance of song when we try to identify these often skulking birds, it is perhaps surprising that, apart from the chiff-chaff, only two European warblers have been named after their sound. The best known of these is the grasshopper warbler, an elusive streaky brown bird that announces its presence via its reeling song, which sounds like a cross between an insect and an angler letting out a fishing-reel at speed.† The other is the melodious warbler, a large yellow-and-green species found in western Europe, which regularly turns up in southern Britain on autumn migration. It does indeed have an attractive song, although to my ears it is no more tuneful than, say, the blackcap or garden warbler.‡

The song thrush, too, is named after its persistent and repetitive melody, which can be heard in our parks, gardens and hedgerows from January through to June. Yet it is not universally popular: although many people (including myself) love the song thrush's chatty tone, others (including my wife Suzanne) find it rather tedious. As with any form of music, an appreciation of birdsong is clearly a matter of personal taste.

*

* Worldwide, there are almost 400 different warbler species, including willow, sedge and reed warblers in Europe, and yellow, blackpoll and magnolia warblers in North America.
† The grasshopper warbler belongs to the genus Locustella, named from the species' sonic similarity to a grasshopper or cricket.
‡ The melodious warbler's scientific name, *Hippolais polyglotta*, is a further nod to its vocal talents.

Of all the birds named after their sound few have a greater claim to the title of the world's greatest songster than the nightingale. The male's extraordinary outpouring of notes and phrases, emerging from the densest thicket at full volume on a spring evening, really has to be heard to be believed.

Although it may not be immediately obvious, the nightingale's name is also a reference to its sound: the 'gale' element derives from a Germanic word meaning 'songstress'. This is also found in the modern German, Dutch and Scandinavian names for the bird, *Nachtigall*, *nachtegaal* and *nattergal* – all of which mean 'night singer' – and all of which are, as can be seen by their similarity to one another, very ancient indeed.

The nightingale has always been widely celebrated for its song, by poets, writers and musicians going all the way back to the Ancient Greeks and Romans, and reaching its zenith in the works of the nineteenth-century Romantic Poets such as John Keats.

Two very different poets – John Clare and T. S. Eliot – even attempted to reproduce the specific sounds made by the bird. In 'The Progress of Rhyme', Clare deploys a series of ever more bizarre and eccentric phrases:

> 'Chew-chew chew-chew,' and higher still:
> 'Cheer-cheer cheer-cheer,' more loud and shrill
> 'Cheer-up cheer-up cheer-up,' and dropt
> Low: 'tweet tweet jug jug jug,' and stopt
> One moment just to drink the sound
> Her music made, and then a round
> Of stranger witching notes was heard:

'Wew-wew wew-wew, chur-chur chur-chur,
Woo-it woo-it': could this be her?*

In T. S. Eliot's masterpiece *The Waste Land*, the poet also uses onomatopoeia to convey the nightingale's song:

. . .yet there the nightingale
Filled all the desert with inviolable voice
And still she cried, and still the world pursues,
'Jug Jug' to dirty ears.

In some ways, though, our long and fervent admiration of the nightingale's song strikes me as rather odd. For when people hear one singing for the very first time, they are sometimes shocked. The nightingale's curious outpouring of grunts, tweets and whistles can take a while to get used to – especially if you are used to the more tuneful, sedate, and above all predictable songs of the song thrush, blackbird and robin.

Especially on first hearing, listening to a nightingale is a bit like trying to appreciate modern jazz: you have to relax, forget your preconceptions and allow the sound to wash over you, rather than trying to follow individual melodies. After a while you get used to the bird's improvisational technique, and can at last begin to enjoy what you are hearing.† Then, as has happened ever

---

* Oddly, Clare – who as an expert field-naturalist would surely have known that only the male bird sings – followed poetic convention by depicting the bird as a female in his sonnet 'The Nightingale'.

† Unlike, it must be said, modern jazz.

since human beings first listened to this small, brown and rather unprepossessing-looking bird, you can simply admire one of the most extraordinary of all the world's natural sounds.

Both the nightingale and the cuckoo, the bird with whose sound we began our story, are long-distance migrants: travelling back and forth each spring and autumn between their African winter quarters and their breeding grounds in Britain and Europe.

In the past few years, many of the mysteries surrounding these incredible global journeys have been solved. One major break-through is that scientists are now able to place tiny, ultra-lightweight transmitters on the birds before they leave our shores, which have allowed us to track their movements in forensic detail.*

When the British Trust for Ornithology decided to promote their cuckoo-tracking scheme by giving names to the individual birds being followed, they named one bird after the lead character in a children's book by John Miles. This literary cuckoo was called 'Gowk', after the folk name for the species that goes all the way back to Old English.

Sadly, after a promising start, in which Gowk safely crossed the Channel in mid-July, the tag transmitted only a few low-quality signals, which then disappeared. The conclusion was inescapable: that this particular cuckoo had failed to make it to Africa, and died en route. But his name lives on; and in doing so reflects the

---

* For both the nightingale and the cuckoo, this new information cannot come a moment too soon. Both species are suffering steep declines in numbers, and both are in serious danger of disappearing from large swathes of their former haunts during the next decade or so.

extraordinary persistence of bird names in our language – especially those derived from the sound the bird makes.

For me, it also shows why we should continue to cherish these ancient names: both those that are still in everyday use, like cuckoo, and those, like gowk, that survive only as folk names in certain parts of the country. The wonderful variety of names we give to birds is a reflection of the crucial importance of nature, in both our language and in our lives.

When we delve into the origins of a bird's name, and discover how it first came into being, we discover something vital about ourselves, about our history, and most of all about our relationship with the natural world. At a time when so many species of birds are under threat, we should cherish that deep and lasting connection: not only for what it tells us about our past, but also how it can inform our future, allowing us to better appreciate our interdependence with global biodiversity.

Which brings me back to the cuckoo – or, as I should perhaps say, the gowk. For had it not been for one cataclysmic event, almost a thousand years ago, this is the name we would still be using for this annual harbinger of spring. That event, which took place on a fine autumn day in the year 1066, would forever alter the course of our nation's history and culture. It would also change the very language we speak – including, of course, many of the names we give to birds.

In the next chapter, I shall explore the profound consequences of the final and most momentous invasion of our island nation: the Norman Conquest.

INVASION AND CHANGE

The Beginnings of English

We need words to name and designate things. But we only have a static language with which to express ourselves.

Piet Mondrian

1: *The Ravens' Lament*

Sunday, 15 October 1066 dawned bright, clear and cold across the rolling Sussex landscape. Soon after sunrise, the autumn mists began to melt away, revealing a scene of utter devastation. Six thousand men – two-thirds of them English, the rest Norman – lay dead.

The only movement came from the hordes of glossy, blue-black ravens descending on the stiffening corpses, plucking out their eyes and stabbing at their open wounds to feed on the exposed flesh. The only sound to pierce the deathly silence was the occasional deep, hoarse cry, as one raven pushed a rival away from its own gruesome plunder.

Later that day, the victorious Normans and defeated English returned to the battlefield to claim their dead. Two monks from Waltham Abbey, which had been re-endowed and rebuilt by King Harold Godwinson just six years earlier, began the grisly task of looking for the body of their deposed ruler amongst the accumulated piles of human remains.

Finally, after hours of searching, they came across what they believed to be his corpse. According to one contemporary source, rather than being slain by the proverbial arrow through his eye, as famously depicted in the Bayeux Tapestry, Harold had been brutally hacked to death by four Norman knights:

The first, cleaving his breast through the shield with his point, drenched the earth with a gushing torrent of blood; the second smote off his head below the protection of the helmet and the third pierced the inwards of his belly with his lance; the fourth hewed off his thigh and bore away the severed limb: the ground held the body thus destroyed.*

Harold's body had been so badly mutilated they had to summon Harold's first wife, Edith the Fair (known also, because of her grace and beauty, as Edith Swan-neck) to confirm his identity. Her reaction to seeing her former lover's corpse in this terrible state is not recorded.

His mother Gytha, stricken with grief after losing three of her sons in the battle, requested that Harold's body be returned, allegedly offering his own weight in gold in exchange. Initially William of Normandy, leader of the invading Norman forces, refused, curtly adding: 'Harold mounted guard on the coast while he was alive; he may continue his guard now he is dead.'

But eventually William did relent, and Harold's body – or what was left of it after the ravages inflicted by the Norman army and the ravens – was taken back to Waltham Abbey for a Christian burial. Meanwhile William the Bastard, Duke of Normandy, rode to London to claim the English throne.

On Christmas Day 1066, after several months of skirmishes and political wrangling, he was finally crowned in Westminster Abbey as King William I. The Norman Conquest had well and truly begun.

Historians love to dwell on what they call 'counterfactuals' – speculating on what might have happened had the outcome of a particular

---

* As described by William of Jumièges, writing just four years after the event, in 1070.

historical event been different from what actually transpired. Of all the many alternative scenarios, one of the most intriguing is to consider the history and development of the English language had Harold, rather than William, triumphed at Hastings.

One thing can be said for certain: English would be far less varied, in both syntax and vocabulary, than the language we speak today. Modern English benefits from 'hybrid vigour': the amalgamation of the Norman French spoken by the invaders, and the Old English spoken by the defeated Anglo-Saxons. As the journalist and literary critic Allan Massie points out:

> If you were to begin by asking, in Monty Python style, 'What have the Normans ever done for us?' you might first reply that the most enduring consequence of the Conquest is the richness of the English language, with its Anglo-Saxon base and Franco-Latin superstructure.[1]

Thanks to its mongrel origins, modern English is a fabulously varied and flexible language: not hidebound by complex and unnecessary grammatical rules, and containing a wealth of alternative words for each object or concept – well over twice as many as other languages.

But this linguistic transformation did not happen overnight. At first, just as had occurred between the Roman invaders and the Ancient Britons, the invading Normans and defeated English kept themselves to themselves. Socially – and more importantly for our story, linguistically – the two groups lived separate lives, fuelled by mutual resentment and suspicion.

English remained purely a spoken language, 'an uncultivated

tongue', fit only for labourers, servants and peasants. Norman French, on the other hand, enjoyed a far more elevated status. It was spoken by the nobles, but importantly it was also a written language, used in legal documents, and in the popular genre known as 'Romance' literature. Meanwhile, a third language, Latin (at this point still a spoken as well as a written language), was primarily used in the religious and educational spheres. The end result was a kind of linguistic and social apartheid, with English firmly at the bottom of the pecking order.

The clearest indication of this is the language spoken by kings. Many 'English' monarchs of this period not only spoke French, but also spent most of their time on the other side of the Channel, where they still controlled vast areas of land. Henry II was away from England for almost two-thirds of his reign, while his son Richard the Lionheart (more accurately known as Richard Coeur de Lion) never actually learned to speak the language of his new realm of England.

The fact that royalty – and by extension, the nobility – spoke French, while the labourers continued to speak English, is reflected in the very different words we still use today for farm animals and for the meat they produce. If you walked into a restaurant and ordered a 'cow steak' you would get some pretty funny looks; as you would if you asked for a pig pie, sheep shank or deer casserole.

This is because, while we use names derived from Old English for the creatures themselves – cow, pig, sheep and deer – we call their meat by French names: beef, pork, mutton and venison. This is a direct consequence of the relative social status of two groups of people in the post-conquest world: the English peasants, who tended the animals, and the French nobles, who ate their meat.

Not surprisingly the new arrivals – and their new and unfamiliar language – also influenced bird names. In Old English, the bird we know as the kingfisher was called an *isen* or *isern*, from a word meaning iron-coloured – i.e. blue – which survives in several modern European names for the species, including the German *Eisvogel* and Dutch *ijsvogel*.

From roughly the year 1000 the name 'fisher' first appears (as *fiscere*) in Old English. Sometime in the fourteenth or early fifteenth centuries the compound name 'king's fisher' emerged, probably as a direct translation of the French *roi pêcheur*. This in turn may be linked to the Fisher King, the mythical figure of the Grail legend, the last in the long line of those charged with safeguarding the holy relic. The new name soon gained dominance over any older ones.

Occasionally, instead of the old Anglo-Saxon name giving way to the new Norman one, they both survived. We still use the names 'dove' and 'pigeon': 'dove' mainly for smaller members of the family Columbidae, and 'pigeon' for the larger ones. But their origins are very different. As we have seen, dove probably derives from an Old English word based on the bird's sound, while pigeon comes from the Old French word *pijon*,* and does not appear in English until the late fourteenth century.

Not surprisingly, given the influence of the conquerors, several other bird names we still use today derive directly from Norman French. These include mallard and wigeon, pheasant and partridge, kestrel and merlin, eagle and peregrine.† At first sight these names

---

* Which ultimately derives from the Latin *pipion*, meaning 'young bird', a word that also comes from its sound (from 'pipiare', meaning 'to cheep').

† Peregrine is from a Latin word meaning 'coming from foreign parts'. This first appeared in its Latin form *peregrinus* around the year 1250, when the writer Albertus

– and indeed the birds themselves – do not appear to have much in common with one another; so we might easily assume that their common French origin is simply a linguistic accident.

But take a closer look. All these species are either wildfowl or gamebirds, which would have been pursued for food and sport; or raptors, used for falconry and hunting. In exactly the same way that beef, pork and venison have French names because they were too expensive for the commoners to eat, so the invading Norman aristocracy gave names to all these birds, as these were the ones they encountered most often in their day-to-day lives. The new names rapidly displaced the Old English ones that had been used until then, which have long since fallen into disuse.

So even at this early stage in our society, the differences between the elite nobility and the labouring classes that would come to define English society were already beginning to show.

You might reasonably assume that as Old English gradually merged with Norman French to create Middle, and later Modern, English, then the now mostly incomprehensible Anglo-Saxon names would vanish too, to be replaced by those with a Latin origin. But as we shall see, the opposite proved to be the case. A surprisingly large proportion of the names we still use today – including redstart, yellowhammer, fieldfare, lapwing and wheatear – have their origins in the pre-Conquest tongue.

Yet if you assume you know what these names actually mean, you may need to think again. For in that change from Old to Middle,

Magnus noted that young birds caught on migration proved better for falconry than those taken straight from the nest. It has since gained the more general meaning of 'wandering', as in the word peregrination, which originally referred to a lifelong spiritual journey or pilgrimage, but now usually refers to any kind of meandering voyage.

and later to Modern English, something very strange happened – something that reveals that names, and other proper nouns, behave in a significantly different way from other words in our language.

2: *Red Tails and White Arses*

What is the commonest surname in Britain, and indeed throughout much of the English-speaking world? It is, of course, Smith. More than half a million people in the United Kingdom, and over two million in the United States, are called Smith, which is also the commonest surname in Australia and the second commonest in Canada.*

The name Smith means 'one who works with metal' – and dates all the way back to Anglo-Saxon times, when men were often named after the job they did. It is not the only profession-based surname still in widespread use today: others include Cooper (meaning barrel-maker), Mason (as in stonemason), Miller (of grain), Turner (of wood) and Taylor (of clothes), all of which feature in the list of the top hundred commonest surnames in England and Wales.

Given that none of these professions is widely practised today (though some of us like to think of ourselves as 'wordsmiths'), their survival is clearly down to the longstanding custom of giving children the same surname as their father, however irrelevant the

---

* It is also a very common name in German (*Schmidt* or *Schmitt*) and Dutch (*Smid* or *Smidt*), and has direct parallels in Romance languages, such as the Italian *Ferrero* (meaning ironworker) and the French *Fabre*. The pseudonym 'John Smith' is also the one most frequently adopted by British men who do not wish to reveal their true identity for personal or nefarious reasons.

original meaning of that name may now be; a practice that began far back in the thirteenth and fourteenth centuries.

Many common place names in Britain also contain elements that reveal their pre-Norman origins. So we still use the suffix '-by', an Old Norse word meaning 'settlement', as in Selby and Whitby, '-ham', the Old English for farm or homestead, and the ubiquitous '-chester', which originally came into our language from Latin, indicating a Roman fort. As with surnames, once a name of a particular place has become established in common use, it proves remarkably resistant to change.

You might not be surprised to learn that the names we use for birds are no exception to this rule. But to discover their original meaning requires a degree of linguistic detective work, because they are effectively 'in disguise'. Over the centuries many have changed into a completely different word, by means of a process that linguists call 'folk [or false] etymology'.

Take two well-known British birds: the redstart, a close relative of the robin, and the yellowhammer, a canary-coloured member of the bunting family. We use these names so frequently that we no longer even notice just how peculiar they are. Yet if we think about them, they make absolutely no sense at all: redstarts are not especially jumpy, and nor do yellowhammers have a particularly percussive call.

These names, along with many others, including fieldfare, lapwing and wheatear, are classic examples of the peculiar propensity for archaic words to survive in names far longer than they would in other aspects of our language. But as their original meaning became less and less clear, the Anglo-Saxon names were eventually transformed into more familiar words. These usually have little or no connection with the original meaning, and so can mislead the unwary.

Thus the Old English word *steort*, meaning tail, transmuted into 'start' (hence redstart, and its scarcer cousin, the black redstart). Likewise, the 'hammer' in the name of our most colourful bunting is nothing to do with tools, but is a corruption of *Ammer*, the word still used for bunting in German today.*

Yet even by the late eighteenth century, the name yellowhammer, while widely used as a folk name, was still not fully established as the official name for this species. The naturalist Thomas Pennant preferred the alternative 'yellow bunting', in a tidy-minded attempt to bring the yellowhammer in line with its cousins the reed, corn and snow buntings. But less than a century later, the Victorian ornithologist William Yarrell changed the name back again, adding a helpful explanation of its origin for his readers: 'I have ventured to restore to this bird what I believe to have been its first English name, Yellow Ammer. The word Ammer is a well-known German term for Bunting.'

Other familiar birds provide further examples of how folk etymology can mislead us. Around my Somerset home, the first sign that winter is on its way comes with the arrival each autumn of large flocks of redwings, fieldfares and lapwings, refugees from the north. These birds travel here to enjoy the benefits of our relatively mild winter climate and the plentiful food this brings.

Their names, at least at first glance, appear to make perfect sense.

---

* Confusingly, though, in German the yellowhammer is the *Goldammer*, while several English folk names also prefer gold to yellow, as in 'golden amber' and 'gladdie' or 'go-laddie', now obsolete West Country names which probably derived from the phrase 'gold laddie'.

The redwing is a small, dark thrush from Iceland, sporting a rufous patch on its flanks. The fieldfare, its larger, more colourful cousin, arrives each November from its breeding grounds in Scandinavia and northern Russia, greedily feasting on berries in hedgerows and probing for worms as it 'fares over' muddy fields. And the lapwing, also known as the peewit from its distinctive piping call, has a very distinctive flight action; as flocks pass overhead on a fine winter's day, the alternating flashes of dark upperwing and white underwing appear to 'lap' through the sky like swimmers in a calm blue sea.

And yet of this trio of winter visitors to my own corner of the West Country, only the redwing's name actually means what it suggests: a bird with a red coloration on (or near) its wing. The other two have far more complex origins, and very different meanings from the obvious ones.

The linguist W. B. Lockwood made short work of the *OED*'s more prosaic interpretation of the fieldfare's name: 'The name is clearly corrupt; the explanation that the meaning is somehow field-farer is just the obvious guess – and quite as obviously improbable . . . for dozens of species fare over fields.'[2]

He had a point. As an alternative, Lockwood proposed that the name of what Chaucer called 'the frosty feldefare' comes from a long-lost Old English phrase meaning 'grey piglet', a reference to the bird's colour and its harsh, grunting call. Only once Old English gave way to the more modern, French-influenced language, and this meaning had become obsolete – just like the suffixes 'start' and 'ammer' – did this ungainly thrush gain its misleading modern name.*

---

* The first written reference to 'fieldfare' – with the modern (and etymologically incorrect) spelling – appears in John Florio's pioneering dictionary, *Worlde of Wordes*, in 1598.

To most people, the meaning of the name 'lapwing' appears equally obvious. Yet, once again, Lockwood disagreed with the easy explanation. Digging down into Old English, he discovered a reference from before the Norman Conquest to the bird as the 'hléapewince'. He believed that the name refers to the prominent tuft of feathers on top of the bird's head, and translated it as 'movable crest'.*

We can trace the gradual changes in the bird's name through time: from 'hléapewince' (first noted in AD 1050), through 'lhapwynche' (1340), 'lappewinke' (1390), 'lapwyng' (1430) and finally the one we use today, lapwing (1591). Soon afterwards, in 1604, that name appeared in the climactic final act of Shakespeare's *Hamlet*, in which Horatio taunts the hurried departure of Osric by comparing him with a newly hatched chick:

This Lapwing runs away with the shell on his head.

This casual insult reveals that Shakespeare had more ornithological expertise than we might give him credit for: he clearly knew that lapwing chicks are precocial, meaning that they are able to leave the nest almost immediately after they are born.

The best known of what my old French teacher Mr Schrecker used to call 'faux amis' (false friends, because they mislead the unwary) is the name 'wheatear'.

---

* The *OED* dissents from this view, however, maintaining that the original name was a combination of two words meaning 'to leap' and 'to totter, waver or wink', and so does indeed refer to the bird's flight, in which the alternating dark upperwing and white underwings look rather like a winking eye.

Wheatears are showy members of the chat family – cousins of the robin and nightingale – with roughly two-dozen representatives, mainly found in the arid, stony deserts of North Africa and the Middle East. Just one species (officially known as the northern wheatear to distinguish it from its heat-loving southern cousins) has managed to extend its range northwards into the temperate regions of Europe, including Britain.

Wheatears are one of the earliest spring migrants to arrive back from Africa, turning up in fields of short-cropped grass from the middle of March onwards. Even though this kind of grass and wheat are not the same plant, people have tended to assume that the bird's name must be somehow connected with our most widespread arable crop.

But this perky little bird has nothing whatsoever to do with ears of wheat. The Anglo-Saxon name, which unfortunately has not survived in print, was probably 'wheteres'. The final 's' on this singular noun provides a crucial clue to its real meaning: 'white-arse'. This is a reference to the wheatear's most prominent feature, its bright white rump, which is revealed as soon as the bird takes to the wing and flits away from you. To confirm this, we need look no further than two dialect names for the species: 'white rump', from Northumberland, and the blunter 'white ass' from Cornwall.

By the seventeenth century the origin of the wheatear's name had already been long forgotten, as can be seen from two contemporary accounts. In *Worthies of England*, published posthumously in 1662, the historian Thomas Fuller pronounced with great authority that: 'It [the wheatear] is so called, because fattest when wheat is ripe . . . whereon it feeds.'[3]

The other comes from the English poet John Taylor who, in August 1653, set out on what he called 'The certain travailes of an uncertain journey', 'for no other intent or purpose, but to plea-sure himself, and to please his friends in the first place'. Taylor's perambulations coincided with the start of the autumn bird migra-tion season, during which he came across 'rare Birds I never saw before', adding in a dreadful example of doggerel:

> Th' are called wheat-ears, less than lark or sparrow,
> Well roasted, in the mouth they taste like marrow.

Having never actually eaten a wheatear, well-roasted or not, I cannot attest to Taylor's culinary tastes, but I do know that his ornithological knowledge was severely limited, as this later couplet reveals:

> The name of wheat-ears, on them is ycleap'd,
> Because they come when wheat is yearly reap'd.[4]

We can only hope that the rest of his account was more accurate than this entirely false piece of speculation (and rather bad poetry).

But what is puzzling is how the English language could have changed so radically that these contemporaries of Marvell and Milton could no long decode the names that had been coined a thousand years earlier, back in Anglo-Saxon times. *When* this rift in understanding happened is easy to answer – some time during the thirteenth century. *How*, and especially *why* it did so, is a little trickier. And the explanation helps to solve a puzzle that may have already occurred to you: why is a blackbird called a blackbird, when so many other birds are also black?

3: Sex, Chaucer and Blackbirds

The way English evolved from an obscure and rather inflexible Germanic tongue into the rich, fluid, complex language we all speak today comes down, as with so many things, to sex.

Fortunately for the future of the English language, the initial stand-off between Normans and Saxons could not last for ever. The mutual attraction between noble French lords and comely English maidens (and perhaps also between aristocratic French ladies and muscular sons of the soil) inevitably led to social and sexual interactions between the two groups. Soon afterwards, these turned into more formal and permanent liaisons. Thus by the late twelfth century one chronicler could observe: 'Now that the English and Normans have been dwelling together, marrying and giving in marriage, the two nations have become so mixed that it is scarcely possible today . . . to tell who is English, who of Norman race.'[5]

Then, as the English monarchs withdrew from their possessions in France following successive military defeats, something rather odd happened. In other countries where two or more languages are habitually spoken, such as Switzerland and Belgium, they usually remain clearly separate, each used by a different community. Alternatively, as in Scotland and Ireland where English displaced Gaelic, the conquerors' language eventually triumphs at the expense of the original one.

But in England, the competing tongues of what had started off as Old English and Norman French underwent a kind of mutually agreed merger, creating a completely new language with features from both its parents: what we now call Middle English.

This new language was in many ways more complex than those it replaced, with a far more extensive vocabulary, thanks to the borrowing of 'loan words' from Norman French and Latin. Some of these displaced the Old English word entirely, but more often than not the old and new words co-existed alongside one another, endowing our language with a plethora of synonyms. Thus today we can choose between words of both Germanic and Romance origin, which mean more or less the same thing: for example, 'kingly' and 'royal', 'pretty' and 'beautiful', or 'wed' and 'marry'.

But crucially, this new language was also more straightforward than its parent tongues, in several important ways. Technical aspects such as inflexions (sets of endings added to words to indicate grammatical case, number and gender) were either lost or greatly simplified.* It is not unreasonable to suggest that this, along with the rich extra vocabulary provided by merging the two different languages, was one important reason for the eventual adoption of English as a global *lingua franca*.

Of course, as we have seen in the previous chapter, this process had actually begun long before the Norman Conquest, with the Viking invasions of northern and eastern England, from the late eighth century until around the time of the Norman invasion, leading to many of the Scandinavian invaders settling on this side of

---

* Modern English does still uses some inflexions, for example the possessive – 'the girl's book' – and to indicate the difference between singular and plural – 'boy' and 'boys'.

the North Sea. Not only did Old English borrow many loan-words from Old Norse, but the shifting grammar also began at this point, with the system of grammatical inflexions being streamlined. 'In order to facilitate communication', notes Professor Simon Horobin from the University of Oxford, 'the two groups of speakers must have placed less stress on the inflexional endings; as a consequence, the Old English system of inflexions began to break down.'[6]

But the most revolutionary change was the almost total disappearance of grammatical gender. Old English, like modern German, had three different genders – masculine, feminine and neuter – but during the transformation into Middle English these distinctions gradually disappeared. Interestingly, this process appears to have begun in the north of England, under the influence of the Vikings; gender disappeared there some time during the twelfth century, earlier than it vanished in the south.

The impact of this cannot be overstated. As we British discover to our cost when we come to learn a foreign language, what must seem perfectly natural to generations of French, Spanish and German children – the use of gender to qualify nouns, as in 'le chat', 'el perro' and 'das Auto' – is a real struggle for native English speakers, for whom gender in language effectively disappeared almost a thousand years ago.

By the time of Geoffrey Chaucer, who was writing in the closing years of the fourteenth century, the competing claims of Old English and Norman French were over, and Middle English was firmly established – a language that, with a little effort on the part of the reader, can still be understood today.

*

Although Chaucer is rightly celebrated for his classic works, most notably *The Canterbury Tales*, we should not forget that he also contributed to the slow but steady growth in the understanding of Britain's birdlife. The ornithologist and broadcaster James Fisher described him as an 'ornithological hero', and while this may be a slight overstatement, it does have some validity. As Fisher points out, Chaucer not only knew the names of more than forty species of birds, he also added several others to the embryonic list of birds seen in Britain, which by the time of his death in 1400 had reached the landmark 100 species.

One of Chaucer's best-known works, 'The Parlement of Foules', features more than thirty British birds, which have gathered together to choose their mates. These range in size from the robin to the swan, and include resident species like the lark and the lapwing, and migrants such as the turtle dove, cuckoo, nightingale and swallow, along with more exotic visitors (perhaps commoner in those days), including the stork and the crane.

But one common and widespread bird is missing from this otherwise comprehensive catalogue of species: the blackbird. Its absence conceals a fascinating story of one of the most profound changes of all: the switch from 'fowl', the standard word for all birds in Chaucer's time, to the one we use today: 'bird'.

Bird names don't come much more basic than that of the most familiar member of the thrush family: the blackbird. It's a bird, and it's black. End of.

Except that, when you start to think about it, lots of other birds are black, too. Crows, rooks, ravens and jackdaws would also have been common, widespread and very familiar to our rural ancestors. So out of all these 'black birds', why did they choose just one species for this epithet?

This is only confusing because we are looking at the name from the wrong angle. For the key word here is not 'black', but 'bird'. This goes back to the Anglo-Saxon word *brid*, which comes from the same root as the words 'breed' and 'brood'. It had a very different meaning from the modern word 'bird', and referred purely to baby birds or fledglings, as the *OED* explains in its primary definition of the word:

> Bird, *n*. The general name for the young of the feathered tribes; a young bird; a chicken, eaglet, etc.; a nestling. *The only sense in Old English; found in literature down to 1600.* [My italics]

So what were adult birds called? Until long after the Norman Conquest they were known as fowls, from the Old English 'fugol' (or in *Beowulf*, 'fugle').*

But gradually, around the time Chaucer was writing (towards the end of the fourteenth century), the original meaning of 'bird' was starting to change. Indeed, Chaucer himself occasionally uses the word in its modern sense: in his poem 'The Legend of Good Women', written around the year 1385, he makes a passing reference to 'whanne the brid began to synge. . .'

The title 'Parlement of Foules' is one of the last recorded examples of fowl being used to refer to all shapes and sizes of bird, large and small. About this time, 'bird' started to be used to denote the

* Closely related to the modern Dutch and German words for bird, *Vogel*.

86

smaller species – those that today we call songbirds, although the name 'foules' persisted for larger birds.

So whereas today the meaning of the spoken phrase 'there's a black bird' could be unclear, referring perhaps to a crow or raven rather than a blackbird, in those days such ambiguity was not a problem, as those larger species would have been known as 'foules'.* So the name 'blackbird' made perfect sense.

The use of 'fowl' to mean all birds persisted well into the seventeenth and eighteenth centuries, as in the *King James Bible* of 1611, which in the opening chapter of the Book of Genesis refers to 'every fowl of the air'. But the new distinction between the two words was becoming more established. In Dr Johnson's epic *Dictionary of the English Language*, first published in 1755, the great lexicographer defines the word 'bird' thus:

A general term for the feathered kind; a fowl. In common talk, fowl is used for the larger, and bird for the smaller kind of feathered animals.

This distinction can still be found in some parts of Scotland, where larger birds are known as 'fowls' and smaller ones are 'birds' – as in 'muir [moor] fowl', a common Scots term for red grouse. But elsewhere the use of 'fowl' is today mostly confined to domestic birds such as chickens, or other groups of larger birds. These include 'wildfowl' and 'waterfowl' (ducks, geese and swans), and

---

* In practice, as David Crystal has pointed out, we can still tell the difference, as 'black bird' is stressed equally on both syllables, whereas in 'blackbird' only the first syllable is stressed.

the names guineafowl and peafowl (the correct term for the species we usually call the peacock).*

Given the very specialised original meaning of the word 'bird', it is perhaps not surprising that the first recorded use of the name 'blackbird' is as recent as 1350, as 'blacbrid'.

So what would the blackbird have been called before this time? A clue lies in the name we still use today for its upland counterpart, the ring ouzel. Alternatively spelled 'ousel' or 'wosel', this derives from the same root as the modern German word for the blackbird, *Amsel*. Also known as the mountain (or moor, fell or hill) blackbird, the male ring ouzel can be told apart from its commoner cousin by the distinctive white band across its upper breast – hence the name ring ouzel.

A further clue to the blackbird's old name comes in Act 3 of Shakespeare's *A Midsummer Night's Dream*, when Bottom refers to 'the Woosell cocke, so blacke of hew, with orange-tawny bill. . .' This must be the blackbird, as ring ouzels have pale edges to their feathers and a pale lemon-yellow bill, whereas male blackbirds are indeed all black, and their bill is a deep orange-yellow shade. Even though the name 'blackbird' has been around for more than 600 years, in some parts of northern England and the Midlands blackbirds were still widely referred to as 'ouzels' well into the twentieth century, in another example of the remarkable persistence of folk names. The Nottinghamshire-born author D. H. Lawrence certainly used the

---

* It also survives in a handful of ancient folk names, such as 'rain fowl', for the green woodpecker, whose ringing call is supposed to herald a change in the weather; and 'gare-fowl', for the now extinct great auk.

name 'black ousel', having learned it from his mother, who would often lapse into archaic words and phrases from her childhood.*

Not surprisingly, given our fondness for this common and familiar species, the name 'blackbird' has spread around the world. Today it is used for several close relatives of our species, such as the grey-winged, Indian, Tibetan and white-collared blackbirds of Asia, and also for a group of entirely unrelated birds found in the Americas, the family Icteridae, which includes the colourful New World orioles and oropendolas as well as the crow-like grackles, parasitic cowbirds and colourful meadowlarks.

The New World use of the name 'blackbird' dates back to the earliest settlers in North America. In 1602, the Norfolk clergyman turned adventurer John Brereton wrote of the birds he encountered in northern Virginia: 'We saw in the country . . . Doves, Sea-pies [Oystercatchers], Blacke-birds with carnation wings.'[7]

This refers to the most abundant North American bird, the red-winged blackbird, which does indeed superficially resemble our own species – until it takes flight, to reveal bright crimson epaulettes on each shoulder.

In this strange new world, it is perhaps no surprise that when homesick settlers such as Brereton encountered a new species of bird, they looked for any superficial resemblance to a more familiar species back home, and named it accordingly – something we shall investigate further in Chapter 4.

---

* Another, unrelated species also retained the name 'ouzel' until at least the middle of the nineteenth century, as this line from Charles Kingsley reveals: 'The startled water-ousel, with his white breast, flitted a few yards.' The mention of the white breast immediately gives away the bird's identity: the author of *Westward Ho!* and *The Water-Babies* is of course referring to the dipper.

4: Fifty Shades of Green?

The blackbird is just one of over 130 species on the official 'British List'* (totalling just over 600 species in all) whose names feature at least one colour.

Not surprisingly, given their prominence in the plumage of so many birds, red and black are the top two colours, with thirty-two and thirty species respectively. Bird names we have already come across featuring these colours include redstart, red grouse and redwing, along with blackcap, blackbird and – with two for the price of one – black redstart.

Next on the list comes yellow, with fourteen species, including yellowhammer and yellow wagtail, then white, with thirteen species, including whitethroat (and of course lesser whitethroat). Grey is surprisingly high on the list, in fifth place, with twelve species, including grey heron, phalarope, wagtail and plover, while gold/ golden and green have nine and eight species respectively, including several 'golden' plovers, golden eagle, goldfinch, greenfinch and green woodpecker.

One colour that comes surprisingly low on the list, with just seven species, is blue. Yet while blue may be a ubiquitous colour in the human world, when it comes to the plumage of birds it is fairly

* The official British List of birds accepted as having been seen in a truly wild state in Great Britain (England, Scotland and Wales and associated waters) has been maintained by the British Ornithologists' Union (BOU) since 1879. The current figures were taken in spring 2017, but do change as new birds are added and/or their names are revised.

rare. Of common British birds only the kingfisher is predominantly blue, and is named after its feeding habits rather than appearance; the blue tit, on the other hand, has a prominent blue crown and tail, but is in fact mainly yellow and green.*

It may seem obvious to name a bird after its colour, but it is a system not without pitfalls, and colour-based names can sometimes confuse the unwary. For instance, female and young male blackbirds are brown, while the female blackcap has a chestnut-coloured crown. Grey wagtails are indeed grey, but they also show prominent flashes of lemon yellow, and so are often mistaken for their cousin, the yellow wagtail.†

Later on, as ornithologists began to explore further afield, they soon found that, as they discovered more species, they needed more and more subtle ways of telling them apart. And so a second tranche of colour-based names began to emerge. These go beyond the usual reds, blacks, whites, greens, blues and yellows to encompass more complex and subtle shades. The best known of these is 'pied', as in pied flycatcher and pied wagtail. Others include roseate (tern), snowy (owl), tawny (owl and pipit), dun (meaning brown, as in dunnock and dunlin), buff (buff-bellied pipit and buff-breasted sandpiper), coal (tit), rose (-ringed parakeet) and ruddy (duck).

* The remaining colours that appear in the names of birds on the British List are brown and purple, with four each, including brown shrike and purple heron; and finally pink, with just one: pink-footed goose. Incidentally, the reason no British bird has the name 'orange' is that this colour did not enter the English language until the late Middle Ages, by which time most common birds – including the robin redbreast – had already been named.

† Any 'yellow' wagtail seen in winter – or on a fast-flowing river at any time of year – is definitely a grey wagtail, as yellow wagtails are spring and summer visitors to Britain, usually found in wet meadows.

Heading north, the globe-trotting ornithologists came across two Arctic species of seabird, whose pallid plumages led to them being dubbed ivory and glaucous gulls – the latter from the Greek *glaukós* (via Latin *glaucus*), and meaning pale bluish-grey or green.

As they explored other bird-rich continents such as Africa, Asia and South America, they discovered various reddish-yellow species, including an antshrike, babbler, owl, wren and whistling duck, all of which were given the Latin-derived epithet 'fulvous'. Darker, more reddish-brown ducks, hawks, partridges and pygmy owls were described as 'ferruginous', from the Latin for iron-coloured or rusty; while a tiger heron and imperial pigeon, whose colour can best be described, in the wise words of the *OED*, as 'of a colour tending to reddish; somewhat rufous. . .' were named 'rufescent'.

Within a particular family, too, many different subtleties of colour and shade are needed in order to name a host of similar-looking species. Take the Old World Warblers: a family comprising roughly 280 species found in Europe, Asia and Africa (including, of course, Mrs Moreau's eponymous bird). These birds are famously tricky to identify in the field, mainly because very few (with the exceptions of the blackcap and whitethroat – both named after their most obvious plumage feature) are easy to tell apart from their cousins. Indeed, most appear to be basically brown, green or yellowish in shade: what birders often contemptuously dismiss as 'LBJs' or 'little brown jobs'.

If we just look at two colours, yellow and green, there is a plethora of subtly different ways of naming a species after its shade. Some are obvious, such as yellow-breasted and lemon-throated. Others are far more refined, among them the descriptors olivaceous, sulphur-bellied and icterine – the last deriving from the Greek *ikteros*, meaning jaundiced, from the erroneous belief that a sighting of a yellow bird was supposed to cure this medical condition.

In the Americas there is another family of superficially similar-looking birds, known as wood-warblers, which like the American blackbirds were named by homesick settlers after familiar species they recalled from back in Britain. This family includes even more birds whose names feature a green, gold or yellow hue, such as black-throated green, citrine (meaning lemon-coloured), golden-cheeked, green-tailed, grey-and-gold, olive-capped, yellow-rumped and a dozen different species of yellowthroat.*

There are some species whose colours and shades are so subtle they can only be described with what the ornithologist and author Jeremy Mynott called 'a nice note of ruminative hesitation'.[8] These include *greenish* warbler, *reddish* egret, *yellowish* flycatcher and the rather sad-sounding *greyish* mourner, a South American flycatcher.

But of all the names of birds on the British list named after colours and shades, the most fascinating story of all is the supposed origin of a name given to two rare vagrants, a shrike and a wheatear: each of which rejoices in the name Isabelline. The story of how they acquired this unusual epithet takes us to the next stage in the story of how birds got their names: the beginnings of modern ornithology.

---

* Although most New World warblers are named after the predominant shades of yellow or green, there are also cerulean, a deep shade of blue, and plumbeous, meaning lead-coloured.

3

HISTORY AND SCIENCE

The Birth of Ornithology

'What's the use of their having names,' the Gnat said, 'if they won't answer to them?'

'No use to them,' said Alice; 'but it's useful to the people that name them, I suppose. If not, why do they have names at all?'

Lewis Carroll, Through the Looking-Glass

1: Dirty Underwear

12 August 1566 was an auspicious day for the Spanish royal family. It saw the birth of Princess Isabella Clara Eugenia, a little girl whose royal pedigree was second to none. She was not only the daughter of the mighty King Philip II of Spain, but also the granddaughter of the two most powerful rulers in the Renaissance world: the Holy Roman Emperor Charles V and the French king Henry II.

Princess Isabella's arrival was a triumph of hope over experience. Her 21-year-old mother, Elisabeth of Valois, had previously miscarried twin girls, and had also survived a bout of smallpox, which nearly killed her. So Princess Isabella's father greeted his daughter's safe delivery with more than the usual relief and joy.*

During her long and eventful life, Isabella did her best to live up to her distinguished royal antecedents. She was a strong and determined woman, and more than held her own in this male-dominated world. Indeed, her stubbornness is at the root of a curious legend: one that links her with the names of several species of bird and mammal.

The adjective 'Isabelline' is found in the English name of three species of bird: a shrike, a wheatear and a bush-hen (a type of rail from the Indonesian province of Sulawesi), and in the scientific names of several others. It has also been used to describe a

---

* Sixteen months later, Elisabeth gave birth to Isabella's younger sister Catherine; less than a year later, after miscarrying another daughter, she was dead. Isabella was just two years old.

distinctively pale form of the Himalayan brown bear, *Ursus arctos isabellinus*, and several breeds of horses and dogs.

All these creatures have one thing in common: their predominant coloration is a dirty greyish-brown, as though they need a good wash. Given the legend of how this very unusual shade got its name, this is rather apt.

From infancy, Isabella was expected to marry for strategic and political reasons, rather than for love. At just two years old, she was betrothed to her cousin, the future Holy Roman Emperor Rudolf II. But when she reached maturity, it became clear that the eccentric, depressed and probably homosexual Rudolf was never going to honour his original agreement to wed her.

In 1599 – at the relatively advanced age of thirty-two – she finally married Rudolf's younger brother, Archduke Albert of Austria. A later portrait, by the artist Peter Paul Rubens, shows the couple posing side-by-side, for, despite the somewhat inauspicious start to their married life, they remained devoted to one another until Albert's death in 1621.

Back in 1598, a year before the couple wed, the dying Philip II had installed Albert and Isabella as joint rulers of the Netherlands. Saying that they were in charge of this far-flung corner of the vast Spanish Empire was one thing; maintaining control over it proved quite another. To combat the growing threat from Spain, the English and Dutch joined forces to defend the city of Ostend, and Archduke Albert was sent to win it back.

In a gesture of marital devotion and self-sacrifice, his loving wife Isabella vowed not to change her undergarments until the siege was over. But unfortunately for her, Albert and especially the belea-guered people of Ostend, there was no quick resolution to this bloody conflict. The siege lasted another three long years, during which more than 100,000 people perished, in what was described by one contemporary as 'a long carnival of death'.*

After the eventual Spanish victory, in the autumn of 1604, Isa-bella was finally permitted to remove her underwear. By then, it had turned a rather unpleasant shade of greyish-brown, duly dubbed 'Isabelline', after the defiant monarch.

There is only one teensy little problem with this rather repugnant, yet strangely touching, tale: the word 'Isabella' had been used to describe exactly the same colour several years before the siege ever took place. It first surfaces in 1600, in an inventory of royal garments, amongst whose pages we find 'one rounde gowne of Isabella-colour satten . . . set with silver spangles'.[1]

Confronted with this troublesome fact, proponents of the legend quickly switch their attention to another famous queen: Isabella of Castile, who reigned jointly with her husband Ferdinand of Ara-gon during the latter years of the fifteenth century. Conveniently, Ferdinand also took part in a siege – of the Moorish stronghold of Granada. Although this conflict lasted less than just nine months, from April 1491 to January 1492, there would still have been plenty of time for his spouse's underwear to turn that rather dingy shade of greyish-brown.

I hate to contradict such beguiling tales, but both these stories

---

* In the words of the historian Anna Simoni, 'the Spanish assailed the unassailable; the Dutch defended the indefensible'. *Ostend Story* (2003).

may have arisen as a convenient way to explain an etymological coincidence. It appears that 'Isabelline' is more likely to be a corruption of the Italian word *zibellino*. This name was given to a pelt of an animal such as a marten or sable, worn as a fashion accessory by wealthy women during the sixteenth century. It may originally derive from an Arabic word meaning 'lion' – and therefore mean 'lion-coloured'.*

The theory goes that when this term was first heard in England, it somehow became associated with Queen Isabella, and the word changed as a result. I must say, though, I still prefer the royal underwear theory.

2: *Folk and Fowls*

Whatever the truth about its origins, the use of the name 'Isabelline' marks the beginning of an era that saw an explosion in the number of species given English names.

According to James Fisher, from 1460 to 1776 the 'British List' doubled from roughly 114 species at the start of this period, to 228 species by the end. Given that about 250 or so species of breeding, migrant and wintering birds are found in Britain today, we can see that by the late eighteenth century the vast majority of common birds had been given English names – or, to put it more precisely,

---

* We may never know the true origin of a word that does not appear in the *OED* until as late as 1859, in a description of desert-dwelling birds in the journal *Ibis* written by the distinguished ornithologist Henry Baker Tristram (see Chapter 5): 'The upper plumage of every bird, whether Lark, Chat, Sylvian, or Sand-grouse . . . is of one uniform isabelline or sand colour.'

official English names. Most familiar species already had a wealth of folk names: some widely used throughout Britain, others confined to particular localities or regions.

Folk names are just that – everyday names coined by everyday folk. Many, though quaint and wonderfully descriptive, have long since vanished through disuse. Others, though – including robin, dunnock and wren – ultimately became the accepted name for the species.

As we have already seen, colour and shade feature in many early bird names, often dating back to well before the Norman Conquest. But there's a problem with naming birds after an aspect of their appearance. And that is that, unlike sounds, colours are not unique to a single species. So it's not surprising that the same name was often used to describe several different, and often unrelated, species.

Take the name 'blackcap'. Today this refers solely to the greyish-brown warbler *Sylvia atricapilla*, whose males sport a prominent black crown. But over time the name has also been used for other species of bird with black on their heads, including marsh, coal and great tits, reed bunting, and even black-headed gull. One name for several species.

The opposite was also true. The proliferation of folk names up and down the country meant that a single species was often called completely different things in different places, a recipe for muddle and misunderstanding.

So in parts of Scotland and northern England the yellowhammer (which, as we have already seen, might be called the 'golden amber', 'gladdie' or 'go-laddie') was known as the 'yoldring'.* Even more confusingly, in other parts of Britain it was called the 'goldfinch', the name normally given to the small, tuneful member of the finch family with a red face and yellow flashes on its wings.

In turn, the goldfinch also had a wealth of alternative names (as you might expect for such a common and colourful bird). These included 'red cap', from its crimson face patch; 'thistle finch', an allusion to its diet of thistle seeds; and the sartorially inventive 'proud tailor', referring to its smart plumage. More obscure names included 'sheriff's man', after the black and gold livery worn by sheriffs, and 'King Harry'. As Lockwood suggested, the latter was probably a cheeky reference to King Henry VIII: 'that monarch's ostentatious attire being linked with the ornate plumage of the bird'.[2]

Sadly, the vast majority of these alternative folk names are now long forgotten. However, despite the fact that modern English is becoming more homogenous, due in part to the influence of television and the Internet, a handful of folk names have managed to survive to the present-day. Across much of Britain people still call lapwings 'peewits' (or in Lincolnshire, 'pyewipes'), after their plaintive, penetrating call; while the green woodpecker is still occasionally known as the 'yaffle', in reference to the laughing sound it makes as it flies away from you.†

But the drive towards coining official names would inevitably lead to a simplification in the plethora of different folk names for

---

* Alternative spellings include youldring, yowdring, yoldrin, yaldrin, yaldran, yeld(e)rin and yieldrin.

† It can, of course, be argued that many of the names of birds we use today are simply folk names that won the battle to be recognised as the 'official' name! For what are 'whitethroat' and 'blackcap', 'robin' and 'blackbird', if not folk names?

the same species, as well as a reduction in the potentially confusing use of the same name for different species. This coincided with a much deeper understanding of Britain's birds, our knowledge of which would increase dramatically during the period in question, from 1500 to 1750.

The impulse behind the giving of standard names to birds was the great outpouring of learning taking place at this time: from the sixteenth-century Renaissance, through the seventeenth-century Age of Reason, to the eighteenth-century Age of Enlightenment, during which, as the historian Roy Porter has noted, 'the key . . . concept was Nature'.[3]

This period also saw great advances in the way we perceived, catalogued and categorised what Shakespeare called 'nature's mysteries', with the seismic shift from what historian Keith Thomas termed 'the cruelty of indifference' to a far more modern and enlightened approach to the natural world.[4]

Until this time, mankind's dominion over nature was more or less absolute. Indeed, as this verse from the *Book of Genesis* shows, it had been sanctioned at the highest level of authority, the Old Testament: 'And God blessed them, and God said unto them, be fruitful, and multiply, and replenish the earth, and subdue it: and have dominion over the fish of the sea, and over the fowl of the air, and over every living thing that moveth upon the earth.'

We humans have never quite managed to shake off the notion that we can and should exploit, without compunction or consequence, the Earth's natural resources. But during this period from 1500 to 1750 we did at least begin to move away from a primarily exploitative relationship between human beings and wild animals, and towards a more inclusive, benevolent approach – what the environmental historian Dr Rob Lambert calls the shift 'from use to delight'.

One consequence of this change in attitudes was that we began to appreciate the natural world for its own sake, rather than simply as a resource for us to exploit. Very gradually – and through intermediate stages such as the Victorian mania for shooting, collecting and stuffing specimens of wild birds – this would ultimately lead to the rise of popular, nature-based hobbies including, of course, birdwatching.[5]

For the very first time in history, we were finally beginning to regard other creatures with a combination of empathy, understanding and curiosity – not all that different from the outlook millions of us have towards nature today. Birds, being more ubiquitous and visible than any other creatures, were at the forefront of this new approach. And this led to a slew of new, and now very familiar, names.

3: Pioneers and Puffins

The movement towards standardising the official names of birds (along with many other species of animals and plants) was begun by a cohort of people who, for the first time, called themselves 'naturalists'.[*] Amongst these pioneering men (and a few exceptional women like the seventeenth-century lepidopterist Eleanor Glanville) was

---

* The term 'naturalist' is first recorded in 1581, in a work by the controversial Scottish Catholic John Hamilton. However, the first use of the word in its modern meaning is not until 1600, in Christopher Sutton's popular devotional work *Disce Mori: Learne to Dye*, in which he writes of 'A lion, of whom the naturalist writeth, that he is of such courage. . .'

the herbalist, natural historian and theologian William Turner (1509/10-68).

For an academic scholar and scientist, Turner led a turbulent and often dangerous life. He held controversial, reformist views, at a time when every change to the holder of the English throne dictated the prevailing religion. Thus in 1538, towards the end of the reign of Henry VIII, he was imprisoned for preaching without a licence. When he was released he left England to travel around Europe, where his radical opinions found a more receptive audience. After Henry's death in 1547, and the accession of the more sympathetic King Edward VI, Turner returned home to become Dean of Wells in Somerset.

But unfortunately for both Turner and his brand of radical Protestantism, Edward's reign was soon cut short by chronic ill health. When the young king died in 1553, aged just 15, his Catholic half-sister Mary succeeded him. Turner's life was now in mortal danger, and he fled abroad once again. He escaped just in time, narrowly avoiding the dreadful fate of his contemporaries Nicholas Ridley and Hugh Latimer, both of whom were burned at the stake by Queen Mary for heresy.

After Mary's half-sister Elizabeth acceded to the throne in 1558, and the Catholic faith gave way to Protestant beliefs for the final time in this unsettled period in our history, Turner could at last return permanently to England.

I include these biographical details as we cannot separate the religious crusader from the pioneering naturalist; indeed, in his fiery personality the two vocations fused, as the editor and translator of his ornithological writings noted:

'It must be understood that, his scientific work apart, nearly the whole of Turner's life was spent in religious controversy. . .'[6]

Perhaps it was this love of argument and desire to go against the grain that allowed him to make such advances in our ornithological knowledge. For Turner was in every sense a true 'Renaissance Man', in the modern meaning of the phrase: both as a polymath, straddling different fields of learning, and also in his constant striving to advance the boundaries of human knowledge about the world – in his case, the natural world.

William Turner certainly did that, taking a particular interest in the classification and naming of birds. *Avium Praecipuarum*, written in Latin and published in 1544, was the first printed book entirely devoted to ornithology. As its full title suggests,[*] he relied heavily on the classical works of Pliny and Aristotle, who had been the last people to attempt to classify birds, between 1,500 and 1,900 years earlier. Incredibly, in all that time virtually no progress had been made in our ornithological knowledge.

Turner set out to systematically record the names of every known bird in Greek, Latin, English and German – a daunting task, given that hardly any prior research had been done on the naming of species. He obtained much of his information by talking to bird-catchers and wildfowlers, for whom a working knowledge of the range of names used for different kinds of birds was essential.

James Fisher notes that Turner listed more than a hundred different kinds of British bird, of which no fewer than fifteen were

---

[*] *Avium praecipuarum, quarum apud Plinium et Aristotelem mentio est, brevis et succincta historia*, which roughly translates as: 'A Short and Succinct History of the Principal Birds Noticed by Pliny and Aristotle'.

named for the first time. These included the hen harrier, woodlark and brambling – the latter with the unusual spelling of 'bramlyng'. According to Lockwood, this is a corruption of 'brandling', and refers to the brindled plumage of this handsome finch, rather than having anything to do with the blackberry-producing plant. If so, then the modern name 'brambling' is yet another of those 'faux amis': unwary linguistic traps set to confuse us.

Turner also first coined the name 'creeper' for the species we today call the treecreeper.* This minuscule bird, often seen moving jerkily around a gnarled tree trunk as it searches for tiny insects, already had a wide range of folk names, including 'tree climber', 'tree clipper', 'tree speeler' (from a Scottish word meaning climber), 'bark creeper' and 'bark runner'. The most evocative example, perhaps, was the Somerset name 'tree mouse'. But a word of caution: the suffix 'mouse', as used in the old name for tits, 'titmouse', is thought to derive from the Old English word 'mose', simply meaning 'small creature', so does not necessarily refer to the treecreeper's rather rodent-like habits.

Turner also either found or coined the name 'nut jobber' for the nuthatch, deriving from the now obsolete word 'job', meaning to peck or jab at something. The modern suffix, 'hatch', derives from the word 'hack', from the bird's habit of jamming a nut into a crevice in the bark of a tree, and then pecking at it to break off morsels to eat.

Turner was not simply naming the birds; he was also trying to distinguish genuine accounts of their behaviour from purely

---

* Treecreeper is a relatively recent coinage, first noted in 1814, and not officially adopted by the BOU until as late as 1883. It soon caught on: one popular Victorian nature-writer, George Rooper, extolled 'the pretty lady-like tree-creeper [which] ran like a mouse up the tree.'

spurious and inaccurate ones, many of which had gained currency through continued repetition down the centuries. Given how little was known about Britain's birdlife at this time, it is remarkable how accurate many of Turner's observations were. He wrote that 'Cranes . . . breed in England in marshy places', and noted that bitterns 'can easily be driven into nets by the use of a stalking horse'.

Not surprisingly, Turner did repeat several long-held errors and misinterpretations. He confused the osprey with the sea eagle, repeated the hoary old myth that barnacle geese hatch from goose barnacles, and claimed that the heron 'screams while it couples and (they say) emits blood from its eyes'. He also thought – along, to be fair, with many others – that male and female hen harriers were separate species, a confusion not cleared up until more than 250 years later, by George Montagu (see Chapter 4).

But given the virtually blank slate from which he was working, William Turner did remarkably well to begin the long process of unravelling the complexities of the multiple names given to Britain's birds. He died peacefully in London in 1568, secure in the knowledge that not only had his once radical religious beliefs now entered the mainstream of English society, but he had also made substantial advances in our knowledge and understanding of English bird names.

During the following hundred years or so, progress in the naming of birds almost ground to a halt – perhaps because Englishmen and women had other things on their minds during these turbulent times. First, there was the transition from the last of the Tudors, Elizabeth, to the Stuart kingship of James I and his unfortunate son

Charles I. Then came the period leading up to and after the English Civil War during the 1640s and 1650s, during which one king was beheaded and another deposed, and Britain was briefly run as a republic by Lord Protector Oliver Cromwell. As the title of a book by historian Christopher Hill puts it, this really was a time when 'the world turned upside down'.

Not until the decade following the Restoration of the English monarchy, under Charles II in 1660, was any real progress made towards giving official, widely accepted names to the remainder of Britain's birds. The impetus for this came from two men from very different social classes, who nevertheless shared a passion for all things ornithological: John Ray and Francis Willughby.

John Ray (1627–1705) came from humble beginnings. He was a village blacksmith's son from Essex, who has been described as 'solitary, modest, principled, persistent. . . The last of the heroes whose work gradually shifted the study of plants away from superstition and towards science'.[*]

Ray's life changed dramatically at the age of sixteen, when he won a bursary to study at Cambridge. He remained at Cambridge as a fellow, and later taught Francis Willughby (1635–72), a handsome young country gentleman whose family seat, Middleton Hall in Warwickshire, is now the site of an RSPB nature reserve. Despite their very different backgrounds, the two men soon discovered that they shared a mutual interest – the new science of ornithology – following which they became firm friends and trusted colleagues.

---

[*] In Anna Pavord, *The Naming of Names* (London, 2005). Ray's modesty was underscored by his deep religious beliefs, revealed in the title of his 1691 work, *The Wisdom of God Manifested in the Works of the Creation.*

After touring Britain and Europe to watch and study wildlife, they returned home with ambitious plans to publish a masterwork summarising their observations and conclusions. But in 1672, at the age of just thirty-six, Willughby caught pleurisy and died. Grief-stricken at his friend's passing, Ray wrote that Willughby's death was 'to the infinite and unspeakable loss and grief of myself, his friends, and all good men'. In tribute, he pledged to publish their joint work posthumously, and soon afterwards did so, first in Latin (1676) and then in English (1678).

Willughby's *Ornithology*, as it is usually called,* was the first volume devoted entirely to birds to be written in English. As a result, it had an enormous influence on later ornithologists and writers. Ray's modesty in ascribing authorship solely to his late friend is typical of the man hailed by James Fisher as 'the greatest of all field naturalists'.

Some bird names appear for the very first time in Willughby's *Ornithology*, yet we know the species themselves were recorded far earlier. One example is the name crossbill, whose name refers to the way the upper mandible of the beak crosses over the lower one.

Crossbills are neither exclusively resident nor migratory, but nomadic in their habits, wandering long distances after the end of the breeding season in search of the conifers on whose cones they feed. In some years, large flocks of crossbills arrive in Britain from continental Europe, turning up in locations where they have not previously

---

* The full title is the rather unwieldy, *The ornithology of Francis Willughby of Middleton in the county of Warwick, Esq. In three books: wherein all the birds hitherto known, being reduced into a method sutable* [sic] *to their natures, are accurately described: the descriptions illustrated by most elegant figures, nearly resembling the live birds, engraven in LXXVIII copper plates.*

been seen. When they do, they can be easily identified, thanks to that unique physiological feature commemorated in their name.

So although the name 'crossbill' does not appear in written form until Willughby's *Ornithology*, we know that they occurred in Britain more than 400 years earlier – all because of a sharp-eyed Benedictine monk and historian named Matthew Paris.

Sometime in the autumn of 1251, Paris observed a flock of unfamiliar birds feeding in the grounds of his monastery at St Albans in Hertfordshire: 'About the fruit season there appeared, in the orchards chiefly, some remarkable birds, which had never been seen in England, somewhat larger than larks. . .' This could have referred to any number of fruit-eating species, including redwings and fieldfares; but the clincher to the species' identity comes in the next line: 'The beaks of these birds were crossed, so that by this means they opened the fruit as if with pincers or a knife.'

This observation is accompanied by a line drawing in the book's margin, which clearly shows a crossbill feeding on a large seed, using the specialised bill unique to this group of birds. This is also the first known reference to its unusual migratory habits, and reminds us that long before the great explosion in learning from the sixteenth to the eighteenth centuries, led by men like Ray and Willughby, perceptive individual observers like Matthew Paris had been gradually adding to our accumulated knowledge of Britain's birds.

Ray and Willughby finally brought to an end the obsession with classical observers such as Aristotle and Pliny who, although they made some remarkable observations for their time, had also made serious mistakes. Aristotle, for instance, had believed that the redstart turned into the robin during the winter months, and that swallows hibernated under water (a belief that endured surprisingly late, well into the eighteenth century, and was even given credence by Gilbert White).

By discarding many of the classical world's false assumptions, which had so hindered the progress of modern ornithology, Ray and Willughby opened the door to a new, more rigorous and scientific, approach to bird study.

One of their simplest yet most revolutionary methods was to classify birds first according to habitat (Land and Water Birds), and then further subdivide these into smaller categories, such as birds that swim, and those that wade; or birds with hooked bills, and those without. In so doing, Ray and Willughby managed to produce a classification that, with a few exceptions, looks remarkably like the one we still use today.

They also sorted out various areas of confusion. As we have seen, until this time, the same name might be used for two completely different and unrelated species. One such was the word 'shoveler'. We might reasonably assume that any reference to a shoveler (or its variants, 'shoveller' and 'shovelard') would refer to the familiar and colourful duck of that name, which uses its specialised, shovel-shaped beak to filter tiny items of food from the surface of the water. Yet until the late seventeenth century the name applied to a very different species: the bird we now call a spoonbill. As its name suggests, the spoonbill also has a peculiarly spatula-shaped bill, which like the shoveler it uses when feeding.

This long-legged waterbird was once common in England, found in the vast, soggy wetland known as the Great Fen that covered much of East Anglia. But some time during this period, as the fens were drained for farming and settlement, and the birds were hunted for food, the spoonbill disappeared as a British breeding species.

As late as 1796, one observer, Captain J. G. Stedman, could still write that 'the shoveler, or spoon-bill . . . is about the size of a goose'. But by then, as the species became less and less familiar, the name shoveler had been transferred to the large, colourful duck with a similarly shaped bill. The first reference to this comes from John Ray, in 1674. Four years later, in Willughby's *Ornithology*, Ray confirmed the new name spoonbill (from an older term, 'spoon-billed heron'), with the explanation: 'The Bill . . . is of the likeness of a Spoon. . .' – which indeed it is.

The confusion between the names spoonbill and shoveler is far from the only one to emerge from this key period in our history, when the names given to different species were in constant flux. Contestants in pub quizzes are easily misled by the answer to the apparently simple question: which British seabird has the scientific name *Puffinus puffinus*? To most people's surprise, it is not the puffin, but the Manx shearwater.

The origin of the name 'puffin' is a mystery; it has been suggested that it might derive from a Cornish word (perhaps via another Celtic language, Breton), but this cannot be confirmed. What we do know is that it originally referred to the young Manx shearwater.

Like puffins, shearwaters nest in underground burrows on remote offshore islands such as Lundy and Skomer.* For centuries, sailors would stop off at their breeding colonies to harvest the plump chicks, whose bodies have a very high fat content. These would

---

* Shearwaters do exactly what their name suggests: glide low over the waves, their stiff wings almost touching the surface of the sea.

then be salted for food to sustain the mariners on their long sea voyages, when fresh meat would be scarce.

Later this was turned into a thriving and profitable trade, no doubt helped by the convenient classification of shearwaters as fish, which could therefore be eaten during the period of Lent, when meat was forbidden. As Thomas Moffett observed in the late sixteenth century, this custom was sanctioned at the highest level of the Catholic Church: 'Puffins, whom I may call the feathered fishes, are accounted even by the holy fatherhood of Cardinals to be no flesh but rather fish.'[7]

At this time the bird we now call the puffin was known as the 'sea parrot', because of its large, colourful beak. But some time during the seventeenth or eighteenth centuries, confusion arose between the two species. This presumably occurred because both nest in burrows, and the young superficially resemble one another, being grey, plump and rather fluffy (and in the case of the puffin chick, lacking the distinctive bill it develops in adulthood). So the common name transferred from one species to the other; yet the Manx shearwater retains the scientific name *Puffinus puffinus* to this day.

The puffin's generic name, *Fratercula*, comes from the Latin word meaning 'friar', which one commentator has suggested arose 'perhaps as a reference to the bird's habit, when rising from the sea, of clasping its feet as though in prayer'.[8] The name was coined by the Swiss ornithologist Conrad Gessner. Writing to his English friend John Caius,* he joked that 'If you imagine that this bird was white, and that you then put on a black cloak with a cowl, you

---

* Physician, medical pioneer and co-founder of my old college, Gonville and Caius, Cambridge.

could give this bird the name of "little friar of the sea" (*Fratercula arctica*).' The name stuck.

The origin of the name of another seabird, the storm petrel, has given rise to another confusing myth. W. B. Lockwood noted that when feeding, these tiny birds (barely larger than a house martin) tap the water with their feet as they fly low over the surface of the sea. He suggested that this 'pitter-patter' action led to the name, though the *OED* again demurs, suggesting that although the origins are now long lost, it may come from the sounds these bird make while mating, or even their smell.

The explorer and naturalist William Dampier, writing in 1703, went a step further, forging an entirely spurious link with the New Testament account of St Peter miraculously walking on the waves: 'As they fly . . . they pat the Water alternately with their Feet, as if they walkt upon it; tho' still upon the Wing. And from hence the Seamen give them the name of Petrels, in allusion to St Peter's walking upon the Lake of Gennesareth.'[9]

This story has taken root in many other European cultures, as can be seen from the folk names *Petersvogel* (German), *Søren-Peder* (Norwegian), and *ave de San Pedro* (Spanish), all of which assume the same entirely spurious Biblical connection.

But perhaps the most intriguing mystery surrounds the name 'scoter'. Scoters are a group of sea ducks found across the higher latitudes of the northern hemisphere. All have one thing in common: they are predominantly black in colour. It is this characteristic that might explain the origin of their peculiar name, which like so many others was first noted by John Ray in the late seventeenth century, when he referred to 'the black Diver or Scoter: *Anas niger*'.

The theory goes like this. In other European languages, and in the English folk name 'black diver', the scoter is named after its appearance. Thus in German, *Russente* translates as 'soot duck', while the Dutch *zwarte zee-eend* means 'black sea duck'. It is hardly far-fetched to suggest that this species was originally known in English as a 'sooter', and that sometime during this period the name was mistranscribed as scoter. Sadly we shall never know if this is correct: the word 'sooter' used in reference to the bird's name has never been found.

In his book *Lapwings, Loons and Lousy Jacks*[10] Ray Reedman offers an alternative explanation: that 'scoter' may derive from the phrase 'sea-coot'. This name has in the past been used for several birds with a predominantly black plumage, including the cormorant, guillemot, scoter and American coot, but its supposed link with the name scoter is pure conjecture.

Ray and Willughby were not only well travelled, but well-read too, so were keenly aware of the work of earlier writers. These included the sixteenth-century Swiss ornithologist Conrad Gessner, brilliantly described by Anna Pavord as 'a one-man search engine, a sixteenth-century Google'.[11]

One of Ray's rare errors came about through a mistranslation of Gessner's name for the species we know today as the waxwing. Gessner had named this bird the Bohemian jay, because of its superficial resemblance to that species, and also its irregular autumnal wanderings south and west from its Scandinavian breeding grounds in search of the berries on which it feeds. Unfortunately, Ray mistranslated 'Bohemian jay' as 'Bohemian chatterer', which, as Lockwood notes, 'is especially unfortunate seeing that the waxwing is a very silent bird' (though it does sometimes call in flight, making a tinkling call rather like a 1980s Trimphone).

A now obsolete name for the waxwing, the 'silk-tail', refers to the bird's smooth, silky plumage, and also finds an echo in its current scientific name, *Bombycilla garrulus* – which translates as 'noisy silk-tail' (another confusing reference to the bird's sound). The modern name 'waxwing' was not coined until 1817, which strikes me as surprisingly late in the day, given that those strange red markings on the bird's wings really do look like the wax once used to seal up envelopes.

Another misleading name, this time chosen by Willughby, for one of our most enigmatic birds of prey, is honey buzzard. He chose the name when he discovered combs of wasps in the bird's nest, and a century later Thomas Pennant adopted it as the official English name for the species.

But both Willughby and Pennant were mistaken: honey buzzards do not feed on the sweet and sticky honey; what they are actually after are the juicy grubs hidden away in the cells of the comb. The species' scientific name – *apivorus*, meaning 'bee-eating' – is much closer to the mark, as is the Dutch name *wespendief* (meaning 'wasp thief'), a reference to the way the bird steals the comb away from those pesky insects, in order to consume the grubs at its leisure.*

Overall, though, despite these few errors, Ray and Willughby

---

* Several other British birds are named after what they eat, including bee-eater (bees), mistle thrush (mistletoe berries) and linnets (flax seeds – *linum* in Latin). But sparrow-hawks rarely catch sparrows, goshawks don't usually hunt geese, and hen harriers don't eat poultry. Thanks to fish shortages, herring gulls now snatch ice creams from the hands of unwary holidaymakers, while oystercatchers don't often get the chance to feed on luxury shellfish. Hartlepool fishermen used to call this black-and-white wader 'mussel cracker', which is far more appropriate.

set the course for the major advances in the standardisation of bird names, which would continue apace in the coming century.

4: *A Little Latin*

Meanwhile, a second linguistic revolution was occurring – not in English names, but in Latin ones.* And while this may at first appear to be an arcane and scholarly by-way in our story of the origin of English bird names, nothing could be further from the truth.

For like other great sea-changes in history – from the invention of printing to the advent of the Internet – the system known by the tongue-twisting phrase 'binomial nomenclature' changed the world, by allowing knowledge and understanding of living things to progress internationally without being held back by linguistic complexity and confusion, as had been the case until then.

This approach, which would eventually create the system of classification still used by scientists around the world today, was pioneered by a Swedish scientist widely known by the Latinised version of his name, Carl Linnaeus.

Linnaeus has been memorably described as 'Sweden's most important contribution to world culture until Abba'.[12] Born in a small southern Swedish town in 1707, he came from relatively humble beginnings: his father was a Lutheran pastor of peasant stock. But he went on to become one of the most famous men of his time, acclaimed as the 'father of modern taxonomy'. The Swiss-born

* Or, as they are more correctly known, 'scientific' names, because they frequently derive from Greek as well as Latin.

French philosopher Jean-Jacques Rousseau put it more simply: 'tell him I know of no greater man on Earth'.

Later scientists and writers – along with amateur naturalists and birders – also owe Linnaeus an enormous debt of gratitude. As one saying goes: 'God created the world, Linnaeus put it in order.'*

So how did Linnaeus achieve such universal admiration and praise? He did so by simplifying the existing, and ludicrously cumbersome, method of naming species, and introducing a system we still use today to classify every single one of the world's millions of living organisms.

Before Linnaeus, plants and animals, including birds, were usually classified using an ornate and increasingly unwieldy system, which formed the Latin name from complex descriptions, sometimes many words long. Thus the common plant hoary plantain, whose current Latin name is *Plantago media*, was lumbered with the ludicrous epithet *Plantago foliis ovato-lanceolatus pubescentibus, spica cylindrica, scapo tereti* (which roughly translates as 'plantain with pubescent ovate-lanceolated leaves, a cylindrical spike and a terete scape').

Nor did birds escape this fate: the shoveler, now *Anas clypeata*, laboured under the seven-word phrase *Anas platyrhynchos altera sive clypeata Germanis dicta*, which the ornithologist Professor Tim Birkhead translates as 'another duck with a broad bill, or, according to the Germans, with a shield-like gorget'.[13] Not only was this far too complicated for general use, it also confuses the modern reader by its reference to *Anas platyrhynchos* – the Latin name for the mallard.

At a single stroke, Linnaeus did away with such unnecessary complication. With the publication of his masterwork *Systema Naturae*,

---

* Professor Å. Gustafsson of the University of Lund, writing in 1979.

produced during the middle decades of the eighteenth century, he set in motion the modern science of taxonomy. At its heart was a new method of classification: the concept of binomial nomenclature.

As the phrase suggests, binomial nomenclature uses two words to do the job that had previously required whole phrases. The first name of the two is the genus (or grouping) to which the organism belongs; the second the specific (or species) name. Taken together, the binomial distinguishes that species from any other. Thus we have *Passer domesticus* (house sparrow), *Troglodytes troglodytes* (wren) and *Turdus merula* (blackbird).*

Before I go on, however, one important misconception should be laid to rest. Linnaeus did not actually invent binomials. That honour goes to the Swiss botanist Caspar Bauhar, who lived and worked more than a century earlier, and who began pruning the over-ornate compound names into those with just two elements. However, Bauhar did not seek to adopt this as a universal system; Linnaeus did. Linnaeus's genius was to recognise that, if widely used, binomial nomenclature would revolutionise the study and classification of living things forever, as Anna Pavord points out: 'The binomial system worked . . . because it effectively mirrored the way that common names had evolved. Hoary plantain is, in effect, a binomial tag. . . In the English language the describing word comes before the generic one. In Latin it's the other way around.'[14]

Linnaeus's simple but ingenious approach transformed the infant

---

* Should a species of bird (or any other plant or animal) need to be further subdivided into different races or subspecies, then a third name (trinomial) is added. So the white wagtail, found over much of Europe and Asia, is called *Motacilla alba alba*, while the pied wagtail, which we see here in Britain, is *Motacilla alba yarrelli*.

science of taxonomy, allowing all the world's organisms to be neatly classified in relationship to one another, and removing the room for error and confusion caused by over-complicated compound names.

Binomials are not simply used in academic or scientific circles. Even today birders, especially if they are amongst a multilingual group from several different countries, will often refer to a bird by its scientific name, in order to make it clear which particular species they are talking about.

I can still recall my first visit to Spain in the mid-1980s, when I was lucky enough to go to the Coto Doñana with the late Tono Valverde, the man who had done so much to save this extraordinary wetland, one of Europe's last great wildernesses. We travelled south from Seville in his dilapidated car on a warm spring day, finally reaching the edge of the vast reserve in the late afternoon. Birds were simply everywhere: herons and egrets, geese and flamingos, and many, many more. My Spanish was poor, and his English worse, but we soon found a workable means of communication by using binomials. Our conversation that day largely consisted of phrases such as '*Gelochelidon nilotica*', '*Glareola pratincola*' and '*Sturnus unicolor*', allowing us to communicate easily through this universal language.*

Even today, scientific names continue to play a crucial role with regard to changing English bird names. At a time when many species still labour under a range of different local names, depending on where you are in the world – such as 'diver' and 'loon', 'skua' and jaeger', and 'bunting' and 'longspur', in Britain and North America

---

* Gull-billed tern, collared pratincole and spotless starling respectively.

respectively – scientific names help provide stability and continuity.

Or at least they did. However, now that the classification of all the world's birds is undergoing a major revolution, thanks to advances in our understanding of DNA, there has been a drive to change scientific names to reflect these new relationships; a move laudable from a scientific point of view, but likely to cause great confusion in the future (see Chapter 7).*

Notwithstanding this current complication, scientific ornithologists and ordinary birders the world over owe a massive debt to Linnaeus, for dragging the classification of birds and other living things into the modern age. As John Wright notes: 'It [binomial nomenclature] was by no means perfect . . . but it was good enough for the moment and, more importantly, became accepted by nearly everyone.'[15]

One other important consequence arose as a result of the new Linnaean system of classification: several scientific names were translated more or less directly from Latin into English, and became the standard name for the species. These included oriole, from *oriolus*, which Lockwood suggests derives from the golden oriole's tuneful, whistling call, but may also be a nod to *aureolus*, meaning 'golden-coloured'.

Another Latin-based name is phalarope. Two of the world's three species of phalaropes occur regularly in Britain: the red-necked, which breeds in Shetland and the Western Isles; and the grey, an

---

* For example, the black-headed gull has been transferred from the genus Larus to a new one, Chroicocephalus, and so is now known by the tongue-twister *Chroicocephalus ridibundus*. Meanwhile the blue, coal and crested tits (once in the genus Parus, along with the other British members of their family), are now in the genera Cyanistes, Periparus and Lophophanes respectively, while the marsh and willow tits have been moved to the genus Poecile. Only the great tit (*Parus major*) remains unchanged.

autumn passage migrant. Their name derives (via French) from the Latin *phalaropus*, which means 'coot-footed'. This refers to the lobes on phalaropes' toes that enable them to swim, and which resemble those on the feet of coots and moorhens.

As Lockwood points out, because phalaropes are so scarce and localised in most parts of Britain, neither species ever acquired an English folk name. But there is one notable exception. On Shetland, where it breeds, the red-necked phalarope is known in the local dialect as the 'peerie deuk', meaning 'little duck', from its tiny size and habit of swimming on shallow lochans when feeding. Intriguingly, the *Scottish National Dictionary* defines the noun 'peerie' as 'a child's spinning-top', and this certainly fits the frantic feeding action of these tiny waders, which revolve like wound-up clockwork toys as they stir up tiny aquatic invertebrates.

On 10 January 1778, Carl Linnaeus, the man who began this revolution in the world of science and naming, died at his home in Hammarby, near Stockholm. He was seventy years old.

Linnaeus's final years had been blighted by illness, yet his scientific discoveries had also brought him fame and fortune. In 1761 he was ennobled by King Adolf Frederick (as Carl von Linné), creating a coat of arms divided into three, featuring what he considered to be the three kingdoms of nature – animal, vegetable and mineral – and after his death he was buried with great honour in Uppsala Cathedral. His continuing legacy, though, is the 4,400 species of animals and 7,700 species of plants to which he gave scientific names; including, of course, many species of birds.

5: A Correspondence Course

In 1789, just four years before his death, Gilbert White, a country vicar in a rural parish in Hampshire, published *The Natural History of Selborne*,* which eventually became one of the best-selling books of all time.†

Yet despite his enduring fame, when it comes to the story of the naming of our birds, White is something of a footnote. His correspondent Thomas Pennant, to whom many of the 'letters' in *Selborne* are addressed, was far more important and influential in this regard.

Whether or not White actually sent his letters to Pennant (and his other correspondent, Daines Barrington), or simply used them as a literary device to impart information to the reader, is not especially relevant. What is significant – especially for our story – is that at the time the book was published, Pennant was far better known than White. He was one of the leading scientists of his day, and influenced, amongst others, that great man of letters Dr Samuel Johnson. So when he coined new names, or popularised existing

* In keeping with the pedantry of this age, its full title reads: *The Natural History and Antiquities of Selborne, in the County of Southampton. To which are added The Naturalists Calendar; Observations on Various Parts of Nature; and Poems.*

† Whether *Selborne* can claim to have sold as many copies as *Quotations from Chairman Mao* (better known as *The Little Red Book*), or various works by Tolkien, J. K. Rowling and Agatha Christie, is hard to tell, as reliable sales figures were not available back in the eighteenth and nineteenth centuries. But it has never been out of print, has been translated into many foreign languages, and in the two-and-a-half centuries since it was first published has appeared in almost 300 different editions.

ones, they were likely to be widely adopted and used by others.

Born in 1726, Thomas Pennant lived his whole life at the family estate in Flintshire, in his native Wales. Here, as a twelve-year-old boy, he was given a copy of Willughby's *Ornithology*, an event to which he later ascribed his lifelong love of natural history. Pennant may have been true to his Welsh roots, but during a long and busy life he also travelled extensively around the British Isles, writing detailed notes on the plants, animals and landscapes he encountered.

His findings appeared in a series of highly influential books. The best known of these, *British Zoology*, was published in several editions from the 1760s onwards, and soon became the definitive zoological work of its time.[*] This combination of scholarly rigour and wide readership meant that Pennant performed a crucial role in both developing new names and authorising existing ones. Indeed, he was so successful that we continue to use many of his chosen names today.

When it came to classifying birds, Pennant's approach broadly involved taking Linnaeus's classification of a group of related species into a genus or family, and then giving each member an English name within that grouping, to make these relationships more apparent. This was very helpful, as names such as 'sparrow' and 'wren' had until then been used interchangeably for several species from very different families.

Previously, for example, the reed bunting had often been called 'reed sparrow', which confusingly was also used for other small birds sharing the same habitat, including reed and sedge warblers. Pennant decided on the name reed bunting, along with 'common

---

[*] In 2008 a copy was sold at the London auction house Christie's for over £16,000.

bunting' (later renamed corn bunting), and 'yellow bunting', the logical term for the yellowhammer, which nevertheless failed to catch on (as we saw in Chapter 2). The name of our hardiest species, the snow bunting, also emerged at about the same time.

The name 'bunting', which initially referred only to the corn bunting, goes back to the fourteenth century, and as a surname (meaning 'plump or thick-set person') is recorded as early as 1275. That original meaning also survives in the nursery rhyme 'Bye baby bunting', which first appears in print in 1784, but whose origin is almost certainly far older. So Pennant's role was more about organisation than innovation: it had long been known that these species were members of the bunting family but, as with so many other familiar species, their vernacular names had arisen by a series of accidents. The tidy-minded Pennant was not the first person, and will probably not be the last, to try to render bird names more logical.

During his career, he developed a number of compound names, combining a colour or shade with a part of the bird's body. These included white-fronted goose ('front' derives from the French for forehead, and refers to the white patch around the bird's bill), black-throated and red-throated divers, red-necked grebe, red-breasted merganser and red-backed shrike. And he either coined or popularised several other names derived from key plumage features, such as spotted flycatcher, ringed plover, long-tailed titmouse (later simplified to 'tit'), and long-eared and short-eared owls.

Pennant also adopted 'bearded titmouse', a direct translation from the French. The bearded tit, as we now call it, is an attractive bird found almost exclusively in reed beds, with a butterscotch and blue-grey plumage, long tail, and distinctive black markings on the sides of the male's bill. Yet these are more reminiscent of the fictional Chinese villain Fu Manchu's drooping moustaches than of any kind of beard. 'Tit' is also misleading: the species is entirely unrelated to the true tits, and indeed has now been placed in its very own family, Panuridae.

Avocet, bean goose, little egret, eider, linnet, night heron, oystercatcher, pochard, ruff, sanderling, tawny owl and wood sandpiper are just some of the many other species for which Pennant either invented the current name, or chose it from the various ones already in use.

Thanks to his influence, these are the names we still use today, even though perfectly acceptable alternatives (for example 'brown owl' instead of tawny owl, 'sea-pie' for oystercatcher) were available at the time. Pennant's choice of names did not always prevail: he preferred water ouzel instead of dipper, eared grebe (still used in North America) for black-necked grebe, golden-crested wren for goldcrest, goatsucker for nightjar and land rail for corncrake.* And in the early editions of *British Zoology* he called the stone curlew the 'Norfolk plover', but later wrongly decided that this curious wader must be from a different family, and so gave it the wonderfully evocative name 'thick-kneed bustard', which also failed to catch on.† But by and large, when Pennant named a bird, that name prevailed.

---

* Some of these alternative names, such as dipper (1388), corncrake (1455) and nightjar (1630), were already in use; but goldcrest was not officially adopted until 1883, and black-necked grebe as recently as 1912. And of course 'Brown Owl' is still used today for the leader of a Brownie pack!

† In some ways Pennant was ahead of his time: in most of the rest of the world the nine species in the same family as the stone curlew are known as 'thick-knees', after the bony protuberances on their legs. Oddly, even though this species is not closely related to the curlews, we still prefer the inaccurate and misleading name 'stone curlew'.

Popular and widely respected – he was described by one observer as an 'elegant scholar and refined gentleman' – Pennant died at home in 1798, aged seventy-two. In the centuries since, his fame has, as one early twentieth-century writer put it, 'suffered somewhat by the lapse of time'.[16] But although he may no longer be a household name, like his friend and contemporary Gilbert White, Thomas Pennant's influence on the development of English bird names remains unmatched.

And what of Gilbert White? Perhaps I have been a little harsh on him; after all, he did famously sort out the confusion between three species of summer visitor to our shores: the chiffchaff, willow warbler and wood warbler.

To the modern birder, the very notion that these three superficially similar little birds might be impossible to distinguish from one another seems absurd. But we are forgetting two things: first, that during the late eighteenth century our knowledge of birds was both limited and piecemeal, as very few people took any interest at all in the natural world; and second, that the kind of sophisticated optical aids we now take for granted, such as binoculars, telescopes and digital cameras, were simply not available.

So as he wandered the highways and byways of his rural Hampshire parish, Gilbert White had to rely on his ability to observe bird behaviour at a distance, with his naked eyes. When it came to telling small, flighty warblers apart, this was fairly limited in its use and efficiency.

But White had another weapon up his sleeve, or rather, on the sides of his head: his ears. Today birders often use the sound of these birds, rather than their appearance, to tell them apart; White may not have been the first person to do so (surely the distinctive two-note sound of the chiffchaff would have aroused interest long before this?), but importantly he was the first to point out the key differences between the three species.

He set out his findings in Letter XIX of *The Natural History of Selborne*, written on 17 August 1768, though presumably relying on evidence gained earlier that spring, when all three would have been singing: 'I have now, past dispute, made out three distinct species of the willow-wrens, . . . which *constantly* and *invariably* use distinct notes.' White had also noticed that

> The yellowest bird [which we now know to be the wood warbler] is considerably the largest, and has its quill-feathers and secondary feathers tipped with white, which the others have not. This last haunts only the tops of trees in high beechen woods, and makes a sibilous grasshopper-like noise, now and then, at short intervals, shivering a little with its wings when it sings.[17]

As a description of the wood warbler's distinctive song, this could hardly be bettered. But if you are thinking of praising the good parson for his acute observations of the bird's plumage, you may have second thoughts when I tell you that he did have the advantage of having examined dead specimens, which he had presumably asked some local marksman to shoot – or perhaps even killed himself.

The other two species, both smaller and less distinctive than their scarcer relative, are the chiffchaff and willow warbler. Again, they are only superficially similar: as a long-distance migrant to and from southern Africa, the willow warbler needs longer wings, which give it a more elegant appearance. The marginally smaller, shorter-winged and more olive-plumaged chiffchaff is a short-distance migrant, with most of our breeding birds wintering in Spain, Portugal or North Africa.

For most birders, by far the easiest way to identify the chiffchaff is by the distinctive song that gives the species its onomatopoeic name, as White himself noted: 'The smallest uncrested willow wren, or chiffchaff . . . utters two sharp piercing notes, so loud in hollow woods, as to occasion an echo, and is usually first heard about the 20th of March.'

White does not appear to have got to grips with the third species – the one we now call the willow warbler – until some time after he identified the other two. At first this may seem rather odd, for the willow warbler is by far the commonest summer visitor to Britain, with well over two million pairs breeding here.[*] Yet although its silvery song, descending the scale like water running down a slope, is very distinctive, the bird's habit of avoiding parks and gardens means it is far less well-known than its cousin the chiffchaff.

Incidentally, the name 'warbler', with which we are so familiar today, does not appear in print until – you've guessed it – the 1773 edition of Thomas Pennant's *British Zoology*. Although the new name eventually gained the upper hand over earlier epithets, the name wood-wren continued to be used for the wood warbler, and was stubbornly resistant to change. It was still preferred by William MacGillivray as late as 1839.

---

[*] To put this figure into perspective, that means there are three times as many willow warblers in Britain as swallows, and the same number as the next two commonest migrants – chiffchaff and blackcap – combined.

Gilbert White has many claims to fame, but two are especially pertinent to this story. First, there is his contribution to the pastime millions of us enjoy today. James Fisher called him 'the man who started us all birdwatching',[18] and for me, this sums up his crucial contribution to the modern world. Before White, people had 'watched birds' so they could hunt and kill them for food, to observe their migratory journeys to try to predict the weather and the seasons, or as objects of superstition, folklore and worship. A few pioneers, such as William Turner, John Ray and Francis Willughby, had begun to carefully observe the habits and behaviour of birds in order to advance the cause of science. But Gilbert White brought a new and different viewpoint: clear, scientific inquiry, of course, but also a pure delight in the way birds *are* – an attitude that laid the foundations for the way we continue to watch and enjoy birds in the present day.

Gilbert White's other, more minor, distinction is that he is one of that small and select band of Britons who have had a bird named after them. Sadly, though, he never got the chance to see his eponymous species, an Asiatic relative of our own song and mistle thrushes that was named for him posthumously: White's thrush.

White's thrush breeds across a wide swathe of Asia, in the forests of central and eastern Siberia and the Himalayan foothills, and usually spends the winter in India or China. But in autumn, young birds occasionally go astray, heading in exactly the opposite direction from their usual migratory course, in a phenomenon known as 'reverse migration'. Most perish, but a tiny handful make it as far as Europe, which explains how one of these large and distinctive thrushes was shot near Christchurch (now Dorset, but at that time part of Hampshire) in January 1828, twenty-five years after Gilbert White had died.

This bird nearly escaped its fate, as this later account reveals: 'It attracted his attention, on disturbing it, in passing through a plantation, where it appeared to have established a haunt in a high furze brake, as it returned to it repeatedly before he could succeed in shooting it.'[19]

The eagle-eyed marksman was none other than James Edward Harris, 2nd Earl of Malmesbury. Recognising that the bird was unusual, he sent it to Thomas Eyton, who in his 1836 work *A History of the Rarer British Birds* named the species 'in memory of one with whom everybody is familiar by name',[20] his ornithological hero Gilbert White.

The choice of this species may not be particularly apt – the only connection being that White lived in the county where the bird was shot – but at least he does have a British bird named after him. It is deeply ironic that the name of his contemporary Thomas Pennant, who gave so many birds the names we still use today, can only be found in two now obsolete bird names that never made it to British shores: Pennant's parakeet (the common Australian species now known as crimson rosella), and the long-forgotten scientific name of the king penguin, which used to be known as *Aptenodytes pennanti* (since changed to *Aptenodytes patagonicus*).[*]

But the naming of White's thrush did signal a new and growing trend that had begun in the eighteenth century, and would reach its

---

[*] As some consolation, Pennant does have three species of mammal named after him, including the North American carnivore, and relative of the pine marten, the fisher *Martes pennanti*.

zenith in the nineteenth: eponymous bird names, those named after a deserving (or occasionally undeserving) human being.

This is the theme I shall be exploring in the next two chapters. These stories – and a fascinating cast of characters – reflect a new era of competition: the race to give names to the last remaining regularly occurring British species that, until then, had remained anonymous and unknown.

4

TAMING NATURE

The Organisation of Bird Names

A named thing is a tamed thing.
Joanne Harris, *Runemarks*

1: A Man of Kent

A thin layer of hoar frost coats every available surface, turning all to white. Ground, trees, bushes and sky merge into one, the sparse vegetation etched onto the landscape like a medieval engraving. In such intense winter cold, surely no small bird can survive – let alone a tiny warbler that depends on insects for its food?

So it is hardly surprising that the vast majority of this bird's relatives are far away to the south. Some, like the willow warbler, have flown all the way to Africa, where they now flit about on the parched savannah, feeding amongst elephants, lions and vast herds of wildebeest. Others, such as the blackcap, have stayed closer to home, on this side of the Sahara, and are foraging amongst the maquis bushes around the Mediterranean Sea. A few chiffchaffs, meanwhile, have remained in Britain, mostly heading to the south-west to take advantage of the milder winter climate in recent years.

But one kind of warbler has chosen a very different way of life. Instead of evolving to migrate each autumn, when the temperature drops and its food supply runs low, this species has chosen to remain right here on the Dorset heath where it was born – the landscape of Thomas Hardy's *Tess of the D'Urbervilles*.

Staying put is a big gamble. For this is one of our smallest and lightest birds, measuring just twelve centimetres from the tip of its bill to the end of its long, cocked tail, and weighing a mere ten grams – about the same as an old one pound coin.

It may be bone-chillingly cold, but according to the calendar, today is the equinox marking the start of spring – which means the start of the breeding season. With the passing of each day, there are a few more minutes of daylight; and in response to this, hormones are produced that encourage this warbler – indeed force it, for it has no real choice in the matter – to sing. So it hops up onto a sprig of gorse, whose custard-yellow flowers are just visible beneath a thick layer of frost, and bursts into song. A harsh, hesitant rattle of rapid-fire notes, rather like a speeded-up recording of a jammed machine-gun, floats over the heath, before evaporating in the chill March air.

This minuscule bird spends its whole life here, on this blasted heath. It is usually either perched on top of a gorse bush, or hidden inside the spiky foliage, searching for tiny insects, which it grabs and despatches with its small, pointed bill.

Given the bird's deep attachment to this one plant, and a plant itself so characteristic of its heathland home, you might imagine that it would be named after its habitat: heath warbler, perhaps, or gorse warbler. Indeed, one folk name is 'furze wren', after an old name for gorse. Instead, though, this species carries a misnomer so bizarre that when people hear it, they often assume they must be mistaken. For this bird is a Dartford warbler.

Yes, Dartford. A town that is famous for its tunnel and bridge, and for traffic snarl-ups during rush hours and on bank holiday weekends. Famous – amongst historians of rock music – as the childhood home of Mick Jagger and Keith Richards of the Rolling Stones. And famous, at least in the world of ornithology, as the place that gave its name to this tiny, and undeniably charming, little bird.[*]

---

[*] Even those who come from Dartford have never thought of the place with much affection. In 2010, the comedian Mark Steel returned to his home town to perform a live

Many birds are named after the habitat where they live: from marsh harrier to sand martin, and tree sparrow to wood pigeon. Some are named after buildings: house sparrow and barn owl, for example; others sport a name associated with farming, such as corn-crake and corn bunting. And a few – less than a score of regularly occurring British birds, including the Scottish crossbill, Canada goose and Mediterranean gull – are named after a country or region. But of all the 600-plus species on the British Ornithologists' Union's official British List, only three are named after an English town or county: Kentish plover, Sandwich tern and Dartford warbler.

As you may have noticed, all three names originate in the same county – Kent. This is no coincidence, for the names of the plover, tern and warbler go back to one man: the eighteenth-century physician and amateur ornithologist Dr John Latham. It was he who first came across these three species, and gave them their fascinating – but utterly inappropriate – names.

John Latham was born in Eltham (now in south-east London, but then a village in Kent), on 27 June 1740. His father was a surgeon, while his mother was descended from the Sotheby family, the founders of the famous London auction house.

As the eldest son, it was inevitable that John Latham would follow his father into a medical career, and indeed he did. But like many professional gentlemen of this era, he used his ample leisure

show for BBC Radio 4. He was not very flattering, but the locals were even less so: one audience member said that if Dartford were a three-course meal it would be 'McDonald's, KFC and a kebab'. Writing at the turn of the nineteenth century, William Cobbett made an equally barbed comment: 'After you leave Dartford, [the county of Kent] becomes excellent.'

time to pursue his passion for nature, becoming a distinguished ornithologist, and doing much to extend our knowledge of British (and later Australian) birds.

Like all ornithologists at this time, Latham practised his science down the barrel of a gun. Optical aids such as telescopes were still in their infancy, and the first book that might enable observers to identify birds in the field – Thomas Bewick's *A History of British Birds* – would not be published for another quarter of a century. So the only way to be absolutely sure of identifying any unusual bird was to shoot it.

Thus it was that early on a fine spring morning, in April 1773, John Latham left his home with his gun over his shoulder, to take a walk around Bexley Heath, near Dartford.*

During John Latham's day, both Dartford and Bexley Heath were still very rural in character, with a large area of trees and scrub extending between the two towns. It was here that he came across a pair of birds he could not even recognise, let alone identify. So he did what he always did under such circumstances: lowered the barrel of his gun and discharged a volley of lead shot towards the unfortunate creatures. Being a practised marksman, he hit both his targets, and they fell lifeless to the ground.

He examined the corpses carefully. Superficially they resembled the common whitethroat: small and slender, with a thin bill and long tail. But the colour was like no bird he had ever seen. The male

---

* Today, Dartford has long been joined to the urban sprawl of London – though officially, at least, it remains in the county of Kent. Bexleyheath, as it has now become, lies on the other side of the border, in Greater London, having been sucked into the metropolis following boundary changes in 1965.

had deep magenta underparts, the shade of a fine red burgundy, a greyish-brown back and head, and a few tiny pale spots around the throat and bill. The female was more drab and browner in shade, but shared her mate's basic plumage pattern.

Excited but mystified by his find, Latham took the specimens home and showed them to his fellow bird collectors. These included Thomas Pennant, the man who, as we have seen, had already made such a huge contribution to the naming of Britain's birds.

Pennant agreed that this was indeed a new bird to science, and granted Latham the honour of naming it. Even though the birds had actually been shot on Bexley Heath, he decided for some unknown reason to call the species *Sylvia dartfordiensis*:* Dartford warbler.

Unlike its cousins, most of which have large breeding ranges stretching across Europe, western Asia and the Middle East, the Dartford warbler is confined to a small area of maritime western Europe. Its range runs from southern England, through western France, Spain and Portugal, to the north-western tip of Africa. With such a restricted distribution, and a declining population, the species has been categorised as 'Near Threatened' by the global conservation organisation BirdLife International.

Being on the very northern edge of its range here in Britain, the Dartford warbler is vulnerable to anything that might threaten its survival. In the two centuries or so since Latham's discovery, its primary habitat – lowland heath – has been largely destroyed. Today, less than one-fifth of England's original heathland remains, mostly in the southern counties of Dorset and Hampshire, with a

* Now *Sylvia undata*.

few outlying patches in Devon, Surrey, Sussex and East Anglia.

But habitat loss is only one problem faced by this tenacious little bird. As a resident rather than a migrant, and with a diet of small insects, it is very susceptible to hard winters. This is particularly problematic during long spells of ice and snow, which make it hard to find food, and also weaken the birds by lowering their body temperature.

The cold winters of the first few decades of the twentieth century gradually reduced the population and range of Britain's Dartford warblers. The crunch came during the infamous 'Big Freeze' of 1962–3. For more than two months, from late December through to early March, Britain froze solid, with a thick layer of snow covering the ground, in conditions more severe than had been seen for over 200 years.

The winter of 1962–3 was horrendous enough for the human inhabitants of the British Isles; but for our birds it was, quite simply, a disaster. The ornithologist and broadcaster James Fisher summed up the enormity of the situation when, towards the end of the worst winter in living memory, he announced that 'It seems likely that at least half the wild birds living in this country before last Christmas are now dead.'

For the Dartford warbler, the situation was critical. Its population had already been heavily reduced by the previous year's cold winter, which had left just a hundred breeding pairs on the heaths of Dorset and the New Forest. But following the winter of 1962–63, numbers plummeted: in spring 1963 only a dozen pairs could be found, mostly on the coast around Poole Harbour, where temperatures had stayed marginally higher than elsewhere.

From this tiny and unpromising base, however, the fortunes of the Dartford warbler at last began to turn. Thanks to a long run of mild winters from the 1970s onwards, numbers steadily grew, to reach a peak by the mid-1990s of well over 3,000 breeding pairs. The two hard winters of 2009–10 and 2010–11 stalled the recovery a little, but the Dartford warbler is now thriving in a way that no-one could have predicted after those terrible events of the early 1960s.

As for the Dartford warbler's discoverer, John Latham, he lived a long and productive life, dying at his home in Hampshire on 4 February 1837, in his ninety-seventh year. And he certainly enjoyed the freedom he gained after his retirement from practising medicine. Having stopped working in 1796, he devoted the remaining four decades of his life to ornithology.

Like other pioneering ornithologists of his day, many of whom we shall encounter in the next chapter, he gave his name to a number of birds around the globe, such as Latham's snipe (sometimes known as Japanese snipe). Other species, including the glossy-black cockatoo, Australian brush-turkey, grosbeak starling and forest francolin, were also originally named after Latham, but have since been given new names.

Yet even he might be surprised to discover that the deeply unsuitable epithet he gave to the Dartford warbler has survived so long. And it's not the only one. Latham named two other British birds after his adopted county, Kent: the Sandwich tern, discovered by his fellow-ornithologist William Boys in 1784, and described and named by Latham three years later; and the Kentish plover, a small wader also discovered by Boys, when he shot three unfamiliar birds on the East Kent coast in May 1787.

Both names are, like that of the Dartford warbler, totally unsuited to the species that bear them. The Sandwich tern (named after the town, not the foodstuff) is found along the coasts of five continents, only being absent from Australasia and Antarctica; while the Kentish plover is also globally widespread. At least the Sandwich tern does regularly occur in Kent, whereas the Kentish plover no longer even breeds in Britain, having disappeared during the second half of the twentieth century. Yet their names survive: a reminder that the most suitable name for a bird is rarely the one by which it is known.

Latham spent many of his later years attempting to bring together the many new ornithological discoveries being made at that time, which he published in a massive ten-volume work, *A General History of Birds*, which appeared in instalments between 1821 and 1828.[1]

However, his advanced age unfortunately meant that the work contained many basic mistakes, as the Revd Charles Swainson, a Victorian parson-ornithologist and the author of a seminal book on the folk names of birds,[2] pointed out: 'His memory was not good; hence he has frequently described the same species by different names; and he placed too much faith in drawings, which led to the same error.'[3]

To be fair on Latham, he was doing his best to clarify a very confusing situation. The late eighteenth and early nineteenth centuries had seen a huge proliferation in the number and variety of bird specimens brought back to Britain from across the globe, thanks to the boom in exploration led by the expansion of the British Empire from roughly 1783 to 1815. 'The museums of Europe', Swainson also commented, 'became crowded with new birds, quite unknown to Linnaeus, without any one naturalist to describe them'.[4]

John Latham had set himself the mission of categorising and classifying all the world's birds; a daunting task for a man by then in his eighties. But although he did not fully succeed, he did at least try. And of all the new places being investigated at this time, and the new species of birds discovered, none were more exciting than the exotic specimens from that newly discovered land far away in the southern hemisphere: Australia.

Decades earlier, these extraordinary birds had captivated Latham, who by examining specimens had written the descriptions of many new species in *The Voyage of Governor Phillip to Botany Bay*, by Arthur Phillip, the first governor of New South Wales, which was published in 1789. And although he never visited Australia himself – indeed, never actually set foot outside Britain – he was nevertheless instrumental in naming many of Australia's best-known birds, including the superb lyrebird, wedge-tailed eagle and the sulphur-crested cockatoo. His fascination with birds down under ultimately led to him being widely called 'the grandfather of Australian ornithology'.

Latham's fascination with Australia's birds was a consequence of a series of historical events, which make a fascinating diversion in our story of how birds got their English names. The coincidence of several factors brought it about: a rise in crime, the loss of a war, and the convenient and timely discovery of a new land on the other side of the globe.

Since the early 1700s, in an increasingly lawless Britain, it had made economic and political sense to send convicts abroad – a process known by the euphemistically benign word 'transportation'. During the middle years of the eighteenth century, more than a thousand people had been sent across the Atlantic Ocean to America, but after the War of Independence ended with the triumph of the rebel colonists in 1783, that avenue was closed. As a result, a new destination had to be found for these unfortunate prisoners. That place was just about as far away from Britain as you could get: Australia.

2: Flaming Galahs and Fairy-Wrens

It had been a long, and at times unspeakably horrendous, voyage. The fleet of eleven ships had left Portsmouth on 13 May 1787, and sailed across the world's oceans for more than eight months, until the first vessel finally made landfall at Botany Bay on 18 January the following year. During the 15,000-mile journey, almost 1,500 crew and passengers had endured baking heat, freak storms, food and water rationing, an aborted mutiny, the company of rats, lice, bedbugs, fleas and cockroaches, and the deaths of almost fifty of their fellow men and women through sickness, violence and the occasional drowning.

The story of the First Fleet has become the stuff of legend. For these were no ordinary passengers, but convicts, being deported from England to this new and unknown land, in what would eventually become one of the greatest mass movements of people in the whole of history: the colonisation of Australia.

Along with the earlier settlement of North America by the Pilgrim Fathers, and the later expansion of the British Empire into Africa and Asia, this would extend the influence of English bird names around the world. But for the people being taken to the other side of the globe, the naming of the birds in this new land was probably the very last thing on their minds.

In *The Fatal Shore*, his eloquent and moving account of the history of transportation, Robert Hughes points out that crew and convicts alike were being sent into the complete unknown:

> Never had a colony been founded so far from its parent state, or in such ignorance of the land it occupied. There had been no reconnaissance. In 1770, Captain James Cook had made landfall on the unexplored east coast of his utterly enigmatic continent, stopped for a short while at a place named Botany Bay and gone north again. Since then, no ship had called: not a word, not an observation, for seventeen years, each one of which was exactly like the thousands that had preceded it. . .[5]

It is no wonder that, as the ships finally made landfall, the over-riding emotion amongst the passengers was one of relief at having survived the voyage at all. But this was swiftly followed by bafflement: at the unforgiving sandstone landscape with its unusual greyish-green vegetation, the terrifying appearance of the indigenous peoples, and especially the truly bizarre wild creatures they encountered as they began to explore their new and utterly unfamiliar surroundings.

There were peculiar animals that jumped along on their hind legs, egg-laying mammals sporting a beak and webbed feet, and an astonishing array of impossibly colourful and noisy birds. As his ship *Lady Penrhyn* was making her way up the narrow channel towards Port Jackson (now Sydney), the ship's surgeon Arthur Bowes Smyth made this excited entry in his journal: 'The singing of the various birds among the trees, and the flight of the numerous parraquets, lorrequets, cockatoos, and maccaws, made all around appear like an enchantment. . .'[6]

He may have been wrong about macaws (they are only found in the Americas) but, as Hughes points out, there were still plenty more birds for him to marvel at:

Several dozen kinds of parrot thronged the harbour bush: Galahs, bald-eyed Corellas, pink Leadbeater's [now Major Mitchell's] Cockatoos, black Funereal [now Yellow-tailed Black] Cockatoos, down through the rainbow-coloured lorikeets and rosellas to the tiny, seed-eating budgerigars which, when disturbed, flew up in green clouds so dense that they cast long rippling shadows on the ground.[7]

These birds can still be seen in the Sydney area, and across much of the rest of this vast nation, though sadly in far lower numbers than when the First Fleet arrived. But from the awestruck accounts of those early settlers, through later generations of Australians, right up to today's visitors from abroad, that sense that Australia's birds – and their names – are truly unique has never really gone away. I discovered this for myself more than two centuries later, in 2008, when I visited this strange and beguiling land.

The plains-wanderer may sound like the jolly swagman out of 'Waltzing Matilda', Australia's unofficial national anthem, but it is actually one of that country's rarest, least-known and most sought-after birds. About the size of a song thrush, and with the physique of a pot-bellied quail, its nearest relatives are the South American seedsnipes.

On that trip to Australia I had a rare opportunity to connect with this almost mythically elusive bird. Nervous with anticipation, a small group of us gathered under a clear, star-filled sky in a paddock in rural New South Wales. I say 'paddock' but, being Australia, it covered an area of more than 80 square miles, and its perimeter was comfortably longer than a marathon course.

Torches at the ready, we set off. It was a chilly night, and I was soon wishing I had worn warmer clothes, as it looked set to be a long one. Yet barely five minutes after we began our search, one of the guides caught a pale, moth-like creature in her spotlight beam. Fluttering on long, slender wings, it plummeted to the ground – surely never to be seen again.

The torches swept around like anti-aircraft lights, and then I heard a clear warning voice: 'Stephen . . . *don't* step forward.'

As the torch beam reached me, I looked down, to find a small, brown creature crouching motionless, exactly where my foot was about to tread. It was a male plains-wanderer, staring right back at me with a mixture of fear and bafflement. Although at that point I had been watching birds for over 40 years, and seen almost 2,000 different species around the world, this truly was the most extraordinary, heart-stopping moment of my entire birding life.

The appreciative noises coming from the darkness around me suggested I was not alone. We stood and stared at this extraordinary creature like members of some minor religious sect until, a few moments later, it flew away into the darkness, never to be seen again.

This was my very first visit to Australia and, despite my long years of watching birds, on each of the other six continents, it was like starting birding all over again in some kind of weird parallel universe. That was because of the 200-plus different species of bird I saw on my whistle-stop tour, more than eighty per cent were completely new to me.

Before I go birding in a new place, I like to do my homework; looking up the birds I hope to see, and trying to learn the key plumage features that will help me identify them. But this time, the very act of doing so left me more confused than ever. What on earth were galahs and gerygones, currawongs and pardalotes, blue bonnets and bronzewings? What was a weebill, or a dollarbird? What was the difference between an apostlebird and a mistletoebird, apart from their vaguely festive names? And what – or perhaps who – was a Jacky winter or a Willie wagtail?

Some species – along with their names – were far more familiar. I was hoping to catch up with one of the largest of the all the world's birds, the emu, and one of the best known, the budgerigar. I knew that the brolga was a species of crane, and a cockatiel a kind of miniature cockatoo. I was well acquainted with bowerbirds and lyrebirds from David Attenborough's television programmes, and could guess that a varied sitella might look rather like a nuthatch (Sitta is the generic name for nuthatches) – as indeed it does.

But I had no idea that the bell miner, the noisy friarbird, and the eastern spinebill are all members of the vast honeyeater family, whose seventy-plus species covered page after page of my field guide. Gazing at their names, many of which appeared to be some combination of a colour and a part of the body – yellow-faced, white-eared, black-chinned, blue-faced, and brown-headed, together with scarlet, black, dusky, banded, striped and painted – I began to suffer from blurred vision, and wondered whether I would be able to cope when faced with this bewildering array of new birds.

The reason that Australian bird names seem so odd is that many of the birds themselves are confined to this particular part of the world. Australasia finally broke away from the much larger landmass of Gondwanaland about 100 million years ago; that's an awfully long time for its fauna and flora to have evolved along a very different path from the rest of the planet.

As a result, more than four-fifths of Australasian mammals, 90 per cent of reptiles, and 93 per cent of amphibian species are endemic – found only in Australasia, and nowhere else in the world. Because birds can fly, and therefore colonise new lands across the sea, a far lower proportion is endemic: even so, about 350 out of the 800 regularly occurring species of bird in Australasia – almost one in two – are only found here. Compare this to Britain, with just one endemic species (the Scottish crossbill), or Europe, with about a dozen.* Yet despite the fact that many of Australia's birds cannot be seen anywhere else in the world, their names often seem strangely familiar to a British birder. So where did these names come from?

---

* Under current taxonomic rules there are thirteen: Balearic shearwater, Spanish imperial eagle, Caucasian snowcock, rock partridge, red-legged partridge, Marmora's warbler, Balearic warbler, crested tit, Corsican nuthatch, Scottish crossbill, parrot crossbill, citril finch and Corsican citril finch. However, as more and more species are 'split' (see Chapter 7) there may well be more – though nothing like as many as can be found in Australia.

On my week-long trek from Melbourne to Sydney, via the eucalypt forests, wetlands and mountains of Victoria and New South Wales, I came across the welcome swallow, Australian raven and black swan, all of which are indeed cousins of our own species.

But the woodswallows, fairy-wrens, robins, treecreepers and the Australian magpie are not at all closely related to their Eurasian counterparts. The magpie-lark, a black-and-white bird about the size of a blackbird, is neither a magpie nor a lark, but a monarch flycatcher – one of a family of small, insectivorous songbirds. Despite their familiar sounding names, many of these birds – including the fairy-wrens and robins – are more closely related to one another than they are to the groups of birds they superficially resemble.

The reason they have such unsuitable and misleading names is, of course, a legacy of those early settlers. Convicts – and many of the sailors – were forced to make a new life in this new land, but that did not mean that they forgot their former existence. And so when one homesick colonist came across a small, plump, perky bird with a red breast hopping across the ground in front of him, it was only natural that he should name it after a favourite bird from home.

This explains why a family of almost fifty species, taxonomically sandwiched between the birds-of-paradise of New Guinea and the picathartes (bald crows) of West Africa, is still known today as the 'Australasian robins'. Some, like the scarlet, rose, pink and flame robins, do indeed have that familiar red breast. But others, including the eastern and western yellow robins, the smart black-and-white hooded robin, and the skulking, greyish-coloured mangrove robin, sport a wide range of different colours. And none of them is even vaguely related to our own robin redbreast.

Not every Australian bird was named out of a nostalgic yearning for the English countryside and its native wildlife. Some were given names based on what they were called by Australia's indigenous population. But even though the aboriginal peoples had been on the continent for at least 30,000 – and perhaps as long as 60,000 – years before the western settlers first arrived, precious few Australian bird names derive from their languages.

Those that do include the gang-gang cockatoo, a greyish-brown and scarlet-headed bird confined to south-east Australia; and its noisy and colourful grey and shocking pink cousin, the galah, one of the most familiar of all Australian birds. This sociable, noisy species has given rise to the slang phrase 'flaming galah', still widely used as an insult to describe a simpleton or fool.

One of Australia's best-known birds also bears an aboriginal name. The laughing kookaburra is a dry-country species of king-fisher whose ringing call does indeed sound like hysterical human laughter. The name 'kookaburra' – clearly onomatopoeic in origin – has been traced back to several indigenous languages. Yet such was the prejudice against 'native' names that, despite being widely used for almost a century, kookaburra was only adopted as the species' official name in 1926. Before then it was known as the 'great brown kingfisher', a rather prosaic name originally coined by Latham.

Such an extrovert bird was also bound to attract its fair share of folk names – perhaps more than any other Australian bird. Many of the names listed by Ian Fraser and Jeannie Gray in their defini-tive work on the subject, *Australian Bird Names*,[8] including 'Jacky', 'Jacko' and 'laughing John', derive from the English word 'jackass', referring to the kookaburra's donkey-like call. Others, such as 'alarm bird', 'breakfast bird' and 'clock bird', all acknowledge the impossibility of staying asleep when a kookaburra is calling outside your bedroom window, while 'woop woop pigeon' and 'ha ha duck' acknowledge the sound's similarity to human laughter.

The most famous of all aboriginal bird names is – thanks to its worldwide popularity as a cagebird – budgerigar.* The name is supposed to come from a phrase meaning 'good cockatoo'. 'Good' in this case refers to these birds' uncanny ability to find precious sources of water out in the bone-dry outback, a crucial aid to nomadic people in times of drought.

But other names which to our untrained ears may sound aboriginal, in fact have a very different origin. The word 'cockatoo', used for a family of birds closely associated with Australia, is actually from the Malay language – hence its early appearance in Arthur Bowes Smyth's 1788 journal. Likewise the names of Australia's tallest bird, the emu, and the heaviest, the southern cassowary, are not aboriginal either, but derive respectively from Portuguese and Malay, the latter coming into English via Dutch or French. In both cases, this is because members of the cockatoo and cassowary families had previously been discovered in south-east Asia, and so had already been given names.

Australian bird names are also distinguished by their frequent use of nicknames, and some over-the-top – yet often very appropriate – epithets. These include noisy (pitta, friarbird and miner), magnificent (riflebird), graceful (honeyeater), rainbow (lorikeet, bee-eater

---

* Also sometimes spelt as *betcherrygah*, *betshiregah*, *bougirigard* and *budgeragar*.

and pitta) and elegant (parrot). But for sheer hyperbole, it is hard to beat a quartet of fairy-wrens, tiny yet colourful birds with cocked tails, whose names get more and more elaborate as they go up the scale: from variegated, through lovely and splendid, to superb.

As for those originally based on nicknames, my favourites are Jacky winter, another member of the Australian robin family, and Willie wagtail, a species of fantail. Jacky winter may have arisen from the bird's habit – like its European counterpart the robin – of singing during the winter months. Willie wagtail, as Fraser and Gray point out, is the 'most archetypal of Australian bird names'. Yet it seems more likely that when the colonists came across a slender black-and-white bird with a long tail they simply named it after a bird familiar from back home, the pied wagtail ('willie wagtail' was already used as a folk name in Britain, especially in Scotland).[9]

Despite their informal and unscientific origins, a handful of other names coined by those early colonists have somehow managed to escape the tendency of modern ornithologists to 'tidy up' bird names, and are still used today. These include the Cape Barren goose, a peculiar-looking bird with a grey body and lime-green bill, named after an island off the north-east coast of Tasmania; the brush-turkey, a member of the megapode family, which incubates its eggs by burying them in a huge mound of earth and leaves; and the lyrebird, whose fan-like tail does indeed closely resemble that ancient stringed instrument.*

---

* The lyrebird also managed to acquire a wide range of alternative names, including 'pheasant', 'paradise-bird' and 'peacock-wren' – the latter aptly described by Fraser and Gray as 'surely one of the most creative or desperate of the many compound names coined in Australia'.

Despite the awful start to their new life, those unfortunate convicts transported to Australia on the First Fleet, and the sailors who accompanied them, did ultimately manage to create a new home in this forbidding and quintessentially foreign land, many thousands of miles from their old lives.

In doing so, they began the process of globalisation that led to the world we know today, in which shrinking horizons have seen the sharing of knowledge and the homogenisation of culture and language. At the same time as these new names were springing up in Australia, successive revolutions were occurring in the way we understood the natural world, leading inevitably to slow but steady standardisation in the English names given to birds.

Not everyone was able to take advantage of this expansion in travel and knowledge. Back in Britain, the vast majority of people – especially those living in rural areas – led a virtually sedentary life, rarely travelling more than a few miles from where they were born. For them, the world was bounded by a few familiar places and people, and also by a few well-known and frequently encountered birds.

So despite the best efforts of pioneering ornithologists from Turner to Pennant – and of course Linnaeus – to standardise the names being used for birds, there was still a powerful pull in the opposite direction. Well into the nineteenth century, and sometimes beyond, ordinary folk still preferred to use folk names: those that had been used by their parents and grandparents before them. Many of the new names took a long time to reach rural communities; and even when they did, were unlikely to gain acceptance over the simpler and more familiar names used for centuries.

This tension between the new and the old names – and between the new science and the old traditions of the countryside — is demonstrated in the life story of one remarkable man: the poet and naturalist John Clare. Although he was courted by literary society, he still retained his rural roots — and the bird names he had learned as a boy — for the whole of his life. And even as ornithology was gaining reputation as a science, these old names were proving remarkably resistant to change.

3: The Nature Poet

No other poet wrote about birds as often — or as well — as John Clare. This nineteenth-century farm labourer turned man of letters was, as the ornithologist and broadcaster James Fisher deftly put it: 'the finest poet of Britain's minor naturalists and the finest naturalist of Britain's major poets'.

Thanks to his field skills, observational talents and hard-won expertise, Clare's writings contain references to at least 120 (and possibly as many as 150) different species. These observations give us a profound insight into the dramatic and often devastating changes to the birds of our farmed countryside over the past two hundred years. Foremost amongst these is the loss of the bird Clare described as a ubiquitous 'summer noise among the meadow hay': the corncrake or, as Clare called it, the landrail.

Patronised by the London literati as a 'peasant poet', Clare, and in due course his poetry and prose, were intimately linked to the place where he grew up, and spent the majority of his life: the village of Helpston. Living on the edge of the flat, watery fens of

East Anglia, but also close to the classic 'Middle England' land-scape of Northamptonshire, the young Clare could explore fields and meadows, streams and rivers, woods and fens, and get to know their birdlife.

Through his rootedness in one place, during his twenties and thirties John Clare produced some of the finest nature poems ever written. However, for over a century these were neglected by liter-ary critics and the general public alike, until from the 1950s onwards his reputation was restored and rehabilitated. Today he is widely hailed as one of the most influential of all writers on nature.

I became hooked on Clare's bird poetry more or less by accident, when studying English Literature at Cambridge back in the early 1980s. My Director of Studies at Gonville and Caius College, the famously enigmatic poet J. H. Prynne, learned of my interest in birds and enthusiasm for the poetry of John Clare, and suggested I meet John Barrell, who I later discovered was one of the world's greatest experts on Clare's writings.

Sitting in Professor Barrell's wood-panelled room in the forbid-ding surroundings of King's College, I nervously explained that I had noticed that the verse structure of Clare's bird poems somehow seemed to mimic the movements and behaviour of the bird itself. Encouraged by his positive response, I went on to write my under-graduate dissertation on this very subject.[10]

I am not alone in my love and admiration of John Clare; he has inspired many of today's cohort of 'new nature writers'. But at the time, not everyone approved of the way he wrote about the natural world. His contemporary John Keats complained that in his verse 'the description too much prevailed over the sentiment.' While that may occasionally be true, it is impossible to dispute Clare's intimate knowledge and understanding of nature, gained from day to day, season to season and year to year, and more importantly his skill in turning these marvellously detailed observations into poetry.*

Yet despite Clare's undoubted influence and popularity today, for the new reader the poems can at first appear rather baffling. This is not just because of the style of writing, which, once you get used to his lack of punctuation and rather eccentric spelling, is actually very accessible – and full of delightful insights into bird behaviour – but also because in many cases the self-taught Clare chose to ignore the official name for the species, preferring to use the folk name he grew up with.

So in his poems we find the land rail and fern owl, butter bump and fire tail, water hen and peewit – now known respectively as the corncrake and nightjar, bittern and redstart, moorhen and lapwing.†

At other times, Clare would use the correct epithet for the species, but ascribe it to the wrong family, as when he referred to the reed sparrow (reed bunting), reed wren (reed warbler) and grasshopper

* Clare was equally contemptuous of Keats's lack of first-hand knowledge of the natural world, pointing out that his more famous rival 'often described nature as she appeared to his fancies and not as he would have described her had he witnessed the things he describes. . .'

† Clare's use of folk names is not some rustic affectation, as can be seen from the sonnet 'The Fern Owl's Nest', in which this alternative name for the nightjar is integral to the experience evoked by the poem:

> The weary woodman rocking home beneath
> His tightly banded faggot wonders oft
> While crossing over the furze-crowded heath
> To hear the fern owl's cry that whews aloft
> In circling whirls and often by his head
> Wizzes as quick as thought. . .

lark (grasshopper warbler). He would also often use names interchangeably for several different species, as in the opening lines of
this sonnet, where 'black cap' refers to the great tit:

> Under the twigs the black cap hangs in vain
> With snow white patch streaked over either eye

The bird we now know as the blackcap – a member of the warbler family – Clare also called the March nightingale, because of its
early return from its winter quarters and melodious song. However,
while he may have titled his sonnet after the folk name, 'The March
Nightingale', within the poem he preferred the official name:

> The rocking clown leans oer the spinney rail
> In admiration at the sunny sight
> The while the Blackcap doth his ears assail
> With such a rich and such an early song
> He stops his own and thinks the nightingale
> Hath of her monthly reckoning counted wrong

Clare's use of folk names is in some ways a throwback to an earlier age, before the standardisation brought about by ornithologists,
when bird names were far more fluid and changeable.

But even Clare could not resist the tide forever. Changes were
afoot, and nineteenth-century ornithologists were busily continuing the work of Thomas Pennant and his predecessors in
standardising the names given to birds. In the longer term the
messy assemblage of folk names so beloved of Clare, with several

alternative names for each species, was simply not sustainable.

This also reflected bigger changes occurring at the time: the growing gulf between the rise of science, epitomised by a new generation of museum-based ornithologists who we shall meet in the next chapter, and men such as Clare, who based their knowledge on hard-won observations in the field, and were often contemptuous of the professionals. According to Clare scholar Eric Robinson, the poet did not have a very high opinion of revered ornithologists such as Pennant, as is evident in this comment on the plucking of geese: 'Mr Pennant says he saw the buisness of Geese pulling baere and that they pulled gosslings that were not above 6 weeks old I have no hesitation in saying that Mr Pennant is a Liar.'[11]

One reason why names had to be standardised was purely pragmatic, and due to the birth of a new publishing phenomenon: books about the natural world. Following the popularity of White's bestselling *The Natural History of Selborne* (see Chapter 3), there was a growing demand for 'guidebooks' enabling ordinary people to identify the wild creatures they saw.

This gap in the market was soon filled by the engraver and political radical Thomas Bewick, with his pioneering *A History of British Birds*, published in two volumes: *Land Birds* (1797) and *Water Birds* (1804). These reached a very wide audience, thanks to their delightful woodcut illustrations and clear, readable prose.

As was the custom of his day, Bewick referred to willow-wrens and throstles, titlarks and ringtails, pied and barred woodpeckers.[*]

---

[*] Willow warbler, song thrush, meadow pipit, hen harrier, great spotted and lesser spotted woodpeckers, respectively.

Many of his readers would have known these, while some would have had their own preferred local versions. But Bewick also used a number of truly obscure names, including cravat goose, ash-coloured sandpiper and castaneous duck,* which would have been baffling to many of his readers. It was clear that from now on the names used for birds needed to be standardised, to enable the reader to know which species was being referred to, whether they lived in Penzance or Penarth, Inverness or the Isle of Wight. Someone needed to take on the thankless and time-consuming task of collating all the different names in use at the time, and making clear and lasting decisions on which should prevail. Such a person would have to be tough and uncompromising, knowledgeable and clear-thinking, assiduous and at times inspired, with the hard-won skills of a field observer combined with the scientific knowledge of the professional ornithologist. On top of all this, they would need the stamina to take on a workload that might defeat a lesser man.

The time was ripe for the entrance onto the scene of one of the least likely of all James Fisher's 'ornithological heroes'; a man who simply got on with the job in hand: 'In his efficient way, he swept up almost the last of our birds that were unknown because unrecognised, and usually unrecognised because undistinguished from some close relative.'[12]

The name of this often misunderstood and underrated man, who gave his name to one of the rarest and most elusive of all Britain's breeding birds? George Montagu.

* For Canada goose, knot and ferruginous duck.

4: *The Military Man*

As I gazed across the field of golden barley, my eyes were momentarily dazzled by the reflection from the sun, high in the clear blue
July sky. Then, in the distance, close to the hedgerow bordering the
back of the field, I saw a movement. This time it wasn't just heat
haze, but – at last – the bird I had come to see.

The female harrier rose up on long, slender wings just a few feet
above the sea of barley, the crop waving to and fro in the gentle
breeze. As she floated effortlessly in the thick summer air I could
see the distinctive white rump at the base of her long, narrow tail,
contrasting with the brownish hue of the rest of her plumage.

For a few moments, I took in her elegant shape and form before,
seemingly out of nowhere, another bird appeared. This was the
male: even slimmer and more aerodynamic than his mate, and
sporting a pale, dove-grey plumage with black tips to his wings,
as if he had just dipped them in a bottle of ink. As the male
approached, she rose higher into the sky, and they began an aerial
dance, twisting and turning in the warm summer air to cement
their bonds of courtship.

Then I noticed that the male was carrying something in his talons
– a vole, or perhaps a meadow pipit or skylark. He flew above his
mate, stalled in mid-air, and dropped his prey; a fraction of a second
later she stalled too, then twisted almost upside-down to grab her
gift from the air, before flying down to her hidden nest.

I had witnessed one of the most intimate of all bird behaviours
and, as the male powered away into the distance, I was left wondering

if I had really seen it at all, so quickly had it happened. But I had – and I'm one of the few lucky ones, for although this elegant harrier breeds across a wide swathe of Europe, western Asia and north-west Africa, barely a dozen pairs of this beautiful creature return each spring to nest in the arable fields of southern Britain.

Yet despite this bird's rarity in the UK, it was in south Devon that, just over two centuries ago, one man identified it as a species new to science; a species that would eventually come to bear his name: Montagu's harrier.

George Montagu first came across what would become 'his' harrier on a hot August day in 1803. A local man had shot and killed a bird of prey and, unable to identify it, brought it to Montagu for him to inspect. As he dissected the bird, discovering that it had a freshly caught skylark in its stomach, Montagu became more and more excited. For although it superficially resembled a male hen harrier, this bird was noticeably smaller and more slender, and also had a longer tail, with reddish-brown markings on its pale grey wings.

Confident that it was a species hitherto unknown to science, Montagu gave the bird its original scientific and English names: *Falco cinerarius*, the 'Ash-coloured Falcon'. Two decades after Montagu's death, the French ornithologist Louis Vieillot and his Dutch colleague Coenraad Temminck commemorated its discoverer by renaming it 'le busard Montagu', from which William MacGillivray coined the current English name: Montagu's harrier.

But George Montagu's contribution to our knowledge and understanding of Britain's birds went far beyond this tribute. His life story reveals much about the stifling formality of the society in which he lived; a society he ultimately chose to reject, so that he could pursue his lifelong passion for birds.

Montagu packed a lot into his six decades on this Earth. Born in 1753, he joined the army at the age of seventeen and was married a year later to Ann Courtenay, the high-born daughter of a nobleman. She gave birth to six healthy children – four sons and two daughters – while Montagu himself rose to become a lieutenant colonel in the county militia of Wiltshire.

But despite his outwardly successful and respectable life, all was not well with George Montagu. He had always been fascinated by the natural world, yet the demands of his military career, and his obligations towards his large and growing family, made him increasingly unhappy and frustrated. By the time he reached his thirty-sixth year he was suffering from what we might now call a mid-life crisis.

A letter survives which sheds some light on his state of mind: written in June 1789 to the Hampshire vicar and naturalist Gilbert White. White had just published his life's work, *The Natural History of Selborne*, which would go on to become the bestselling nature book of all time. In the pages of his letter, the much younger Montagu pours out his heart, telling White that he has 'delighted in being an ornithologist from infancy, and, was I not bound by conjugal attachment, should like to ride my hobby into distant parts'.

Eventually, that's exactly what he did. But not before he faced crisis after crisis: a series of disasters that might have broken a lesser man. For during the following decade, Montagu's life began to fall apart in a quite spectacular manner.

First, in 1797, his unmarried elder brother James died suddenly, leaving George the family estates. There was just one condition:

he must live in one of the houses on the estate with his wife. But by then, Montagu had already separated from Ann, and begun a secret affair with the wife of a London merchant, Mrs Eliza Dorville. The news of their clandestine relationship soon became public, causing outrage in polite Georgian society.

About this time Elizabeth, Lady Holland, a noted society hostess, encountered Montagu at a dinner party. She was clearly not impressed, as she waspishly confided to her journal:

> Colonel Montagu I saw but once . . . and after dinner he gave the natural history of every bird that flies and every fish that swims. He is a man of bad temper, nor does it sound creditable to him that none of his officers speak to him, and they are on the eve of bringing him to Court-martial.

Soon after this inauspicious encounter, court-martial proceedings were indeed begun against Montagu. This was ostensibly because of insulting remarks he was supposed to have made to the wives of his fellow-officers, but he was surely not helped by his scandalous liaison with Eliza Dorville. On 15 October 1799 the tribunal found him guilty, and expelled him from the militia. His military career was over.

Worse was to come. Following the court-martial, Montagu became embroiled in a bitter dispute with his eldest son over the inheritance, which eventually led to the loss of most of the family estates. But with every cloud comes the proverbial silver lining. For George Montagu, it was the freedom to indulge in his twin passions: the love of his mistress and his burgeoning career as a naturalist.

He and Eliza fled westwards, settling at Knowle House, just outside the village of Kingsbridge on the South Devon coast. There, he pursued the study and classification of birds, and she – described by him as 'my friend in science' – provided illustrations of them. His masterwork, the two-volume *Ornithological Dictionary; or Alphabetical Synopsis of British Birds*, was first published in 1802, with several revised editions after his death. A later ornithologist, Elliot Coues, described this as 'one of the most notable of treatises on British birds . . . which has held its place at a thousand elbows for three-quarters of a century'.

The reason the *Ornithological Dictionary* is so important to our story is that – like all good dictionaries – it is both clear and comprehensive. There are long entries on each species, which in taut, closely spaced prose describe the bird and its appearance, plumage details, habitat, habits and other points of interest. But there are also dozens of one-line definitions, most of which give the alternative name for a species together with its official one, as in this series of entries:

CHURCH OWL – A name for the Barn Owl.
CHURN OWL – A name for the Nightjar.
CINEREOUS GODWIT – A name for the Greenshank.
CINEREOUS SHRIKE – A name for the Butcher-bird
[red-backed shrike].

For anyone trying to fathom the confusing morass of alternative folk names of Britain's birds at the time, the book was a godsend. But it was far more than the dry reference work suggested by its title – for, having worked out which species was being referred to, the reader could then obtain a clear summary of the latest knowledge about that particular bird.

A flavour of Montagu's writing can be seen in the opening lines of the entry on the hoopoe, which then as now was a scarce but regular visitor to southern Britain:

> The weight of this beautiful bird is about three ounces; length twelve inches; the bill is black, two inches and a half long, slender, and curved; irides hazel; the crown of the head is furnished with a crest composed of a double row of dull orange-coloured feathers, tipped with black, lengthening from the forehead backwards, the longest of which is above two inches.

This is precision writing at its best: the prose of a man who has looked really closely at the bird he is writing about. In referring to the hoopoe as 'beautiful' he even, rather uncharacteristically, allows himself a personal comment.

With its combination of forensic accuracy and extraordinary attention to detail, Montagu's *Ornithological Dictionary* set the standard for the bird books that would follow during the Victorian era, such as the seminal multi-volume works by William Yarrell (1837–43) and William MacGillivray (1837–52).*

But Montagu did not simply replicate and catalogue the work of others; he made many crucial discoveries of his own. As well as his eponymous harrier, near his Devon home he also discovered

---

* For more on William MacGillivray, the man described as 'Scotland's forgotten genius in the field of natural history', see Chapter 5.

the cirl bunting, a species known from continental Europe but not recorded before in Britain.

The cirl bunting is a handsome yet rather curious-looking bird, which looks as if it has been assembled from different parts of other, more familiar species. Superficially similar to its cousin the yellow-hammer, with a yellowish head, it also sports a streaky back like a reed bunting or dunnock, olive-green underparts like a greenfinch, and a black mask and throat like a house sparrow.

Montagu first came across cirl buntings near his home in the freezing winter of 1800, finding them 'not uncommon amongst flocks of yellow hammers and chaffinches.' Whether the species was there all along, and just needed someone of his skill and experience to notice it, is a moot point; some have suggested that it had only recently colonised England from across the Channel, though it seems far more likely that it had hitherto simply been overlooked. But as with so many other species, it was Montagu who cleared up any doubts as to its status as a British bird, unable to resist a dig at his fellow-ornithologists for their apparently poor observational skills: 'It is remarkable that so common a bird as the Cirl-Bunting seems to be in the west of England, should have so long escaped the notice of British naturalists.'

He himself had no doubt that the species had been present for some time. As he notes in the closing lines of his entry, even when the weather turned so cold during that bitter winter of 1800, the birds stayed put, suggesting that the species was not newly arrived from warmer climes, but had always been living there.

In the 200 years or so since Montagu made his momentous discovery, the cirl bunting's fortunes have waxed and waned. Until the middle of the twentieth century it could be found (albeit locally) across much of southern Britain, but after a rapid and precipitous decline the species retreated to the southern tip of Devon, close to where Montagu had first discovered it, and numbers fell to little more than a hundred pairs. The cirl bunting appeared to be on its way out as a British breeding bird.

Thanks to the efforts of the RSPB and local farmers, however, this curious yet attractive little bird has since made a dramatic comeback. Although, because of its highly sedentary nature and very specific habitat requirements, it is still largely confined to Devon, there are now almost 1,000 breeding pairs in the county. The species has also been successfully reintroduced to Cornwall, in what is thought to be the only example of the successful reintroduction of a songbird in the whole of Europe. I'm sure Montagu would have approved.*

Sadly, George Montagu's later life was beset by tragedy. Three of his four sons were killed in the wars against France, and he never became reconciled with his surviving eldest son, leaving him out of his will. He and Eliza did have three children of their own – Henry, Isabella and Georgiana – and his two daughters with Ann also survived him. But it's not hard to imagine that one

---

* If you're wondering about the meaning of the word 'cirl', John Latham coined it in 1783, as a direct translation of Linnaeus's scientific name *Emberiza cirlus*, which we still use today. It comes from the Bolognese dialect of northern Italy, and may derive from an obsolete verb *zirlare*, meaning 'to whistle like a thrush'. This would make cirl bunting another example of an onomatopoeic name hidden beneath layers of translation. It also means that neither of the two commonly used pronunciations – 'curl' and 'sirl' – is correct, as in Italian the combination of letters 'ci' is pronounced as 'ch'. So next time you come across the bird, confuse your companions by calling it a 'chirl bunting'.

reason this proud, intense and reputedly difficult man may have thrown himself into his work was as one way of mitigating the terrible loss of his sons, and perhaps also assuaging his guilt at deserting them.

On 20 June 1815, just two days after the Duke of Wellington's famous victory over Napoleon at the Battle of Waterloo, the life of George Montagu came to a premature and painful end. A few days earlier, while building work was being carried out on his home in south Devon, he had inadvertently trodden on a rusty nail. Tetanus ensued, and he died in a high fever, aged sixty-two.

Later students of birds had good reason to thank George Montagu, for the *Ornithological Dictionary* was the first systematic attempt to list all the birds found in Britain. It helped to kick-start the still young science of ornithology, and was widely used for at least a century after his death. And of course we still commemorate him – albeit often unwittingly – when a birder sights the rare and beautiful raptor and shouts excitedly to his companions: 'I've got a Monty's!'

For me, Montagu also represents a man who, despite all his many troubles, led a life well lived, eventually managing to fulfil the ambition to 'ride his hobby into distant parts' – albeit only as far as south Devon. Perhaps I also feel a personal connection with a man who, after a mid-life crisis, headed down to the West Country with the woman he loved, to begin a new and fulfilling life devoted to writing about birds.

The species named after George Montagu, Montagu's harrier, is one of a handful of regularly occurring British birds, and many more around the rest of the world, named after people. In the next chapter, I shall examine the golden age of eponymous bird names, during which many of the more obscure species that had not yet been given a common English name finally earned one. It was an era marked by mutual backscratching and backstabbing, as men (and a few women) competed with one another to have a new species of bird named after them – and by doing so, win everlasting fame.

5

EPONYMS AND EXPLORATION

Bird Names go Global

Remember, they only name things after you when you're dead or really old.

Barbara Bush

1: The Museum Man

As the drizzle continued to fall, soaking the rocks, grass and my clothes, I began to regret my earlier enthusiasm for our nocturnal expedition. It was a damp and uncomfortable August night, and a film crew and I were perched on slippery rocks at the top of Hirta, the largest island of the St Kilda archipelago. Our mission: to record the sounds of Leach's petrels returning to their nests.

For several hours, all we could see were mysterious shapes looming out of the murk, caught momentarily in the beams of our torches before disappearing into the darkness. These were Leach's petrels, though I could only be sure because of their extraordinary calls, which sounded like an amusement arcade machine suffering from radio interference: a constant outpouring of squeaks, clicks and yelps that, had I not known what was making them, would have chilled my blood.

Of all Britain's breeding birds, Leach's petrel is one of the hardest to see. That's not because it is especially rare – there are roughly fifty thousand pairs, far more than the UK population of coots, cormorants or grey herons – but because it chooses to nest on a few far-flung islands off north-west Scotland. Even here, in places such as North Rona, the Flannan Isles and St Kilda, this tiny seabird is almost impossible to find, as it only returns to its breeding colonies after dark, to avoid being attacked by predatory gulls.

When Leach's petrels have finished breeding, they head straight out over the open ocean. They then spend the autumn and winter

175

on the high seas, rarely venturing close to shore unless forced to do so by strong gales. So it is perhaps not surprising that this species was not formally described and named until 1820, the year after the birth of Queen Victoria, and long after the vast majority of Britain's breeding birds had already been discovered.

The story of how Leach's petrel acquired its name embodies the changes occurring during this era, and touches on the life of one of the most eccentric men ever to be commemorated in the name of a British bird: Dr William Elford Leach.

Born in 1790, William Leach was for eight years the Assistant Keeper of Birds at what is now the Natural History Museum, though in later life he became better known as a specialist in insects and crustaceans.

A man of small and delicate build, Leach lived in two small rooms in the museum itself, decorated with an array of skulls and stuffed bats, which he dubbed the 'skullery and battery'. To his colleagues' amusement he kept fit by vaulting over the back of a stuffed zebra in the middle of his office. But beneath his unconventionality, Leach had a sharp and enquiring mind, and in between these gymnastic sessions he kept a keen eye out for new specimens to add to the museum's growing collection.

Attending a major auction of bird skins and eggs in May 1819, Leach found his attention caught by Lot 78, which came with an intriguing description: 'An undescribed petrel with a forked tail, taken at St Kilda in 1818; the only one known (with egg)'. Bidding was brisk, but Leach managed to purchase the petrel and its egg for £5 15 shillings, equivalent to about £420 at today's prices.*

---

* To his delight he also acquired a great auk (also with an egg) for £16 – about £1,200

A year after the auction, the Dutch ornithologist Coenraad Temminck (after whom Temminck's stint is named) visited Leach at the British Museum and examined the specimen. He named it in honour of his host: *Procellaria leachii* – Leach's petrel. Although the species now has a different scientific name, *Oceanodroma leucorhoa* (which roughly translates as 'white-rumped ocean-runner'), the original English name still stands.

Leach was undoubtedly flattered by having this newly discovered seabird named after him. But he may also have been slightly embarrassed, because he must have known the species was not a completely new discovery. In fact, it had already been found by another ornithologist: William Bullock – the man who sold Leach the specimen in the first place. Yet although Bullock had obtained the specimen of the petrel on one of his many collecting trips, and must surely have realised it was new to science, he had – either through carelessness or indifference – neglected to give it a name.

William Bullock was, like Leach, an eccentric and extraordinary man. Described by Barbara and Richard Mearns (authors of *Biographies for Birdwatchers*) as 'a naturalist, collector, traveller, antiquary, auctioneer, and showman',[1] he ran a travelling museum that contained well over 30,000 exhibits, including more than 3,000 specimens of birds and their eggs, and attracted hordes of visitors. But in 1819 he decided to sell off this vast collection to fund a characteristically madcap scheme to make his fortune in Mexico. This was how Leach came to purchase the bird that still bears his name.

today. Less than half a century later, this statuesque flightless seabird would become globally extinct.

We have no idea whether Bullock was aware of the fact that he had a prior claim to the naming of this enigmatic seabird, but we do know that three years later, in 1822, he and his son (also called William) finally headed off to Mexico, where they hoped to make a killing by investing in silver mines. However, the scheme was not a success, and the elder William later returned to Britain via the United States, writing several books about his travels along the way. He died in Chelsea, in 1849, at the age of seventy-six.

William Bullock may have been denied his moment of fame by Leach, but he did live to see a bird named after him – and his son. While in Mexico, they had continued their obsession with shooting and collecting birds. Later, another William – Swainson – chose to name a new species of bright-orange-and-black bird discovered there after them, as Bullock's oriole. 'This, the most beautiful of the group yet discovered in Mexico', wrote Swainson,* 'will record the name of those ornithologists who have thrown so much light on the birds of that country'.

However, despite its auspicious start Bullock's oriole has had a rather chequered history: for many years it was considered merely a well-marked race of the Baltimore oriole, but it has now been granted full specific status once again. (This is discussed in more detail in Chapter 7.)

Back in England, William Leach had also thrown himself into the nomenclatural fray, and was busily giving names to a number of new species. Unfortunately, most of these were later quietly

---

* William Swainson is himself commemorated in the names of three North American birds – a hawk, a thrush and a warbler, as well as a host of tropical species, most of which have since been given new names.

dropped, as he had chosen some rather odd naming systems, such as the nine different genera of birds he christened with variations on the name Caroline (or the Latin 'Carolina'), including anagrams such as *Cirolana*, *Conilera* and *Rocinela*. As Barbara and Richard Mearns suggest, although some people took these to be a tribute to Queen Caroline of Brunswick, the wife of George IV, it is more likely that they referred to a mysterious woman with whom Leach was in love.

All this was taking its toll on Leach's already fragile mental and physical health. In 1821 he fell ill, having 'overworked himself to such a degree that his health and mind became affected', and retired to Italy, accompanied by his devoted sister.

But although gone, he was certainly not forgotten. As well as Leach's storm petrel, William Elford Leach's name featured, in one form or other, in the scientific names of well over a hundred species. More importantly, he was ultimately recognised for his efforts in putting museum science in Britain on a more organised and professional basis.

For decades, zoologists on the continent had pioneered the revision of Linnaeus's original method of classifying species into new and different groups, based on a range of different characters, rather than just one. This helped them work out the relationships between different species – along with larger groups such as families – with a far greater degree of accuracy than before. But British scientists, slavishly following the teachings of their Swedish master, had become inflexible in their thinking, refusing to budge from the original approach. As a result, British zoological studies had become stagnant and ossified.

Leach had always corresponded with French zoologists (something both difficult and unpopular at a time when the Napoleonic Wars between Britain and France were at their height), and soon realised that they were onto something. Despite opposition from his peers, through his determination, insight and hard work, he managed to drag the science of zoology in Britain into the modern era, and give it the status it deserved.

In 1836, the year of William Leach's untimely death from cholera, a parliamentary enquiry delivered its verdict on the management of the Natural History Museum. Leach, noted one observer 'was the first to make the English acquainted . . . with the progress that had been made in natural science on the Continent. Thus a new impetus was given to zoology'.*

His career may have been cut short by illness but, by dragging the infant science of zoology into the modern world, William Leach had paved the way for the next generation, and in particular two far more famous men: Alfred Russel Wallace and Charles Darwin. It is fitting that he should be memorialised in the name of one of our scarcest and most elusive seabirds.

2: Eponymous Birds

William Leach and George Montagu are just two of several thousand people commemorated in the vernacular or scientific names of the world's birds – or, as these names are often known, 'eponyms'.[2]

---

* The zoologist John Edward Gray, speaking to an 1836 parliamentary investigation into the management of the British Museum.

The heyday for this trend was during the eighteenth and nineteenth centuries, when new species of birds were being discovered at a tremendous rate.

This was fuelled by the expansion of the British Empire and its associated exploration of the globe, and especially by the rise of a new breed of intrepid gentleman-explorers, whose gung-ho attitudes would lay the foundation for much of our knowledge and understanding of the world's birds.

Appropriately, many of these men (and a handful of women) are still commemorated in the English names of birds. But even at a time when the fashion for eponyms was at its height, getting your name attached to a new species was not quite as easy as it might appear.

First, you had to travel to distant places with a shotgun over your shoulder, and enough supplies to enable you to spend long and arduous periods in the field. Then you had to find a bird that had never been seen before, shoot it, retrieve the lifeless corpse, and preserve this for long enough for someone else to examine it – ideally one of the museum-based ornithologists back home in Britain. They needed to verify that what you had found was indeed new to science, and not simply some aberrant form, or unknown plumage, of an already familiar species.

Finally, you had to persuade them to honour you by giving it your name – either in English or Latin, or preferably both. But this presented a further problem. The protocol was very clear: you were *not* under any circumstances permitted to name a bird after yourself, but you *could* name it after a fellow ornithologist, who would then, perhaps, return the favour by naming another new species after you.

That was the theory. Unfortunately, however, this cosy mutual arrangement did not always work. In 1826, Charles Payraudeau named Audouin's gull, which he had discovered on a visit to Corsica, after his 'excellent ami' Jean Victor Audouin. However, Audouin somehow neglected to return the favour, and so while his own name lives on in the field guides, the unfortunate Monsieur Payraudeau is consigned to ornithological obscurity. I like to imagine Payraudeau writing a series of increasingly desperate letters to Audouin, imploring him to fulfil his side of the bargain.*

Charles Payraudeau was perhaps unfortunate – after all, many other ornithologists of his day did end up being commemorated in eponymous bird names. Yet looking down a list of the 250 or so different birds that occur regularly in Britain, it immediately strikes me how few are named after people. The reason is obvious: by the time it became the norm to do so, from the late eighteenth century onwards, the vast majority of common British birds had already been found, and so already had vernacular names.

Apart from Montagu's harrier and Leach's petrel, only one regular British breeding bird has an eponymous name: Cetti's warbler, named after an eighteenth-century Italian Jesuit priest, Francesco Cetti.

If we include passage migrants, wintering species and occasional breeders, six other species occurring in Britain are named after people: Bewick's swan, Cory's shearwater, Lady Amherst's pheasant, Temminck's stint, Richard's pipit and Savi's warbler. But when we consider vagrants – those rare birds that are occasional wanderers to our shores – then the picture changes dramatically, with another

---

* Actually he is not totally forgotten: Payraudeau's collection of bird specimens can still be seen at a small museum in La Chaize-le-Vicomte in the Vendée.

42 species with eponymous names, making 51 in all.* Again, this makes sense: these mostly live in the more far-flung corners of the globe, so throughout this era were still being discovered and named.

When it comes to nationality, as you might expect, most of those who have given their names to our birds are British – eighteen in all – followed by eight Italians, seven Germans,† five Frenchmen and three Americans, with one Swede and one Dutchman. Some are so obscure we know virtually nothing about them, while others are amongst the most famous naturalists of all time.‡

The vast majority of them – roughly three-quarters – were mainly active during the nineteenth century, though many were born in the eighteenth and did some of their most important work at this time. Spanning such a crucial period in British and world history, their names are not simply a narrative about ornithology and the naming of birds; they also conceal very human stories, which give us a detailed picture of the world in which they lived and worked.

* In taxonomic order, these are: Steller's eider, Barrow's goldeneye, Fea's petrel, Scopoli's shearwater, Wilson's and Swinhoe's storm-petrels, Baillon's crake, Allen's gallinule, Macqueen's bustard, Baird's sandpiper, Wilson's phalarope, Wilson's snipe, Cabot's and Forster's terns, Sabine's, Bonaparte's, Ross's, Franklin's and Audouin's gulls, Pallas's sandgrouse, Tengmalm's owl, Eleonora's falcon, Pallas's, Hume's, Radde's, western and eastern Bonelli's, Marmora's, Ruppell's, Moltoni's subalpine, Pallas's grasshopper, Sykes and Blyth's reed warblers, White's, Swainson's and Naumann's thrushes, Moussier's redstart, Blyth's pipit, Cretzschmar's and Pallas's reed buntings, Blackburnian and Wilson's warblers.
† Including some born in Prussia (part of which is in present-day Poland) – borders were fairly fluid at this time.
‡ At one end of the fame scale we have Gilbert White (White's thrush), while at the other end there is 'Monsieur Richard of Lunéville' (the capital of Lorraine in eastern France). In October 1815 he 'collected' (i.e. shot) the bird that now bears his name, Richard's pipit. Yet today that is the only thing we know about him.

When I look down the list of the forty-three individuals,* however, one thing immediately strikes me: the gender imbalance. Only three are women.

They are Eleonora of Arborea, a fourteenth-century Sardinian princess, politician and military leader (Eleonora's falcon); the eighteenth-century museum curator Anna Blackburne (Blackburnian warbler); and the British aristocrat Sarah Amherst (Lady Amherst's pheasant). All three birds that bear their names are, like the women they honour, fascinating in their own particular way.

Eleonora's falcon is a slim but powerful raptor which has strayed northwards to Britain from its Mediterranean breeding grounds on only a handful of occasions, since the first was seen over Formby Point in Lancashire in August 1977. Uniquely amongst European birds of prey, Eleonora's falcons delay their breeding until late in the summer, so that they have chicks in the nest during September, the peak period for the autumn migration of songbirds. This guarantees a ready supply of fresh food for their youngsters, which having fledged then follow their parents all the way to Madagascar, where they spend the winter. The next spring, they return to the cliffs of islands such as Mallorca, where I have watched flocks of them during late April catching dragonflies in bright blue skies.

Despite its striking appearance – the species comes in two colour phases, with some birds similar in plumage to a hobby, others all dark – Eleonora's falcon was not described until 1839, from specimens

* Forty-three, as opposed to fifty-one, because some people are commemorated in more than one species. Alexander Wilson (1766–1813) – a Scotsman who left to seek his fortune in the United States and became known as 'the father of American ornithology' – and Peter Simon Pallas each have four species named after them, while Edward Blyth and Franco Andrea Bonelli each have two.

shot by the Italian soldier and naturalist Alberto della Marmora (of whom more later) on the island of Sardinia. Della Marmora sent his specimens to his colleague in Turin, Giuseppe Gené, who decided to commemorate the location of the birds' discovery by naming it after Eleonora of Arborea, a Sardinian princess famed for leading her troops into battle. This may at first appear a rather odd choice, until we discover that she is not only still the island's greatest heroine, but also passed a law protecting the falcons, by preventing the young being taken from the nest – an act of benevolence far ahead of its time.

Anna Blackburne, after whom one of the most beautiful of all North American wood warblers is named, cannot claim quite such a heroic life. Indeed, as Barbara and Richard Mearns point out in their companion volume dealing with North American eponyms, *Audubon to Xantus*, 'she is scarcely known at all'.[3] But in her own quiet way she bucked the trend for women of her time, by becoming a professional naturalist in all but name.

Anna was born in 1726 near Warrington in Lancashire (now Cheshire), and after her mother's death spent much of her life looking after her rich industrialist father in his home at Orford Hall. Being both wealthy and unmarried, she could and did devote much of her spare time to studying nature, an interest she inherited from her father, who conveniently was a friend of Thomas Pennant.

To develop her knowledge of the natural world, Anna first learned Latin, and then began a lengthy correspondence with none other than Linnaeus himself. Inspired by the great man, she set up her own museum at Orford Hall, which eventually housed a major collection of birds, plants and insects. Some of these were sent by another of her correspondents, the German ornithologist and collector Peter Simon Pallas, who also had several species of bird named after him.*

Meanwhile, Anna's younger brother Ashton had travelled to North America, where like many young men of this era he indulged his passion for shooting every living thing within range of his gun. Writing in 1784, after Ashton's death, Thomas Pennant was suitably impressed at his dedication and industry:

> To the rich museum of *American* birds, preserved by Mrs.
> ANNA BLACKBURN [*sic*], of *Orford*, near *Warrington*, I am
> indebted for the opportunity of describing almost every one
> known in the provinces of *Jersey*, *New York* and *Connecticut*.
> They were sent over to the Lady by her brother, the late Mr.
> *Ashton Blackburn*; who added to the skill and zeal of a sports-
> man, the most pertinent remarks on the specimens he collected
> for his worthy and philosophical sister.[4]

Sadly, we do not know if the colourful, black and fiery orange specimen that Pennant named Blackburnian warbler was among those shot by Ashton, but, on the balance of probability, we can infer it was. This has led some to believe that the warbler was named after Ashton, and not his sister; but given Pennant's closeness to the family it is likely that in naming the bird he intended to commemorate both.†

* Including Pallas's sandgrouse, Pallas's warbler, Pallas's grasshopper warbler and Pallas's reed bunting – all of which have been seen in Britain.
† Blackburnian warbler has only ever been recorded twice in Britain, both times in October on offshore islands: on Skomer in 1961 and on Fair Isle in 1988. I was the only birder
on Fair Isle at the time who managed to miss the bird!

The third member of this diverse trio of women after whom birds on the British List are named is the redoubtable Sarah, Lady Amherst. Born the Hon. Sarah Archer in July 1762,* she was widowed with three children before she was forty. But less than a year after her first husband's death, she married again, to a man ten years younger than her: William, Lord Amherst.

Despite Sarah's relatively advanced age, she went on to bear him four children, making seven in all, before in 1823 Lord Amherst took up his post as Governor-General of India. Life there was far from easy, marked by war, mutiny and, for Lady Amherst, by then in her sixties, a dose of cholera that would have killed anyone with a weaker constitution.

After Sir Archibald Campbell, commander of the British forces, had made peace with the King of Burma, he presented Lord and Lady Amherst with two stunningly beautiful pheasants, which in 1828 they eventually brought back to England. A year later, the London taxidermist Benjamin Leadbeater named the species Lady Amherst's pheasant, 'as a tribute due to the distinguished lady to whom ornithologists are indebted' – even though all she had actually done was arrange for the birds to be transported back to England.

Sadly, the rest of her life was marred by tragedy. Having lost one son, Jeffrey, to fever in India, two of her remaining three sons also pre-deceased her, before her death in 1838, aged seventy-five.

The bird named after her has enjoyed mixed fortunes, too. Confined to a forested stretch of Asia from Myanmar in the west to

* Sarah was the eldest daughter of Lord Archer, Baron of Umberslade (near Tanworth-in-Arden, Warwickshire).

southern China in the east, Lady Amherst's pheasant would not normally appear in any book on British birds. But from the late nineteenth century onwards, a number of these exotic gamebirds were bred and released in the grounds of stately homes such as Woburn Abbey in Bedfordshire.

For almost a century, the birds quietly got on with their lives in the woods and fields of Bedfordshire, near to where they had originally been released, with a few crossing the county border into Hertfordshire and Buckinghamshire. By the late 1960s, the population stood at between 100 and 200 pairs. But because they were regarded as little more than an escaped cagebird, few birders took any real interest in them.

Then, in 1971, all that changed, with the surprising (and, in hindsight, misguided) decision to elevate Lady Amherst's pheasant to the official British List, where it joined other originally feral species such as the Canada goose, mandarin duck, and its cousin the golden pheasant. This was done on the grounds that the population was thought to be self-sufficient, a decision that now appears to have been based on rather dubious evidence.

Almost as soon as the species gained official status, and birders finally began to seek it out to add to their lists, numbers began to fall. By the 1980s there were perhaps 200 individuals, and by 1990 as few as 60. I recall one day in early 1987 taking a walk around the woods near Ampthill in Bedfordshire where the few remaining pheasants were supposed to be. Having drawn a blank, I returned to where I had parked my car, only to notice a group of birds at the back of a field. Four magnificent male Lady Amherst's pheasants, their impossibly long tails barred with black-and-silver, were feeding unobtrusively along the edge of a wood. It was the only time I ever saw the species in Britain.

Soon afterwards, Lady Amherst's pheasant did make a brief comeback, but at the turn of the millennium the population was down to as few as 30 individuals. By then, its days as a British bird were numbered: genetic bottlenecks meant the species could not recover unless new birds were released, something no one was willing to do. At the time of writing the population is down to a single male, so the species is inevitably doomed to vanish from Britain.

As to why Lady Amherst's pheasant declined so rapidly, there are a number of reasons. According to the acknowledged authority on introduced species in Britain, Sir Christopher Lever,[5] predation by foxes and the taking of their eggs and chicks by magpies may be one factor, as may human disturbance and loss of habitat. But ironically, two other introduced species may also be at least partly to blame. Goshawks, whose native population was augmented through the late twentieth century by birds released by falconers, would surely make short work of such a showy and colourful bird. Meanwhile another species introduced from Asia, Reeves's muntjac, has destroyed much of the woodland understorey where the pheasants find shelter and make their nests.

It's a matter for debate to whether the loss of such a bird is a cause for concern, considering that it should never really have been present in Britain in the first place. But when the species in question is one of just a handful of regularly occurring British birds named after people – and the only one named after a woman – it is, to my mind, rather sad.

So what of the only other regular British breeding bird to be named after a person: Cetti's warbler? It is one of five species of warbler whose names sound like the defensive line-up of an Italian football team: Bonelli, Cetti, Savi and Marmora, with Moltoni on the bench. Perhaps they'll play against a tight German midfield of Pallas, Radde and Ruppell. Or maybe they'll come up against the English forward line of Hume, Blyth and Sykes. This virtual soccer team comprises the men after whom no fewer than thirteen species of warbler on the British List are named (Pallas and Bonelli have bagged two species each).

Unlike the small, relentlessly active and difficult-to-identify birds that now bear their names, most of which are best told apart by their songs, these men were a pretty diverse bunch. Although by definition they were all amateur or professional ornithologists, for the most part they had other professions and callings, too. Francesco Cetti was a Jesuit priest and mathematician; Alberto della Marmora rose to become a general; Gustav Radde was an apothecary (equivalent to a modern-day pharmacist); Colonel William Henry Sykes was an army officer and later MP for Aberdeen; and Allan Octavian Hume – dubbed 'The Father of Indian Ornithology' – served as a colonial administrator in the Indian Raj.

As with the majority of people who have given their names to birds, all but three of the eleven were most active during the nineteenth century, the unofficial Age of Ornithological Discovery. Only Francesco Cetti (1726–78) and Peter Simon Pallas (1741– 1811) lived earlier, while Professor Edgardo Moltoni was born at the tail end of the nineteenth century in 1896, and died in 1980.*

---

* This anomaly is explained by the fact that the bird bearing his name, Moltoni's sub-alpine warbler, was only recently elevated to full species status, having been separated

The circumstances under which these eponymous ornithologists discovered their species were often quite random. On 22 September 1856, while exploring the remote Transbaikalia region of south-east Russia, the German explorer and naturalist Gustav Radde came across a bulky-looking leaf-warbler. Greenish-brown and with a distinctive pale stripe above its eye, it was hiding in the unlikely surroundings of a kitchen garden in a town with the tongue-twisting name of Kulussutajevsk.

Having finally managed to get reasonable views of the bird, Radde confidently declared it to be a new species: *Phylloscopus schwarzi*, named after his friend and fellow-Prussian Ludwig Schwarz, the astronomer to the expedition. Two decades later, in 1881, another pioneering explorer of this region, the Yorkshireman steel manufacturer and inveterate traveller Henry Seebohm, gave the species its vernacular name, Radde's bush-warbler, later simplified to the one we use today.*

Savi's warbler – named after Paolo Savi, another academic who taught at the University of Pisa – was one of the last of Western Europe's breeding birds to be identified, less than 200 years ago. In 1824, when Savi was examining a small, nondescript bird he had shot some years earlier in Italy, he finally realised that he had discovered a species new to science.

Ironically, the first example had been originally found not in Italy but at Limpenhoe, a village along the Yare Valley in Norfolk, but was misidentified – by none other than Coenraad Temminck – as a

from its very similar-looking cousin, the subalpine warbler.
* In France and Spain, however, Radde's warbler retains its link with the man originally honoured: *pouillot de Schwarz* and *mosquitero de Schwarz* respectively.

Cetti's warbler. A decade or so later, the Norfolk bird was correctly re-identified as a Savi's, and the rather tatty specimen remains in Norwich's Castle Museum to this day.

I can still remember my excitement on seeing Cetti's and Savi's warblers at Stodmarsh in Kent back in the mid-1970s. They had recently colonised Britain, and were beginning to establish thriving populations in south-east England. To be honest, I hardly saw them at all, as both are so elusive that I barely glimpsed either species for longer than a couple of seconds.

I did, however, hear them and, though these two unstreaked, brown warblers may look superficially similar, it is hard to imagine two more strikingly different songs. Savi's warbler – like its cousin the grasshopper warbler – produces a low, insistent, buzzing sound, more like some kind of cricket than a bird, or like a fishing reel being rapidly unwound. This seems to melt into the evening soundscape, making it hard to pick out amongst the various chirping and buzzing insects, especially at a distance. The same definitely *cannot* be said of Cetti's warbler, which has one of the loudest and most distinctive songs of any British bird. As writer and self-confessed 'bad birdwatcher' Simon Barnes has noted, there are several mnemonics that mimic its rhythm: including the unforgettable: 'Me – Cetti? If you don't like it . . . FUCK OFF!'

The Greta Garbo of birds, this small, grey and chestnut brown warbler spends its whole life hiding away in dense vegetation alongside water, and is hardly ever seen for more than a moment or two. But when you hear an explosion of notes emerge from a dense thicket of brambles, the identity of the singer is never in question.

These days this is a familiar sound throughout much of southern

Britain, now that Cetti's warbler has firmly established itself as a breeding resident – unlike most other warblers, which migrate south in autumn, Cetti's stays put all year round. Walking around my local patch on the Somerset Levels, I hear its familiar song in every single month of the year. But until spring 2015, when a Savi's warbler unexpectedly turned up near my home, I hadn't heard one singing in Britain for almost forty years.

When I first saw Savi's warbler back in the 1970s I – and most other observers – assumed it would soon establish itself as a regular British breeding bird. But for some unknown reason, although it is a common breeder in the Netherlands and northern France, Savi's warbler remains only a sporadic visitor on this side of the Channel. Perhaps the one I heard in Somerset will be in the vanguard of a new invasion and, like its cousin Cetti's warbler, this elusive species will finally establish itself as a truly British bird, adding a second Italian eponym to the list of our regular breeding species.

3: Into the North

When we think of the great polar explorers, the same names usually come to mind: Scott, Amundsen and Shackleton in the south, and Peary and Nansen in the north. James Clark Ross is not as well-known as any of these legendary men, and yet arguably he did more to pave the way for their achievements than any other early explorer.

Today, James Ross is commemorated in the name of one of the most beautiful and mysterious of all Arctic birds: Ross's gull. Ross's gull gives the lie to the widely held belief that gulls are ugly, boring, and all look the same. Unlike its larger, bulkier and more cantankerous relatives, it is a graceful, delicate creature, wafting buoyantly over the sea ice towards a passing ship like a visiting angel.

During the brief arctic summer, when Ross's gulls gather to breed on the rapidly thawing tundra, their normally snow-white breast acquires a delicate pinkish tinge, almost as if the bird is blushing at its newfound sexual potency. But few people have ever seen a Ross's gull in all its rosy glory. Indeed, given that this species lives in some of the remotest regions of the planet, very few people have seen one at all. James Fisher called Ross's gull 'one of the most mysterious birds in the world',[6] and although more than sixty years have passed since he wrote those words, this enigmatic creature is still one of the most sought-after of all the Arctic birds that occasionally wander south to Britain.

When I was a teenage birder, back in the mid-1970s, this shadowy bird was barely on my radar. But a chance encounter in the summer of 1974 changed all that. A young Ross's gull turned up on the Dorset coast, near the holiday resort of Christchurch – a sighting described at the time as 'the most remarkable ornithological event of the year'.[7]

My school friend Daniel and I were camping nearby in the New Forest and, having heard about the bird's presence, cycled as fast as we could to where it had been seen. After failing to see the bird on the first day, we returned two days later. Finally we were rewarded, with a minute or so's sighting of this Arctic wanderer, as it drifted past us and eventually out of sight.

More than forty years on, I can still remember the sheer thrill of encountering this legendary bird in such bizarre circumstances: next to a beach at the height of the summer holidays, surrounded by families sunbathing and making sandcastles. There and then I resolved to find out more about this mysterious species – and about the man whose name it bears. So who exactly was James Clark Ross, and what connection did he have with his eponymous gull?

Like many of his fellow Victorian explorers, James Ross's life story reads like something out of the *Boy's Own Paper*. Born in 1800, he originally went to sea as a twelve-year-old ship's lad, on a vessel captained by his uncle, John Ross – himself a distinguished polar explorer and decorated veteran of the Napoleonic Wars.

During the next few years, the expedition's ships travelled back and forth through the Arctic seas, on an ultimately unsuccessful search for the legendary North-West Passage. For these early nineteenth-century explorers, the obsessive quest for this sea route from the Atlantic to the Pacific was the equivalent of later generations climbing Mount Everest or landing on the moon, and in its time perhaps even harder to achieve. For although the Vikings had sailed their longboats far into this land of ice-floes, bitter winds and violent seas, no-one had ever managed to find their way through to the other side – and on to the lucrative trade markets of Asia. It was a quest that would ultimately provide new insights into the geography and natural history of this remote and forbidding region, yet one that would also cost the lives of many brave men.

One young explorer determined to make his name by discovering the fabled North-West Passage – or die trying – was James Clark Ross. By the time he reached his early twenties, Ross had already risen to the rank of midshipman (an officer cadet, one of the junior ranks). More importantly for our story, he had also assumed the mantle of the expedition naturalist, and was keen to acquire interesting new specimens.

So when on a fine, cold day in June 1823, Ross spotted an unusual-looking gull flying alongside the ship close to the Melville Peninsula in the northern reaches of Arctic Canada, he was determined to get a closer look. As he approached, and realised that it was something different, he raised his musket and blasted the unfortunate seabird to kingdom come.

The ship's captain William Parry recorded the event for posterity in the expedition's journal:

> Mr Ross had procured a specimen of gull having a black ring round its neck, and which in its present plumage, we could not find described. This bird was alone when killed but flying at no great distance from a flock of [Arctic] tern, which latter it somewhat resembles in size as well as in its red legs; but is on closer inspection easily distinguished by its beak and tail, as well as by a beautiful tint of most delicate rose-colour on its breast.[8]

When the expedition returned home later that year, having once again failed to discover the North-West Passage, Captain Parry presented the distinguished zoologist John Richardson with the bird and mammal specimens the crew had collected during the voyage. Richardson examined the mystery gull, and rightly concluded that it was indeed a species new to science. He named it the 'cuneate-tailed gull' (from the unusual wedge-shaped tail), and gave it the scientific name *Larus rossi*,* after its young discoverer.

And there things might have stood, were it not for what might be charitably called a mix-up or, less generously, an attempt by a fellow ornithologist, William MacGillivray, to grab all the credit for himself. Rather like William Leach a few years earlier, MacGillivray does not come out of the affair with much credit.

MacGillivray was not a man who you would think needed to resort to underhand tactics to cement his position. Later on in life, through his magisterial five-volume *History of British Birds*, published over fifteen years from 1837-52, he would make huge advances in establishing the study of birds as a respectable and proper science. He also gave names to several new species, including the harrier that, following the example of the French ornithologists, he named after George Montagu.

Ironically, for such a key figure in the naming of birds, MacGillivray himself only has a single species named after him: MacGillivray's warbler, a scarce songbird that breeds in the forests of western USA and Canada, and spends the winter in Central America. Not only did MacGillivray never see the species that bears his name, he never even visited the continent where it lives. He owed the dubious honour to his long friendship with the legendary North American bird artist John James Audubon, whom he had helped to write the text to his monumental work *The Birds of America*.†

Despite – or perhaps because of – his fame, MacGillivray was a troubled and difficult man, with a notoriously abrasive personality. This may have been because he had been born with the stigma

* Now in its own monotypic genus, *Rhodostethia rosea*.
† Three species of bird are named after Audubon: a shearwater, a warbler and an oriole.

of illegitimacy, so always saw himself as an outsider. He seemed to challenge himself at every opportunity: at just twelve years old he began his studies at Aberdeen University. Whether through genuine poverty or simple bloody-mindedness – or possibly a combination of the two – he would walk home to the Hebridean Isle of Harris at the end of each academic year: a distance of 180 miles.

Later on, he outdid even that feat of endurance. Deciding it would help his fledgling career as an ornithologist if he visited the British Museum's bird collections in London, he elected to walk there (via a circuitous route in order to see more of England), tramping more than 800 miles in all weathers.

In later life, his temper was legendary, as the American bird collector Elliot Coues later noted:

> MacGillivray appears to have been of an irritable, highly sensitized temperament, fired with enthusiasm and ambition, yet contending . . . with poverty, ill-health, and a perhaps not well-founded, though not therefore the less acutely felt, sense of neglect; thus ceaselessly nerved to accomplish, yet as continually haunted with the dread of failure.[9]

Nor was MacGillivray very tolerant of other people's weaknesses, as Coues went on to explain:

> He never hesitated to differ sharply with any one, or to express his own views pointedly . . . he scarcely disguised his contempt for triflers, blockheads, pedants, compilers, and theorizers.[10]

Whether MacGillivray thought John Richardson fell into any of these categories we cannot be sure; though given that Richardson was later knighted for his contributions to polar exploration and science, that is perhaps unlikely.

John Richardson had named Ross's specimen at a public meeting in Edinburgh (where both he and MacGillivray worked), so might have reasonably assumed that the species' name was now firmly established. But for some reason he neglected to confirm the new name in print until more than a year later, in an appendix to Parry's journal of Ross's voyage.

In the meantime, MacGillivray had also examined the specimen, and before Parry's journal appeared, published its name as 'Ross's rosy gull' (*Larus roseus*). Because MacGillivray's chosen name was the first to appear in print, under the strict rules of scientific nomenclature it took priority, and he took the credit. So to Richardson's frustration his original (albeit rather cumbersome) name was relegated to the footnotes of ornithological history. Meanwhile, at the age of just twenty-four, James Ross had become the youngest person ever to be commemorated in the name of a British bird, an honour he still holds.

In later life, James Ross continued to make pioneering and hazardous expeditions to the High Arctic. His finest achievement, the discovery of Ross's gull notwithstanding, was reaching the Magnetic North Pole in June 1831, a discovery that allowed sailors to fix their position more easily, wherever they were in the world's oceans, and which undoubtedly helped to save many lives in the years that followed. He also explored the southern oceans, circumnavigating the whole of Antarctica, where his voyages are commemorated in place names such as the Ross Sea, Ross Island and the Ross Ice Shelf.

Another of Ross's fellow polar explorers, Edward Sabine, also had a species of gull named after him. Although Sabine was twelve years older than Ross, the two nevertheless became lifelong friends after they met on one of those early expeditions to search for the North-West Passage. During one of these, on 25 July 1818, Sabine and Ross sighted a series of rocky islands 20 miles offshore, and trekked off across the sea ice to investigate. On arrival, the two men noticed some unusual gulls breeding alongside Arctic terns, sporting forked tails, dark grey heads and black bills with canary-yellow tips. True to form, they took aim and shot them, later sending the skins back to London via a passing whaling ship. These ended up in the hands of Edward's elder brother Joseph, who presented them to the members of the Linnaean Society, and named them in honour of his brother: *Larus sabini* – Sabine's gull.

Eventually Ross returned to Britain and was knighted for his achievements. Having reached his early forties, he finally settled down with his new wife Anne, their marriage producing four children. But the call of the Arctic proved too strong, and in the late 1840s he made his last voyage north. On his return, he continued to work as the leading authority on polar navigation, dying at his Buckinghamshire estate in 1862, the same age as the century.

A few years after Ross saw his gull for the very first time, another new species of gull was discovered on an Arctic voyage. Franklin's gull superficially resembles our own familiar black-headed gull, but has a darker grey back, a fully black (rather than brown) head, a white eye ring and a bright red bill and legs, making it appear altogether more becoming than its commoner relative – as if it were wearing make-up.

The gull was named after the man who arguably ranks at the very top of the hall of fame of polar explorers: Sir John Franklin. But unlike Ross, Franklin's distinguished career as a soldier, explorer and politician did not end in comfortable retirement back home in the English countryside. Instead he would suffer extraordinary hardship, tragedy, and a slow and painful death in the remote and frozen Arctic.

Even before he headed northwards, John Franklin's life was marked by extraordinary feats of endurance and suffering. Having joined the Royal Navy at the age of thirteen, he sailed to Australia on a voyage aiming to circumnavigate that vast and unknown land. But his vessel was wrecked, and he and the crew – most of them suffering from scurvy – found themselves marooned on a coral reef for several weeks before they were finally rescued.

Before he reached his twentieth birthday Franklin had fought at the Battle of Trafalgar, during which all but seven of the forty-seven men alongside him on deck were killed. Following this lucky escape, he went on his first voyage to the Arctic, an unsuccessful quest to reach the North Pole; he was then chosen to lead an expedition to try to discover the fabled North-West Passage. He was well aware that polar exploration had never been easy, but the trials and tribulations endured by Franklin and his men on this and later voyages almost beggar belief.

In August 1819, a reconnaissance party led by Franklin left their ship and headed off across the rapidly freezing tundra, where they underwent unimaginable hardships, eventually being forced to eat boiled leather and lichen to avoid starving to death. One member of the party, driven insane by hunger, even shot and killed a fellow crewman so he could eat his flesh.

Incredibly, Franklin, Richardson and a handful of others did somehow manage to survive their terrible ordeal. When they returned home the following autumn, they were given a heroes' welcome. You might imagine that these horrendous experiences would have put them off polar exploration forever, but over the next three decades Franklin continued to go off to search for the North-West Passage, continually being thwarted by the seemingly impenetrable barrier of the sea ice.

It was during one of these voyages, on 6 June 1827, that the bird that would be named after him was found: a male Franklin's gull, shot on the Saskatchewan River. In some ways it is surprising that this species had not been discovered earlier, for it is not a bird of the High Arctic like Sabine's and Ross's gulls. Franklin's gulls breed on the vast open prairies of Canada south and eastwards to Montana and Minnesota, and spend the winter along the Pacific coasts of Central and South America, migrating through much of the United States along the way.

In May 1845, almost two decades after he found his eponymous gull, Franklin and his 133-man crew set sail on what would be their final expedition, again heading north and west to chart the possible route through to the Pacific Ocean. This time the sea ice was so impenetrable that the two vessels became stuck – not just for one winter, but for two long years in a row.

Eventually, the fateful decision was taken to abandon the stranded ships and trek across the ice, in the hope of reaching land and safety.

But this brave attempt was doomed to failure from the very start: already weakened by a combination of starvation, scurvy and the bone-chilling cold, the entire crew perished. Later a stone cairn was discovered, which revealed that Franklin had actually died on 11 June 1847, not long before his men had left the boat.

Today, a dramatic painting of the last days of this doomed expedition hangs in the National Maritime Museum in Greenwich, in east London. Painted by William Thomas Smith, it bears the dramatic title 'They forged the last link with their lives'. Taken from a letter from Sir John Richardson to the Prime Minister Lord Palmerston, this sentence commemorates the fact that, despite their deaths, the expedition had proved enormously valuable in surveying new territory.

These early voyages in turn paved the way for later exploration of both the Arctic and Antarctic, in which ornithologists continued to play a crucial part. The best known of these were both on the fateful expeditions with Captain Robert Falcon Scott. Edward 'Bill' Wilson perished with Scott on his last, doomed expedition to reach the South Pole, but not before he had produced a series of accurate and beautiful sketches of Antarctic birds. Apsley Cherry-Garrard did survive, but had the grim and thankless task of searching for – and ultimately discovering – the bodies of Scott and his men, frozen in their hut just 11 miles from safety.

Cherry-Garrard's legendary quest to collect the eggs of the emperor penguin was later documented in a book aptly titled *The Worst Journey in the World*, in which he famously wrote that 'Polar exploration is at once the cleanest and most isolated way of having a bad time which has been devised.'[11]

The other important ornithological legacy of Captain Scott's ultimately disastrous expedition was the last, almost unbearably moving letter he wrote to his wife Kathleen. Knowing he was doomed to die, Scott sent her clear instructions on how to bring up their infant son, asking her to 'Make the boy interested in natural history if you can, it is better than games.' That young boy would grow up to be the best known naturalist, wildlife artist and conservationist of his, and arguably any other, era: Sir Peter Scott.

As for the legendary North-West Passage, the route through the ice was finally found during the first decade of the twentieth century by the Norwegian explorer Roald Amundsen – later conqueror of the South Pole – using charts made by Franklin and his crew on their final, ill-fated voyage. So Sir John Franklin and his brave men did not, it seems, die entirely in vain.

Yet even though our knowledge of the Arctic and its wildlife continued to expand, the gull discovered by James Ross remained a genuine enigma. As recently as 1938, well over a century after Ross's gull was first described, ornithologist Bernard Tucker could still write that 'Very few . . . have seen this gull alive.'[12]

During the intervening years, other polar explorers had occasionally come across this elusive bird. Their excitement when they did so is evident from this evocative entry from Fridtjof Nansen's diary for 3 August 1894:

Today my longing has at last been satisfied; I have shot Ross's gull. This rare and mysterious inhabitant of the unknown north, which is only occasionally seen, and of which no one knows whence it came and whither it goeth, which belongs exclusively to the world to which the imagination aspires, is what I have always longed to discover.[13]

A decade later, one mystery was finally solved, when the breeding grounds of Ross's gulls were finally discovered – completely by chance. The distinguished Russian ornithologist Sergei Aleksandrovich Buturlin was visiting Yakutia – a vast and remote region of north-eastern Siberia almost as big as India – when he found a colony of Ross's gulls nesting on the tundra outside the village of Pokhodsk.

Breeding colonies have since been discovered elsewhere in the Arctic, including north-east Greenland and the far north of Canada, not far from where Ross made his original find. The gulls probably spend the autumn and winter months somewhere in the North Atlantic, although even with the advances in tracking technology we have at our disposal today, we still do not know exactly where.[14]

4: Scotland's Forgotten Genius

William MacGillivray is Scotland's forgotten genius in the field of natural history. There is no question of his pre-eminence as a naturalist, of his originality of mind, of his skill as a writer and above all his talents as an ornithologist.[15]

This tribute from William MacGillivray's biographer Robert Ralph identifies one aspect of the character of this pioneering nineteenth-century ornithologist. We have already seen aspects of his other, darker side, in the way he took the credit for the naming of

Ross's gull, over the prior (but unpublished) claim of his colleague John Richardson, and in his ability to both offend and to find offence with others. But we have also witnessed his generosity of spirit, as shown in naming Montagu's harrier after his illustrious predecessor.

If MacGillivray is remembered nowadays at all, it is for what should have been the most influential and important ornithological work of the nineteenth century. The fact that he is largely forgotten, except by those few people who have actually read his writings, is partly due to his stubborn character and partly, as so often with the vagaries of fame, simply down to bad luck.

MacGillivray's *A History of British Birds* is rarely referred to nowadays, and read even less frequently: the five stout, leather-bound volumes sit forgotten on library shelves, or linger unsold in the catalogues of antiquarian booksellers, gathering literal and metaphorical dust. After all, why would anyone bother to read a work now almost two centuries old, when so much has been discovered and written about our avifauna since it was published?

I first came across a set of MacGillivray's masterwork in a second-hand bookshop in Cambridge in the early 1980s, when I was writing my dissertation on the bird poems of John Clare. It was priced at a prohibitive £200, way beyond my student pocket, but thanks to the generosity of the bookseller I was able to make detailed notes on the books' contents without actually having to make a purchase.

Almost forty years later, I have finally acquired a set of my own, and have been entranced by the contents. The blend of forensic detail, together with extensive descriptions of each species' habits and behaviour, all wrapped up in that unmistakable musty smell of antiquarian books, take me straight back to this exciting era when so many discoveries about Britain's birds were being made. It also makes me appreciate the efforts of men such as MacGillivray and his English contemporary William Yarrell, who did so much to extend and consolidate our knowledge of Britain's birdlife.*

Like his predecessor George Montagu, MacGillivray was an obsessive completist, as the books' full title bears witness:

> *A History of British Birds, Indigenous and Migratory:*
>
> *Including*
>
> *Their Organization, Habits and Relations;*
> *Remarks on Classification and Nomenclature;*
> *An Account of the Principal Organs of Birds, and*
> *Observations Relative to Practical Ornithology.*

Never let it be said of Victorian writers that they didn't provide enough information for their readers! So how was MacGillivray's work received? It is fair to say that reactions were somewhat mixed, as this comment, written eighty years after publication, reveals:

> To MacGillivray has always belonged the enviable reputation of writing one of the most original histories of British birds we possess. The consensus of opinion accords his *History* the merit of being original and accurate . . . but at the same time his peculiar

---

* In 1830, Yarrell was the first person to distinguish between the two species of 'wild swans', winter visitors from the north. He named the smaller of the pair Bewick's swan, after Thomas Bewick, who had died two years earlier. Later he popularised the name whooper swan for the larger species.

methods of classification and nomenclature (most undoubtedly original) naturally aroused criticism and even condemnation.[16]

Talk about damning with faint praise – rarely can the word 'original' have been used so pejoratively. Yet the co-author of that verdict, William Mullens, was not unsympathetic to MacGillivray's work, considering it superior to that of any of his contemporaries. Mullens was also scathing about the critics who condemned Mac-Gillivray for his eccentric ordering of families and obsession with detailed accounts of each species' anatomy, accusing them of having 'broken the heart of the greatest ornithologist this country has ever possessed', and almost preventing the completion of what he called 'one of the greatest books on British birds'.

It wasn't just MacGillivray's taxonomy that baffled his readers, but also the names he used for so many familiar species. A glance at the entries in the first volume, published in 1837, yields a truly baffling assortment, each invented by MacGillivray to impose some sense of order and logic on avian nomenclature. Fortunately for the modern reader, MacGillivray often added the more widely accepted name (usually the one we still use today) as an alternative:

> The Mountain Finch, or Brambling
> The Black-throated Grosbeak, or Hawfinch
> The Red-fronted Thistlefinch, or Goldfinch
> The Mountain Linnet, or Twite

In the second volume, published two years later in 1839, the names were even more eccentric. The thrushes appeared as black, ringed, chestnut-backed, red-sided and variegated – for blackbird, ring ouzel, fieldfare, redwing and the eponymous White's thrush respectively.

'Shore pipit' (for rock pipit) aside, the pipits and larks retained their more conventional names, but when it came to the pipits' cousins, the wagtails, MacGillivray went off-piste once again. Pied wagtail was the only instantly recognisable name, as the grey wagtail became 'grey-and-yellow', and the white wagtail (the continental race of pied) became 'grey-and-white'. For the yellow wagtail, and its continental relative the blue-headed wagtail, he invented an entirely new name – 'quaketail' – with the respective epithets 'green-headed' and 'blue-headed'.

I can see what MacGillivray was trying to do. A tidy-minded man, borderline obsessive-compulsive by nature, he was simply attempting to add some kind of rationality to bird names, where little or none had existed before. For instance, later in the same volume blackcap appeared as 'black-capped warbler', and whitethroat 'white-throated warbler' – both names are perfectly logical, yet nevertheless utterly inelegant.

MacGillivray created more evocative names for other members of the warbler family. He coined 'grasshopper chirper' for grasshopper warbler, and 'sedge and marsh reedlings' for sedge and reed warblers (the much rarer marsh warbler was yet to be discovered in Britain). But my favourite is 'Provence furzeling' – undeniably a more accurate name than the Dartford warbler, and redolent of the names still used for the species in Dutch, German and the Scandinavian languages, although not, oddly, in French.*

* *Provenceångare* (Swedish), *Provencesanger* (Danish and Norwegian),

For the leaf warblers, he preferred 'yellow, willow and short-winged woodwrens' (wood and willow warblers and chiffchaff), while other new and rather bizarre names included 'long-tailed muffin' (long-tailed tit), 'hedge chanter' (dunnock), 'blue-throated redstart' (bluethroat) and 'white-rumped stonechat' (wheatear).*

It's easy to mock MacGillivray, especially as not a single one of the names he invented has stood the test of time; we might perhaps look on him more kindly if, as with so many of the new names coined by Thomas Pennant in the previous century, they had been adopted into general use. For who is to say that Pennant's 'tawny owl' is better than MacGillivray's 'tawny hooting-owl', or that the former's 'oystercatcher' is superior to the latter's 'pied oystercatcher'.

Sadly, for William MacGillivray, his plans to add rigour and logic foundered in the face of general usage and the mocking ridicule of his peers. In the meantime, Yarrell's shorter and more accessible work, also entitled *A History of British Birds* (but lacking the long and convoluted subtitle), had become a popular bestseller. One of the main reasons for its wide appeal amongst the reading public was the inclusion of attractive woodcuts to illustrate each species.

Ironically, MacGillivray had also planned to have his work illustrated, and had painted many excellent plates himself, which had been praised by no less an authority than John James Audubon as equal to anything that great American artist had achieved himself. But stricken by poverty, as he was throughout his life, MacGillivray simply could

Provencegrasmücke (German) and *Provenceaalse* (Dutch). In French the Dartford warbler's name is *Fauvette pitchou*.

* A hundred and fifty years later, a cabal of late twentieth-century ornithologists attempted to standardise British bird names once again – and, just like MacGillivray, they failed to do so. See Chapter 7.

not afford the cost of including these in the finished work.

Yarrell's chosen method of publication may also have helped promote his writing. Like many novelists of the period, including Dickens and Trollope, he issued his work not in one thick, heavy and expensive volume at a time, but periodically, in thirty-six affordable monthly parts.* Yarrell also managed to complete his *History* by 1843, whereas his rival took almost a decade longer to do so. This gave Yarrell a crucial head start in the market, from which MacGillivray never recovered.

MacGillivray's heartfelt opening words to the Preface of Volume IV, written in March 1852 from the Devon resort of Torquay, sought to excuse the long delay since the previous volume:

> As the wounded bird seeks some quiet retreat, where, freed
> from the persecution of the pitiless fowler, it may pass the time
> of its anguish in forgetfulness of the outer world; so have I,
> assailed by disease, betaken myself to a sheltered nook, where,
> unannoyed by the piercing blasts of the North Sea, I had led to
> hope that my life might be protracted beyond the most danger-
> ous season of the year. . .

This acid blend of bitterness and self-pity, lightened by a soupçon of black humour, is emblematic of MacGillivray's complex character. He was always an outsider, impatient and intolerant of others, and just as rigorous, it seems, at judging himself.

---

* A hundred and thirty years later, from 1969–71, IPC magazines and John Gooders followed in Yarrell's footsteps with the ten-volume partwork *Birds of the World*, a seminal influence on birders of my generation (see Prologue).

Yet the seaside cure seems to have worked – at least temporarily – for soon afterwards he returned north to his home in Aberdeen, where he was Professor of Natural History at the university. Here, on 31 July, he wrote the Preface to the fifth and final volume of his epic work. He once again outlined the case for the *History's* importance, and added a telling comment on the poor reviews he expected to receive:

> He who possesses the greatest contempt for public opinion is always the most anxious for general applause. I should, no doubt, be very well pleased to be commended; but I do not now anticipate great distress from the most virulent censure.

Ironically, MacGillivray never read any reviews of this final volume, whether praiseworthy or critical. For on 8 September 1852, barely a month after his final bitter sideswipe at the critics, he died, at the age of fifty-six. He was buried in Edinburgh's New Calton Cemetery, next to his late wife and two of his children, who had died in infancy. For half a century his grave remained unmarked, until some of his relatives and former students raised the funds for a huge and impressive granite monument that still stands today.

Ironically, after his death his fame grew, with the circulation of his posthumously published book *The Natural History of Dee Side and Braemar*, privately produced with funding from none other than Queen Victoria. Towards the end of the Queen's long reign, the pioneering ornithologist Professor Alfred Newton bestowed upon MacGillivray the grand epitaph that 'after Willughby, MacGillivray was the greatest and most original ornithological genius

. . . that this island has produced'.[17]

William MacGillivray may have lived a troubled life, and died in sad and difficult circumstances. But like the equally irascible George Montagu, he left us a masterwork that – if the critics had not become so hung up on his fanaticism for detail and eccentric names – might have changed the way we look at Britain's birds forever. Instead, it was Yarrell's *History*, written in a less rigorous but undoubtedly more popular style, with more acceptable English names, that went on to influence birdwatchers and ornithologists for almost a century afterwards.[*]

Had things been different, and MacGillivray's view prevailed, birders might even now be referring to furzelings and quaketails, reedlings and hedge chanters, blue-throated redstarts and long-tailed muffins. I have a tinge of regret this never came to pass, and that instead we are saddled with the far more familiar, yet perhaps less imaginative, names we use today.

5: Exploration and Empire

As the nineteenth century rolled on, Britons continued to travel around the world, and discover more and more birds, for which new names had to be found – many of them prolonging the fashion for eponyms. Exploration and empire-building provided plenty of reading material for generations of schoolboys, with the dramatic

* Yarrell's *History of British Birds* was reprinted several times during the remainder of the nineteenth century, and formed the basis for a very popular single-volume work, Howard Saunders, *An Illustrated Manual of British Birds* (London, 1889).

episodes of polar exploration we have already witnessed – packed with adventure, suffering and derring-do – winning an eager audience through a plethora of classic Victorian books for boys.

But other travellers preferred to pursue their quarry at a slower and more gentlemanly pace, and in warmer, more equable climes. Typical of this latter breed was the Reverend Henry Baker Tristram (1822–1906). Tristram spent much of his working life as a country parson, though he eventually became Canon of Durham Cathedral. Yet despite his weighty clerical responsibilities, he still managed to pursue his abiding passion: the collection and study of the birds of North Africa and the Middle East.

He was so enthusiastic about his travels around the Middle East that, like the parody of an absentee clergyman Dr Vesey Stanhope in Anthony Trollope's *Barchester Chronicles*, he appears to have spent considerably more time in the deserts of Palestine than the cloisters of Durham. What his long-suffering wife Eleanor (who bore him seven daughters and a son during their fifty-three-year marriage) thought of his peregrinations is not recorded.

Not for nothing was Henry Baker Tristram known as 'The Great Gun of Durham'.* But he did not simply aim and fire at any bird that moved, like some of his less fastidious contemporaries. As well as being a fine shot, he had a keen eye for the unusual. Moreover, at a time when few ornithologists ventured into these regions, he had the field more or less to himself. As a result eleven species of bird have, at one time or another, borne his name.† The best-known of

---

* He was also, more affectionately, dubbed the 'Sacred Ibis', after the symbol of the British Ornithologists' Union – hence the title of an excellent biography of Tristram by W. G. Hale, *Sacred Ibis: The Ornithology of Canon Henry Baker Tristram* (Durham, 2016).
† Tristram's wheatear, serin, starling, warbler, bunting, scrubfowl, honeyeater,

these is Tristram's starling (often known as Tristram's grackle), a striking, glossy-black bird with orange wing-linings which can be seen over much of Israel, and whose loud, wolf-whistling call is very distinctive.

Canon Tristram lived a long and satisfying life, dying at the age of eighty-three in spring 1906. Before this, however, he had experienced a Damascene conversion. He acknowledged that amassing vast collections of bird skins and their eggs – in his case comprising well over 20,000 different specimens – was not how the study of birds should continue in this new century. Indeed, for the last two years of his life he served in the honorary role of Vice-President of the newly formed bird protection organisation the RSPB, just after King Edward VII had granted the Society its royal charter.

From this point onwards, the pendulum slowly began to swing, away from killing birds with shotguns and towards studying them using binoculars. Tristram was among the last of his kind: gentleman-naturalists and crack shots, with the time, money and inclination to travel to far-flung corners of the world, indulging their passion for killing birds in the name of furthering the science of ornithology.

But just before this, there had been one last hurrah for the old guard. During the final decades of Queen Victoria's reign, history provided the perfect opportunity for ambitious young men to contribute to the naming of the world's birds. It came about because of the most important (and arguably most controversial) institution of that complex and fascinating era: the British Empire.

---

flowerpecker, storm-petrel, woodpecker and pygmy parrot. Only four (the starling, warbler, bunting and storm-petrel) still carry his eponym.

On the last day of July 1912, amidst the searing summer heat, the city of Etawah in the Indian state of Uttar Pradesh came to a standstill. In the usually thriving and noisy bazaar, every shop and stall remained closed for the day, while the people mourned the loss of a man whose death, at the age of eighty-three, had just been announced. Yet this man was not some fêted maharajah – indeed, he was not Indian at all – but an officer of the ruling, and mostly despised, British Raj.

Allan Octavian Hume – the man mourned not just in Etawah but right across the vast nation of India – was by turns a civil servant, political reformer, co-founder of the Indian Congress Party, poet and naturalist.

So how did this modest, hardworking (and for his day surprisingly liberal) man earn such love and respect from the people he ruled? How on earth did he find time, in his busy political and administrative life, to put together the largest private collection of Indian birds ever created, and end up having no fewer than fourteen different species of bird named after him?* And what does his life story tell us about the largest empire the world has ever seen?

At its height, the British Empire's colonies, dominions and protectorates covered almost one-quarter of the globe's land – more than 13 million square miles – and ruled over more than 450 million people, about one in five of the world's population.

From small beginnings, thanks to pioneering expeditions led by men such as John Cabot, Walter Ralegh and Francis Drake during the

---

* Hume's ground tit, wheatear, babbler, hawk-owl, lark, wren-babbler, blue-throated barbet, parakeet, leaf warbler, owl, swiftlet, whitethroat, treecreeper and reed warbler. Of these, only six (the wheatear, hawk-owl, lark, leaf warbler, owl and whitethroat) still bear his name.

fifteenth and sixteenth centuries, the Empire had expanded hugely, to include large parts of the Americas, Africa, Asia and the Pacific. That oft-repeated cliché, 'the Empire on which the sun never sets' was not simply a jingoistic metaphor, but the literal truth: Britain's imperial possessions were so scattered around the world that there was always daylight falling on the Union Flag somewhere.

The vast size of the British Empire was not only its greatest strength, but also a fatal weakness. As other nations grew envious of Britain's powers, they wanted to diminish them and grab a share of the booty for themselves. Even though the British Empire continued to expand until the 1920s, the seeds of its downfall were already sown: the new world order decided at the Treaty of Versailles in 1919 would never allow one nation to be so globally dominant again.

During the second half of the nineteenth century, all this was yet to come. The Empire was still supreme, especially in India, where more than 300 million people lived under British rule, governed by men like Allan Octavian Hume.

Hume's career was certainly a colourful one. Having arrived in India in 1849, at the age of twenty, he had spent the next few years rising up the Indian Civil Service to become the chief officer of a district twice the size of Wales. Then, in 1857, the rebellion known as the Indian Mutiny began nearby. Showing great courage, Hume stormed a temple where the rebels were holed up, and later – despite having recently recovered from cholera – led a charge that forced them to retreat.

During the following decade, as the political situation eventually settled down, Hume finally had time to pursue his passionate interest in Indian birds. He began to amass a vast assemblage of skins, nests and eggs that eventually topped 100,000 specimens, the second largest private collection in the world after that owned by Walter Rothschild at Tring. In one single expedition, Hume collected no fewer than 1,200 skins of 250 different kinds of bird, of which eighteen species were new to India.

To house this extraordinary collection, he spent £20,000 (equivalent to more than a million pounds today) building a large extension on his home, in which row after row of beautifully crafted wooden cabinets housed his precious eggs and skins. He wrote several books on Indian birds, and started his own quarterly journal, entitled *Stray Feathers – a journal of ornithology for India and his dependencies*, in which he wrote racy accounts of his collecting trips around the sub-continent.

In 1879, on what would be his final expedition, he noticed that the feathers in a ceremonial head-dress worn by a local official came from a species of gamebird he did not recognise. After sending hunters out to procure live examples, he named the bird Mrs Hume's pheasant (after his beloved wife Mary), the name still used today.*

In 1882, at the age of fifty-three, Hume retired from the Indian Civil Service and returned to his home in Simla, to begin work on his life's masterwork: a book that would include every species of bird found in India. Soon afterwards, however, disaster struck. Having spent the winter of 1884 at his other residence on the lowland plains, Hume returned to discover – to his unimaginable horror – that all

---

* Sadly, as with so many of that region's birds, it is now threatened by over-population, habitat loss and hunting.

his research papers, weighing several hundredweight and containing more than twenty-five years of detailed notes and information, had been taken down to the local bazaar by his servants to be sold as waste paper. His dream was in tatters, and the world was deprived of what would have been the definitive work on Indian ornithology.

But Hume left another, arguably far more important, legacy. Having been so cruelly thwarted in his ornithological ambitions, he could have retired from the fray. Instead, he chose to devote the rest of his life to politics. Ornithology's loss was India's gain, because in 1885 Hume was instrumental in setting up the Indian National Congress. Guided by Mahatma Gandhi, who became the party's leader in 1921, Congress grew to be India's dominant political force, and spearheaded India's eventual independence from Britain in 1947. Without Hume's vision and hard work on behalf of the Indian people, it could be argued that independence might have come much later, or in a very different form.

In 1890 Hume took a trip back home to Britain, where on arrival he was informed of Mary's death back in Simla. Four years later, he decided to leave India for good, settling in the suburban district of Upper Norwood in south London, where he lived quietly until his death in 1912.

With Hume's passing, an era was over. The days of the British Empire were numbered, and the world was about to change dramatically with the onset of the First World War.

The way birds were named would change too, as the age of exploration drew to a close, and with it the tradition of new species being named after their discoverers, which had lasted for almost 200 years from the early eighteenth through to the late nineteenth centuries.

From now on, new bird names would be decided by committees using pen and paper, rather than by pioneering individuals carrying shotguns. The days when an amateur naturalist such as Allan Octavian Hume could push the boundaries of our knowledge of the world's birds, and give his name to so many species, were finally – and permanently – at an end.

6

TWENTIETH-CENTURY FLOCKS

The Names we use Today

Names are not always what they seem.

Mark Twain

1: Redbreasts and Hedge Sparrows

Max Nicholson – birdwatcher, scientist and pioneering conservationist – spanned the twentieth century like an ornithological Colossus. Born in 1904, the same year as Fats Waller, Salvador Dalí and Cary Grant, he lived to see the turn of the new millennium, before dying in 2003, in his ninety-ninth year. More than any other person, before or since, he witnessed – and to a great extent was also responsible for – the science of ornithology being dragged out of a bygone era and into the modern age.

In a long, active and quite remarkable life, Max Nicholson was instrumental in either founding or reforming many of today's leading conservation organisations, including the RSPB, BTO (British Trust for Ornithology), Natural England and, perhaps most crucially of all, the WWF (World Wide Fund for Nature). He also ran the Battle of the Atlantic shipping convoys during the Second World War and, as a senior civil servant, was at Winston Churchill's right hand at the historic Second World War conference with Stalin and Roosevelt at Yalta.*

Even before Nicholson's birth, however, what he memorably called 'the Victorian leprosy of collecting' was starting to give way to a more benevolent approach to bird study. This new, and very different, way of relating to the natural world would be achieved by looking through binoculars, rather than down the barrel of a

* One can only assume that Nicholson turned down a knighthood and a peerage; both of which were richly deserved but never bestowed.

gun. Developments in technology meant that optics were rapidly displacing firearms, and the time when an unusual bird needed to be shot to confirm its identity was finally coming to an end. The profession of taxidermy, so popular during the Victorian age, would soon become (quite literally) a dying art.

The turning point came in 1901, the year the old queen was finally laid to rest, with the publication of a book by Edmund Selous, simply entitled *Bird Watching*.[1] Remarkable though it may now seem, this is the first recorded use of this phrase in the English language, at the start of a century that would end with birding – as it is now called – having become one of the most popular leisure activities in Britain.

Since Selous's book appeared, what we know about Britain's birds has increased exponentially. Much of this has been achieved through a dedicated cohort of 'amateur' (albeit highly skilled) birders who, even today, provide much of the raw data and field observations used by professional scientists, via surveys conducted by organisations such as the BTO. But from the turn of the last century, in Britain at least, amateurs and professionals alike turned their focus onto known, named species, rather than unknown, unnamed ones.

Changes to bird names remained the province of a small group of men who had the time, energy and inclination to sit on official committees. Top of the tree was the British Ornithologists' Union (BOU), an august body whose pronouncements on matters ornithological were handed down like tablets of stone to the masses below.

The BOU still makes the final decisions on the official 'British

List', now standing at over 600 species,* and also adjudicates on the names we call these different species – or perhaps, I should say, the names we are *supposed* to use. For as we have already seen, bird names have long proved stubbornly resistant to what the mandarins of British ornithology have decreed that we should call them, even to the present day.

Take one of our commonest and most familiar birds, the robin. As late as 1952, the BOU insisted on calling this species by the official name 'redbreast', even though the name 'robin' had been widely used since at least the seventeenth century, and probably for far longer. Astonishingly, 'robin' was not formally adopted by the BOU as the official name for *Erithacus rubecula* until the next check-list was published, in 1971.†

During the course of the twentieth century, an interest in birds – and indeed all of nature – also became far more egalitarian. Once purely the preserve of a small and elite group of professional orni-thologists, it was beginning to be enjoyed by people at every level of society.

Typical of the new breed of birdwatchers was the Cheshire-based ornithologist T. A. (Thomas) Coward. Although the elaborately moustachioed Coward was the middle-class son of a religious

---

* With the addition of the 600th species, a Yelkouan shearwater off the coast of Devon (seen in 2008, but not finally accepted until 2016), the rapid growth of the British List has long confounded James Fisher's 1966 prediction that 'we are . . . unlikely to reach a list of more than 480 wild species by the year 2000, or more than 500 ever' (*The Shell Bird Book*, London, *op. cit.*).

† Other old names also lasted longer than we might imagine. In the 1912 *A Hand-list of British Birds*, compiled by Dr Ernst Hartert, our smallest species of bird was still known by the taxonomically misleading name 'golden-crested wren', even though the BOU had preferred goldcrest almost thirty years earlier.

minister and businessman, he carefully cultivated a 'man-of-the-people' image, with his flat cap, pipe and bicycle. And despite their superficial differences in social class and appearance, both he and Max Nicholson (who came from the Anglo-Irish landed gentry) shared the same mission: to popularise the hobby and pastime of watching birds to the broadest possible audience.

As a working journalist, Coward did this initially as a contributor to the *Manchester Guardian*'s 'Country Diary' column, which he wrote for many years until his death in 1933. But he is best known today for what could arguably described as the first modern 'field guide': a handy, portable aid to enable the small but growing cohort of birdwatchers to identify the species they were seeing.

The Birds of the British Isles and Their Eggs, published in two stout volumes in 1919 (a third, containing background information on bird behaviour, was added in 1926), was ideal. The leather-bound, gilt-embossed books were small enough to fit into a coat or jacket pocket, but packed with enough detail to enable the quick and easy identification of unfamiliar birds. Indeed, they were so ahead of their time that they were still being used by post-war birdwatchers such as Bill Oddie and Ian Wallace well into the 1950s.

Being a forward-looking birdwatcher, you might expect Coward to have jettisoned the old names and embraced the new ones. And apart from a few exceptions, such as calling tits 'titmice', and giving equal weight to 'green plover' alongside lapwing, that's exactly what he did. Browsing its pages, we find that the names are more or less the same as in a modern field guide, and certainly far more familiar than those found in most Victorian bird books.

But there is one notable exception. On page 233 of Coward's first volume, sandwiched between the wheatear and the dipper, there is 'Hedge-Sparrow'. Younger readers may be puzzled by this name, though anyone over fifty years old will surely find it familiar. It refers to the species we now call the dunnock, the only member of the accentor family to occur regularly in Britain.

The name 'hedge sparrow' (with or without the hyphen) has a long and distinguished pedigree, having first been recorded by the Tudor priest and tutor John Palsgrave (as 'hedge sparowe') in 1530. By the early nineteenth century, however, professional ornithologists preferred the more taxonomically correct 'hedge accentor', to distinguish this species from the house and tree sparrows, which are in a completely different family. But despite persistent moves to have this adopted as the official English name, it never caught on, probably because the name 'accentor' is clearly one invented by scientists rather than by ordinary folk, and sounds somehow 'foreign'.*

Yet still the hedge sparrow's clearly unsuitable name continued to be the subject of debate. Writing in 1895, the pioneering bird protectionist W. H. Hudson observed:

> Most people know that a sparrow is a hard-billed bird of the finch family, and that the subject of this notice is not a sparrow, except in name. . . 'How absurd, then, to go on calling it a sparrow!' certain ornithologists have said from time to time, and have renamed it the hedge-accentor. But as Professor Newton has said . . . a name which has been part and parcel of

---

* As W. B. Lockwood acidly remarked, 'This half-Latin book name found little support . . . and quickly fell into disuse'. The name 'accentor' was coined by the German naturalist Johann Matthäus Bechstein in the early nineteenth century, and is derived from the Latin *cantor*, meaning 'singer'.

our language for centuries, and which Shakespeare used,* 'is hardly likely to be dropped, even at the bidding of the wisest, so long as the English language lasts'. Now, as the English tongue promises to last a long time, it seems safest to retain the old and in one sense, incorrect name.[2]

The name 'hedge sparrow' did indeed prove remarkably persistent, as Hudson had predicted. Long after goldcrest had replaced 'golden-crested wren', and willow warbler had supplanted the equally inaccurate 'willow-wren', it remained the standard name for *Prunella modularis*. Even in Phyllis Barclay-Smith's slim volume *Garden Birds*, published in 1945,[3] she referred to the 'hedge-sparrow'; indeed, she did not mention the name dunnock at all.

But moves were afoot to rename this shy and retiring little bird. Ever the iconoclast, in his 1951 Collins New Naturalist volume *Birds and Men*[4] Max Nicholson called for seven changes in the names of common birds. Despite his elevated status, and legendary skills of persuasion, no fewer than six of the seven, including the proposal to change song thrush to 'throstle', never got off the ground.†

However, his final suggestion – to rename the hedge sparrow as the dunnock – was ultimately taken up. As he wrote, in his characteristically no-nonsense style: 'Dunnocks do no harm to us, but

* See *King Lear*, Act 1 Scene IV, in which the Fool warns Lear against his scheming daughters:

For you know, nuncle,

The hedge-sparrow fed the cuckoo so long,

That it's had it head bit off by it young.

† The other proposed changes were: great spotted and lesser spotted woodpeckers to 'pied' and 'barred' woodpeckers, great black-backed and lesser black-backed gulls to 'great blackback' and 'lesser blackback', and common gull to 'mew gull'.

have in return been exposed to the undeserved insult and injury of being miscalled hedge-sparrows by people too stupid to see the absurdity of such a name, or too timid and conventional to revert to the older, briefer and better one.'

As Nicholson was at pains to stress, 'dunnock' has a longer pedigree than the name it supplanted, the first recorded reference coming almost half a century earlier than 'hedge-sparrow', in 1483. It even appeared in Emily Brontë's *Wuthering Heights*, in which the character Hareton Earnshaw is, after his mother's death in childbirth and his grieving father's descent into alcoholism, 'cast out like an unfledged dunnock'. This is, of course, a reference to the cuckoo's habit of laying its egg in a dunnock's nest, whereby after hatching the cuckoo chick then ejects any dunnock offspring from its new home.

Nicholson also pointed out that the yoking of this harmless species with the house sparrow – in those days a major agricultural pest – had led to the inadvertent destruction of dunnocks' nests by members of 'sparrow clubs', who were paid a small bounty for every house sparrow they killed, or whose nest they destroyed.

His sheer persistence, together with the perennial confusion caused by the linking of this species with the unrelated tree and house sparrows, eventually won the day. By the time of the BOU's 1971 book-length publication *The Status of Birds in Britain and Ireland*, the official name had finally been changed to dunnock.

As Max Nicholson confidently predicted, the time 'when the whole company of British bird-watchers will call a dunnock a dunnock' has now arrived. Well, almost. For even today, more than sixty years after he first made his proposal to change the name, some older observers still continue to refer to the little bird creeping around their rockery or garden lawn as the 'hedge sparrow'. A small but significant triumph, perhaps, for the forces of the common man (and woman) against the ornithological Establishment.

Hedge sparrow is just one of many examples of a persistent trend running through our bird names: naming a bird after where it lives. Or perhaps it is more accurate to say, where it is *meant* to live. For even among many of the names we use today, many of these habitat-based epithets are at best questionable, and at worst downright misleading.

Take two closely related species, the marsh and willow tits. Few other British birds are so badly named, for the marsh tit's preferred habitat is not wetlands, but deciduous woodlands, parks and large rural gardens. Willow tits, on the other hand, prefer damp, marshy areas, often nesting close to streams and rivers, or alongside disused gravel pits.*

The story of how these two species acquired their ill-fitting monikers is a salutary reminder of the ingrained 'messiness' of English bird names, however much some tidy-minded people might wish to sort out what we call our birds, so that each species has the name most appropriate to its sound, appearance, habitat or status.

* It has been suggested – not entirely in jest – that the willow tit should now be renamed the 'marsh tit', and the marsh tit given the new name of 'oak tit'.

2: Tit-Willow and Willow Tit

On a tree by a river a little tom-tit
Sang 'Willow, tit-willow, tit-willow'
And I said to him, 'Dicky-bird, why do you sit
Singing 'Willow, tit-willow, tit-willow'
'Is it weakness of intellect, birdie?' I cried
'Or a rather tough worm in your little inside?'
With a shake of his poor little head, he replied
'Oh, willow, tit-willow, tit-willow!'

The opening lines of 'Tit-Willow', from Gilbert and Sullivan's 1885 comic opera *The Mikado*, are still sung today in theatres and church halls up and down the country. When W. S. Gilbert wrote these lyrics, he may have simply chosen the name 'tit-willow' because of its euphonious beauty. But as birders have long been aware, when the phrase is inverted it turns into the name of one of our scarcest breeding birds: the willow tit.

Yet ironically, at the time these quintessentially English lyrics were written, the willow tit was not thought to be a British bird at all. It was an unfamiliar foreign species, whose range stretched from France and Scandinavia in the west, to Siberia and Japan (the setting for *The Mikado*) in the east. For the small band of Britons who were interested in birds, from casual bird-spotters to serious ornithologists, the willow tit might as well have been on another planet.

Then, in 1897 – twelve years after the first performance of *The Mikado* at London's Savoy Theatre – two German ornithologists made a dramatic discovery; one that would send shock waves through the higher echelons of British ornithology. While examining a drawer containing the skins of marsh tits at the British Museum of Natural History, Ernst Hartert and Otto Kleinschmidt came across two unusual specimens, which they immediately realised were not what they seemed.

The two Germans noted subtle anomalies in plumage features, including a pale panel on the wing, a sooty (rather than glossy) black cap and a rather bull-necked appearance. Taken together, these led them to conclude that these birds were not marsh tits at all, but willow tits. A quick check of their provenance revealed that they had been shot in Hampstead in north London, and so they became the very first record of the willow tit in Britain.*

A year later, the news was published in the journal the *Zoologist*, under the intriguing title 'A hitherto overlooked British Bird'. And overlooked it most certainly had been. For unlike new additions to the British List today – which are mostly global wanderers from Asia or North America that are discovered on some remote, windswept offshore island – the willow tits were here all along. They had been hiding, as it were, in plain sight.

Imagine the embarrassment and shame felt by the members of Britain's ornithological establishment, who had hitherto assumed a lordly superiority over their continental rivals. Now that two Germans had made such a momentous discovery right under their noses, some of our most senior bird experts had to eat humble pie.

Yet to be fair on the embarrassed Brits, the observant Germans

---

* Soon afterwards, Lord Walter Rothschild was sent two similar birds shot in a wood in nearby Finchley; these too proved to be willow tits.

had managed to unravel one of the trickiest identification puzzles posed by any regularly occurring British birds. Willow and marsh tits are so similar that, even today, experienced birders using top-of-the-range optical equipment often find it difficult, even impossible, to tell them apart.

Although the two species do show subtle plumage differences, the most reliable method of knowing whether a particular bird is a marsh or willow tit is by listening for their distinctive calls. Whereas the willow tit makes a nasal sound, repeating three or four notes in rapid succession, the marsh tit delivers a short, explosive call, rather like a sneeze.

Even after the discovery of willow tits in Britain, the controversy over the species' true status continued. Sceptics claimed that it was merely a race of the marsh tit, or even that the so-called new specimens were merely the juvenile plumage of that species. But in the first issue of the long-running journal *British Birds*, published in 1907, Walter Rothschild (the bird collector from the famous banking dynasty) comprehensively refuted these arguments, taking a swipe at his critics as he did so: 'Most of our older ornithologists have failed, or rather refused, to see the differences between the English Marsh and Willow Tits, and again, in this instance, the old proverb, "None so blind as those that will not see," has abundantly justified itself.'[5]

He went on to nail his argument in favour of the marsh and willow tits being separate species by pointing out a truism that forms the basis of modern systematics: that 'no two races or subspecies of the same bird [i.e. species] can live side by side; they must either inhabit different geographical areas or be found at different vertical heights.'[6] But willow and marsh tits were indeed living alongside one another throughout much of Britain: conclusive proof that they were indeed two different species. And so the willow tit gained the distinction of being the last 'undiscovered breeding bird' to be added to the British List, from those 1897 specimens, at least until the separation of the common and Scottish crossbills in the 1980s – but more on that story later.

However, it turns out that over half a century earlier there had been a missed opportunity to discover the willow tit in Britain. All it would have taken was for a curious reader to have questioned an assertion by William Yarrell in a supplement to his popular three-volume work *A History of British Birds*, published in 1845. For in the entry for marsh tit, Yarrell wrote: 'Colonel Montagu* says he has seen the Marsh Tit excavating the decayed part of such trees.'[7]

As Mark Cocker points out in *Birds Britannica*,[8] this 'describes with great accuracy the willow tit's burrowing technique' – for, uniquely amongst our songbirds, the willow tit excavates its own nest-hole in the manner of a woodpecker. Had any of Yarrell's readers been familiar with the two species from travels in continental Europe, they would have immediately realised that the birds seen by Montagu must have been not marsh, but willow tits. As it was, a further fifty-two years would pass before the species was eventually discovered in Britain – by the Germans.[†]

---

* See Chapter 4 for more on Colonel Montagu.

† This also makes me wonder whether the bird given the name 'marsh titmouse' by John Ray, back in the late seventeenth century, was also a willow tit – especially as another name from that period was 'fen titmouse'. It's tempting to think that had the early ornithologists spent less time firing off their shotguns and more time studying bird behaviour and choice of habitat, the confusion between the two species might have been sorted out a couple of centuries earlier.

3: Reed Warblers and Roasted Larks

Warblers are one of those groups of birds that beginner birders find very tricky to identify – the classic 'little brown (or olive, yellow or green) jobs'. So it's perhaps not surprising that plumage features are rarely used to tell one species apart from another – with the exception, as already noted, of the distinctive blackcap and whitethroat. And while song is often used to identify them, only the chiffchaff and grasshopper warbler have sound-based names.

But when it comes to birds named after habitats, the warbler family has few rivals. Of the thirteen regular British breeding species, no fewer than six are named after the places where they live: reed, sedge, marsh, wood, willow and garden warblers.

Some of these names are perfectly correct: reed warblers do live in reed beds, from which their chuntering, repetitive song echoes from mid-April when they arrive back from Africa, through to the end of the breeding season in late June. Wood warblers are also aptly named: these lemon-green sprites are denizens of the oak woods of the north and west of Britain, where they sing their delightful song during the spring and early summer, high in the dense canopy of leaves. Likewise the marsh warbler: this now very rare British breeding bird does indeed live in wetlands, usually nesting in dense patches of nettles, willowherb and meadowsweet right alongside the water.*

---

* If we include European warblers that are rare or occasional visitors to Britain, several other names derive from watery habitats. These include river, paddyfield and aquatic warblers.

But the other three habitat-based names are woefully inaccurate. Sedge warblers don't nest in sedges, preferring small bushes in the heart of reed beds; garden warblers are rarely found in gardens, unlike their commoner cousin the blackcap; and willow warblers are not especially attracted to willows, but can be found in a wide range of woodland habitats.*

Many birds named after their habitat, like the warblers, belong to families where several species look and sound the same as one another, so there are few distinguishing calls or plumage features that we can use to tell them apart. The pipits – small, brownish songbirds that look superficially similar, and sound even more so – are a classic example.

Britain is home to four species: meadow, tree, rock and water pipits.† Rock pipits do live on rocky coasts (the only European songbird to have colonised this constantly changing habitat, where they forage for insects along the tideline), while water pipits are indeed usually found in freshwater wetlands. Meadow and tree pipits are less easy to separate by habitat, but can also be told apart by their behaviour: whereas meadow pipits parachute all the way down to the ground after delivering their song, tree pipits tend to return to their original perch – as you might expect, on the branch of a tree.

The larks, too, are well named: woodlarks often breed in young

* Other habitat-based names are more accurate: woodcocks inhabit woods, sand martins nest in sandbanks, and water rails and marsh harriers live in wetlands, as, indeed, do moorhens – the 'moor' part of the name doesn't refer to the heather-covered moors of the Brontë sisters, but is a corruption of the word 'marsh' or 'mere'. (The fact that a widespread folk name for marsh harrier is 'moor buzzard' confirms this, as does the official name for the area around my home, the Somerset Moors and Levels.)
† Despite their obvious behavioural differences and distinct plumage, rock and water pipits were not 'split' by taxonomists from one into two separate species until 1986.

forestry plantations with open heath nearby; shore larks (a scarce winter visitor to eastern Britain) are usually found along or near the coast; and what more appropriate name could there be for the skylark? No other bird spends quite so long simply hanging in the air on a fine summer's day, delivering that extraordinary outpouring of musical notes for what seems like hours on end.

And yet although 'skylark' sounds like a name that has been with us since time immemorial, it was actually coined fairly recently. In 1678 John Ray referred to 'the common or Skie-lark'; before then this quintessential sound of summer was simply known as the 'lark' (from a now long-forgotten Germanic word meaning 'songster').*

Larks were commonly kept as cagebirds – often cruelly blinded, as it was falsely believed this would make them sing more sweetly – and were also killed for the pot. The bestselling *Book of Household Management*, written by the Victorian domestic goddess Mrs Beeton, included a recipe for lark pie, with the immortal instruction to 'roll the larks in flour, and stuff them.'†

We no longer eat larks, but the ubiquity of this familiar rural species has led to its virtually unrivalled prominence in our language and culture (matched only by that other much-admired songster,

---

* Folk names for this familiar countryside bird include 'heaven's hen', 'rising lark', 'sky-flapper' and the widespread 'laverock' – the last most often used in the north of England and Scotland.

† A Roman recipe for larks' tongues outdoes even this:

Get 1,000 larks.

Remove their tongues and set aside.

Discard the larks.

Put the tongues in a pan with a little oil and sauté quickly.

Transfer to a hot platter.

Serves four.

the nightingale). Following Shelley's famous ode to a 'Blithe Spirit', a later poet, George Meredith, was also inspired by the skylark's song. His verse 'The Lark Ascending' is perhaps the best-known bird poem in the English language, and was later the inspiration for one of our best-loved pieces of music, by the twentieth-century composer Ralph Vaughan Williams.

> He rises and begins to round,
> He drops the silver chain of sound
> Of many links without a break,
> In chirrup, whistle, slur and shake,
> All intervolv'd and spreading wide,
> Like water-dimples down a tide
> Where ripple ripple overcurls
> And eddy into eddy whirls. . .

Many people who have never even seen or heard a skylark (which, given its rapid decline over the past fifty years is probably quite a few), may nevertheless refer to the bird in phrases such as 'up with the lark', 'sing like a lark' and 'larking about'.* The idea of 'having a lark' – meaning to have fun – is thought to derive from nineteenth-century naval slang, when sailors might mess about high in the rigging of a ship – just as a lark hangs like a dust-speck up in the sky.†

---

* The phrase 'up with the lark', denoting an early riser, goes back to Tudor times, while 'as happy as a lark' appears a little later, during the eighteenth century. For more examples of the way bird names have influenced our day-to-day language, see Chapter 6, Part 5.
† A poignant example appears in Charles Dickens' novel (and David Lean's film) *Great Expectations*. After Pip has been transformed into a gentleman thanks to an unexpected bequest from the former convict Magwitch, his brother-in-law Joe visits him at his new

Given our long and close relationship with birds, it's hardly surprising that some of our most familiar species are named after an artificial 'habitat', such as an agricultural crop or human habitation. These include the corncrake and corn bunting, house sparrow and house martin, barn owl and barn swallow (the official name for our familiar swallow).

As I look down this list, I am immediately struck by the fact that most of these species are in trouble. Having chosen to make their lives alongside us, and having prospered for centuries, they are now facing serious – and in some cases possibly terminal – declines.

The corncrake and the corn bunting are both named after our main arable crops, corn being a synonym for any staple grain, including wheat, barley or oats. But they have both suffered massively from the post-war move from traditional, mixed farming to more intensive and industrialised modern agriculture.

As we saw in the writings of John Clare, in the early nineteenth century the corncrake – or as he called it, the land rail – was a familiar 'summer noise among the meadow hay'. Yet by the latter part of Queen Victoria's reign, the corncrake's days as a widespread British breeding bird were already numbered.

In the north, the Highland Clearances, and the resulting replacement of arable crops by sheep, led to a steep decline in the bird's population in the Scottish Highlands. Farther south, in lowland Scotland, Wales and England, mechanised mowing was beginning to displace scything by hand. This spelt disaster for this shy and

home. The change in Pip's social status has created a barrier between them, which Joe attempts to overcome by telling Pip what a good time they'll have when he returns home: 'And when you're well enough to go out for a ride – what larks!' Yet sadly, as we – and they – realise, this will never come to pass.

elusive bird, which is very reluctant to abandon its eggs and chicks, even when under threat. Because of its exemplary parenting, not only were many young corncrakes killed but the adults perished too, caught up in the relentless blades of the mowing machines.

As mechanised harvesting spread north and west, so the corncrake began to disappear from much of the countryside. At the start of the Second World War, the species was still common in Ireland and the Northern and Western Isles of Scotland, but had vanished from large swathes of England and Wales. By the time of the first *BTO Atlas*, for which fieldwork took place from 1968 to 1972, the corncrake was virtually absent from the British mainland, having retreated to the islands of the Outer Hebrides, where traditional farming methods still persisted.[9]

In recent years, thanks to concerted efforts from conservationists and farmers, the corncrake has made a modest comeback. Meanwhile, a scheme to re-introduce the species into lowland England, on the Nene Washes near Peterborough, has been a partial success. But the days when the corncrake was as familiar as the skylark are long gone, and are unlikely ever to return.*

Other birds that have thrown in their lot with humans are also in trouble. Barn owls and barn swallows both struggle to find suitable places to nest, as so many rural barns and other farm buildings have been converted into homes. And although house martins and house sparrows are still found across much of Britain and Ireland (in about

---

* The other species named after the food we grow, the corn bunting, is not in quite so dire straits as its near namesake. But 'the fat bird of the barley', as it is affectionately known, has now vanished from large areas of lowland Britain. This includes my own home county of Somerset, where in 2012, for the first time since records began in the nineteenth century, not a single corn bunting was seen.

90% of all 10-km squares) both species have suffered major falls in abundance in recent years, with the biggest declines, ironically, in our towns and cities. This is down to a complex combination of factors, including loss of nest sites, a lack of food and, in the case of the house sparrow, possibly also the effects of air pollution on this very sedentary bird.

For the house martin, it is tempting to wonder where this charismatic little member of the swallow family would have bred before we built houses. I have seen them nesting in crevices in sea-cliffs on the coast of Wales, which must have been their original habitat. They also still nest in crevices in the crags of Malham Cove in North Yorkshire, where they have suffered in recent years from disturbance by climbers scaling the famous cliffs.

But for centuries now, house martins have preferred to build their cup-shaped nests, patiently constructed from hundreds of tiny balls of mud, on the sides of our homes. So it comes as no surprise that the folk names for this species reflect its deep connection with our own lives. They include 'eaves swallow' and 'house swallow', the latter the same as the German folk name *Hausschwalbe* (far more appropriate than the official name *Mehlschwalbe*, which rather oddly translates as 'flour swallow').

Another folk name is 'window swallow' – a direct translation of the French *hirondelle de fenêtre* – which reflects the way house martins often look as if they are going to fly straight through our bedroom windows, before veering off at the very last moment.*

---

* Note that, as with 'pigeon' and 'dove', 'swallow' and 'martin' are more or less interchangeable. For example, in North America the sand martin is known as the 'bank swallow'.

Many centuries ago, this motley group of species chose to throw in their lot with us. They made their nests on our homes and in our outbuildings, and fed in the fields where we grew our crops. In the process, they became some of our most familiar and best-loved birds. Today, though, they face an uncertain future, with global climate change now adding to the problems already brought about by intensive agriculture, pollution and habitat loss. It does not feel too extreme to say that we have betrayed them.

4: Canada Geese and Crossbills

As well as many birds being named after their habitat, some also feature a geographical region or place in their names. And as with habitat, in a tidy, organised world these would be entirely logical: Iceland gulls would breed mainly in Iceland (they don't), and Canada geese in Canada (they do, but having been introduced to Britain there are now an awful lot breeding here too). But given the haphazard way in which birds have acquired their names, you may not be surprised that the vast majority of geographical names are rarely accurate, or even particularly helpful.

Sometimes this is because the description covers such a vague area, as is the case with the Arctic tern, great northern diver and northern wheatear.* Other names are more specific, but just as unhelpful.

The Mediterranean gull is a smart cousin of the more familiar

---

* Northern wheatear is, like barn swallow, a relatively new name. It was deliberately coined in the latter years of the twentieth century to help sort out any confusion between the bird we simply call the 'wheatear' and its many other relatives, most of which live further south, in the Middle East or around the Mediterranean Sea (see Chapter 7).

black-headed variety, with a jet-black head and blood-red bill. Once its name was reasonably accurate: until about half a century ago this was a globally rare bird, found mainly in southern Europe and western Asia, with a significant part of the world population wintering around the Med. In those days the Mediterranean gull was so rare that in 1960 the eminent Dutch ornithologist Karel Voous described it as 'an unmistakable relict . . . probably in the course of becoming completely extinct'.[10]

Yet very soon after Voous made that doom-laden prediction, the species' fortunes began to turn. Like other members of its family, the Mediterranean gull is an opportunistic feeder, and from the 1960s onwards was able to take advantage of the exponential increase in surplus food created by our increasingly wasteful consumer society. Numbers started to increase, and its range began to expand to the north and west.

In 1968 a Mediterranean gull paired with a black-headed gull at a colony in Hampshire and successfully bred; following which several pure-bred pairs of the species became established, so that by the turn of the millennium there were at least 500 breeding pairs in Britain, including a huge colony in Poole Harbour. The global population of this handsome bird is now estimated at between 230,000 and 660,000 pairs,[11] and today its future is well and truly secure.

The same cannot be said for probably the most globally threatened bird regularly seen in Britain, which also has a connection with the Mediterranean Sea: the Balearic shearwater. Like other members of its family, this svelte seabird hugs the waves on narrow, stiff wings. It is named after that trio of holiday islands in the western Mediterranean – Mallorca, Menorca and Ibiza – the only places on the planet where it breeds. Today, there are thought to be just 10,000 individuals of this enigmatic species in the world, some of which can be seen as they fly past our southern coasts each year on their post-breeding wanderings, in late summer and early autumn.

Surprisingly few British birds are named after countries. Indeed, the nation with the most birds named after it on the official British List (with three species) is Egypt – no doubt reflecting our long colonial connection with that North African nation.* The only other British bird named after a nation-state is the aforementioned Canada goose.†

Three other regularly occurring British birds are named after islands or regions. They are the Manx shearwater, named after its breeding colony on the Isle of Man; Slavonian grebe, named either after the region of that name in Croatia, or more likely from Scalovia (also spelt Sclavonia), a part of Prussia, now in modern-day Lithuania; and the Lapland bunting, which is found across a wide swathe of northern Europe, Asia and North America.

As for birds named after the United Kingdom's own nations, the Scottish crossbill, an enigmatic bird which (if it truly exists) is Britain's only truly endemic species, is found here and nowhere else in

---

* However, one of these, the Egyptian goose, was introduced here, and the other two, Egyptian vulture and Egyptian nightjar, are very rare vagrants with just two accepted records of each.

† Some might reasonably argue that 'American' is synonymous with the USA, but I believe that in the case of bird names it refers to the continent of North America, not the country. After recent taxonomic changes, 'American' is found in the name of eight species on the British List: American wigeon, bittern, coot, golden plover, herring gull, kestrel, robin and redstart. The recent addition of Chinese pond heron to the British List, thanks to a record in Kent in 2014, means there are now five 'British birds' named after nation-states.

the world. As we saw in Chapter 3, crossbills sport a unique feature in the form of crossed mandibles, enabling them to extract the papery seeds from pinecones, a food source not readily available to any other species of bird.

Over time, ornithologists observing crossbills in the Caledonian pine forests of the Scottish Highlands began to suspect that there were two discrete populations there, each with a subtly different bill size and shape. This allowed each cohort of birds to exploit two different kinds of food: one feeding mostly on the seeds from larch and spruce cones, the other on a more mixed diet including the cones of Scots pine.

As early as 1975, the ornithologist Alan Knox tentatively suggested that these might represent two separate species, whose divergent diets had led to a permanent change in their bill size. This would, he reasoned, keep their populations ecologically separate, allowing them to live alongside one another in the same forests without interbreeding. Five years later, the British Ornithologists' Union boldly declared that there were indeed two species: the common (or red) crossbill, found across a wide swathe of the northern hemisphere, and the Scottish crossbill, found only in a small area of the Scottish Highlands and therefore an endemic British bird.*

Having 'lost' the red grouse a few years earlier, when the gamebird previously considered to be Britain's only unique species was downgraded to a mere subspecies of the far more widespread willow grouse, the Scots were delighted to have a new endemic species. But as with all complex taxonomic decisions, not everyone agreed

---

* To add to the confusion and complexity of the situation, there is now a third species present, with an even bigger bill, called the parrot crossbill.

with the change. Some observers accused the BOU of jumping the gun, fuelled perhaps by a jingoistic desire to announce the discovery of a genuine British endemic.

That controversy has not fully died down, even though research by the RSPB has recently shown that the Scottish crossbills do indeed have larger bills, and also make a different sound – publicised gleefully in the press as the birds having a 'Scottish accent'. Taken together, these two factors would indeed allow the Scottish crossbills to maintain reproductive isolation from their cousins, even when the two different species are living and breeding cheek-by-jowl with one another in the same place.

Thus, more than a century after the last 'new' British breeding bird, the willow tit, was discovered hiding in our midst, it has been supplanted by the Scottish crossbill – as distinctively Caledonian as single malt whisky, sporrans and Andy Murray.

So could there be any more 'cryptic species' awaiting discovery, somewhere in Britain? Astonishingly, given how well we think we know our birds, there may well be, but it will take a revolution in genetics for us to find out (see Chapter 7).

5: Eiderdowns, Cranes and Kites

I was once told a (possibly apocryphal) tale about a young boy being taken on a visit to the Farne Islands, the thriving seabird colony off the coast of Northumberland.

Just as the boat was leaving the harbour, the youngster spotted a small flock of eider ducks. Most were nut-brown females, with their delicately vermiculated plumage, looking as if someone had painstakingly drawn wavy lines across their wings and body, and etched even finer markings on their head. They were accompanied by a smaller group of males: boldly marked in slabs of black and white, with a strange greenish patch like a birthmark on the side of their necks, and a rosy flush across their breasts.

As the boy watched, to his delight the males began displaying to their mates, each throwing his head back onto his mantle like an over-enthusiastic gymnast. All the while, they were uttering one of the most bizarre sounds in the bird world: a call memorably described by Bill Oddie as sounding like a cross between a shocked old lady and the late Frankie Howerd.

The boy excitedly grabbed his father's arm as he struggled to remember the name of this striking bird. Overwhelmed with excitement, he finally managed to exclaim, 'Look daddy . . . it's . . . it's . . . a duvet duck!'

The great Dr Johnson would surely have been amused by the boy's etymological error. For in an essay in the *Idler* magazine from January 1759, this pioneering lexicographer made the very first published reference to the word 'duvet': 'There are now to be sold . . . some Duvets for bed-coverings, of down.'

The name 'eider' (meaning 'down bird') comes originally from the Icelandic, and the bird's modern French name is *eider à duvet*. 'Duvet' also means 'down', and refers to the small, incredibly soft feathers that female wildfowl pluck from their breasts, to line their nests and keep the eggs snug and warm. Eider ducks produce large amounts of particularly soft and thermally efficient down, which has traditionally been harvested for human use.*

The eider is a common and familiar breeding bird along the coasts of north-west Europe. So it is likely that our prehistoric ancestors, many of whom lived close to the sea, were the first people to begin harvesting the birds' down to keep themselves warm. But the first named individual to do so lived much later, in the seventh century AD, on the remote and chilly Holy Island in Northumberland.

Cut off from the mainland twice a day by the tides, Holy Island – also known as Lindisfarne – was at that time home to a small and isolated community of monks. Amongst them was a man named Cuthbert, who later rose to become the Bishop of Lindisfarne. After his death in AD 687 Cuthbert was canonised, and is now widely regarded as the patron saint of the north of England.

Holy Island was – and still is – home to a thriving population of eider ducks, which hide their nests away deep in the heather and bracken above the tideline to avoid being preyed on by gulls.

---

* Because eider ducks live at such cold northerly latitudes, and mainly hunt for food at sea, their down has a unique structure that traps warm air better than any other material – natural or synthetic. It is also produced in very small quantities: while tens of thousands of tonnes of goose down are sold worldwide every year, the entire annual global production of eider down could fit onto a single truck.

Medieval legend has it that Cuthbert cultivated a special relationship with the eiders, harvesting their down and in turn looking after them by passing laws against the taking of their eggs – the first recorded instance of a nesting bird being given official protection, anywhere in the world.*

Today, St Cuthbert is still honoured in the local name for the eider, which is known as 'Cuthbert's duck', sometimes affectionately shortened to 'Cuddy's duck', in memory of this far-sighted and benevolent holy man.

But what of the eiderdown itself? The idea of making and marketing a quilted bed cover stuffed with duck down was first brought to Britain from Germany by an English diplomat, Paul Rycaut, in 1689 – almost exactly a thousand years after Cuthbert's death. Rycaut sent his friends large bags filled with eider down, instructing them that 'the coverlet must be quilted high and in large panes, or otherwise it will not be warme.'[12]

Some ideas perhaps arise too early for their own good. The British public, it seemed, was not yet ready for this strange European invention, either because it was too expensive, or more likely because they preferred the masochistic practice of sleeping beneath scratchy, flea-ridden woollen blankets.

Gradually, though, things began to change. In 1841, *The Times* included an advert for an 'eiderdown quilt, or duvet', and by 1859, the novelist Wilkie Collins could write of 'a sweet little eider-down quilt, as light as roses'. By the 1950s the eiderdown had become the standard form of bed covering, placed on top of a layer of sheets

---

* Whether he did this out of a desire to protect this vulnerable wild creature, or from a less altruistic desire to keep all the down for himself, is not known.

and blankets to add an extra layer of warmth. But as a stern letter to *the Times* reveals, not everyone approved of the use of this portmanteau word, especially when the filling came from a lesser form of wildfowl: 'I ask you . . . to lend your pen to scotching the unwarrantable term "eiderdown" when applied to the ordinary goose-down quilt.'*

Yet even as this was being written, the days of the traditional eiderdown were numbered. After several false starts, it took the vision of one man, the legendary retail entrepreneur Terence Conran, to consign the eiderdown to the history-books. In 1964, when Conran opened his first Habitat store on London's trendy King's Road, one of the most popular items on sale was the 'continental quilt' – the product we now know as a duvet.†

The eiderdown is just one of many examples of the way bird names have entered our language as similes and metaphors. We may refer to a greedy eater as a 'gannet', a mad person as 'cuckoo', or say someone is 'as bald as a coot'. But how often do we give a moment's thought to the origin of these words and phrases, or how they first came into our day-to-day speech?

---

* *The Times*, 26 April 1950. But the march of the eiderdown could not be stopped, even by such determined ornithological pedantry.

† Many years later, Conran recalled that he had first come across it on a visit to Scandinavia: 'I had been in Sweden in the 1950s and was given a duvet to sleep under. I probably had a girl with me and I thought this was all part of the mood of the time – liberated sex and easy living.' A shrewd businessman, Conran understood that Britain's hard-pressed housewives would be less interested in the erotic possibilities of his new product, and more keen on the practical benefits. So he marketed the duvet as 'the ten-second bed': so much easier to make than the traditional version. It worked. Nowadays, with well over ten million duvets sold in Britain every year, virtually everybody sleeps beneath one.

Sometimes, of course, the link is pure coincidence: when someone is said to 'grouse' (meaning complain), there is no obvious link with the bird of that name; nor does the verb 'to quail' appear to have any connection with our smallest gamebird, unless it refers to its legendary shyness. The chess piece known as the rook has nothing to do with that member of the crow family, and the fungal disease thrush is likewise unrelated to the bird.

But there are many genuine connections between the meaning of a word and its origin as a bird's name. These include 'sniper', meaning a hidden marksman, a nod to the difficulty of shooting this fast-flying wader; and the colour 'teal', a deep, rich shade of bluish-green which comes from the patches on either side of the male teal's head.*

The origin and meaning of another familiar word containing a bird's name, scarecrow, seems obvious – but delve a little deeper, and confusion reigns. When the word was first coined, around the middle of the sixteenth century, it referred to a young boy employed to frighten the birds away from the newly sown seed in a farmer's field, by throwing stones and making a loud noise. Perhaps because small boys tended to get bored and wander off, farmers soon began to use a substitute: a cross-shaped structure hung with clothes and a hat, which was supposed to resemble a human being.

But which species are we actually talking about here? For carrion crows – the commonest species across most of the UK – are frequently confused with rooks. Both are all black, though the rook does have a distinctive greyish-white patch around its beak, and a smaller, more angular head. They also sound subtly different,

---

* The use of the name of the duck for this attractive colour appears to be very recent: the first *OED* reference is as late as 1923.

with the rook's call being less harsh – as the nature writer Dominic Couzens explains, it sounds like a crow that has been on an anger-management course.

One proverbial way of separating the two species is referred to in an old Norfolk rhyme:

> When thass a rook, thass a crow,
> And when thass crows, thass rooks.*

This relies on the fact that while crows are usually (though not always) solitary, rooks are more sociable birds, generally found in flocks. And while we tend to be suspicious of the all-black, rather sinister-looking crow, we take a more benevolent attitude towards rooks. This is perhaps because our relationship with them goes back many thousands of years, as the late Derek Goodwin, an ornithologist who made a special study of the crow family, pointed out: 'The rook is often thought of as one of the most characteristic birds of the British countryside. So it is, at least of the agricultural countryside . . . it is unlikely that there were any rooks in Britain, or indeed in Western Europe, before there were any farmers.'

The farmers themselves might take a less friendly approach, because if the premise behind the Norfolk rhyme is correct, the main threat to their precious crops would not have been the solitary crow but the gregarious rooks, whose large, noisy flocks can strip a newly planted field bare in an hour or two. This being the case,

* Roughly translated, this means, 'If you see one rook, it's a crow; if you see lots of crows, they're rooks'.

the scarecrow should really be called a scarerook; it is just another curious example of how words can mislead us.*

Whether it means rook or crow, it's obvious that the word scarecrow is named after a bird, and not the other way around. Likewise, we know that the Harrier jump jet, the first aircraft capable of vertical take-off and landing, was christened after the low-flying bird of prey; and that the imprint Puffin Books was named after the seabird, whose comical appearance and brightly coloured bill clearly appealed to children.† But in other cases, it can be hard to work out which came first: was it the name of a bird or that of the object?

Take the kite and the crane. You might think that kites were named after the children's toy, while cranes were so called because of their resemblance to the mechanical version. Actually it's the other way around. Like so many of our oldest bird names, these have onomatopoeic origins. Kite – originally 'cyta' in Old English – has no counterparts in any other European language, and so we know it originated in Britain, some time between the sixth and eleventh centuries, as it must have developed after the Anglo-Saxon invasion but before the Norman Conquest. The name comes from an imitation of the bird's high-pitched, whistling call, though W. B. Lockwood suggested that it might have initially been applied to the mewing cry of the buzzard, and only later adopted for its scarcer cousin.

Likewise, 'crane' is also likely to have come about as a representation of the bird's deep, honking call. The name has counterparts in the various Old Germanic and Scandinavian languages, showing

* Even Shakespeare was caught up in the confusion between the two species: *Macbeth* features the memorable but puzzling line, 'Light thickens, and the Crow Makes Wing to th' Rookie Wood. . .'
† And which followed in the footsteps of Penguin and Pelican Books.

that, as with other ancient names such as goose, it almost certainly has a Proto-Indo-European origin.

With both kites and cranes, some have argued that the use of the same names for the birds and man-made objects is simply coincidence. But it is also widely believed that both toy kites and mechanical cranes were named after their resemblance to these particular species of bird.

Kites (the birds) really do look like their namesake: they hang in the air on long, fingered wings with effortless ease, twisting and turning with each new gust of wind, and using their forked tail as a rudder to control their position. So it would be reasonable to assume the name derives from the bird's aerobatic antics.

The evidence for and against this is mostly circumstantial. The *OED* certainly favours a connection, suggesting that the name of the toy derived from 'its hovering in the air like the bird'. And in the first recorded use of the new meaning, in Samuel Butler's mock-heroic poem *Hudibras*, published in 1664, the author conveniently provided a direct comparison between the two:

As a Boy, one night, did fly his Tarsel of a Kite, The strangest long-wing'd Hauk that flies.

With 'crane', the link between bird and object is far more clear-cut. Unlike 'kite', variations of the same word are used in many European languages for both the bird and the machine: *grue* and *grue* in French, *grúa* and *grulla* in Spanish, and *kraan* and *kraanvogel* (literally 'crane-bird') in Dutch. Looking at a crane as it stands tall and stately, its head and bill curving forward at right angles to its long, straight neck, the connection between the two does seem irrefutable.

Another reason why we might query the links between these bird names and their man-made equivalents is that we tend to think of both kites and cranes (the birds, not the objects) as scarce and limited in their range. But this is an illusion, caused by the way we view the historical status of birds through the prism of our own current experience. If a bird is rare or common to us, we tend to assume that it has always been so, in what ecologists call 'shifting baseline syndrome'.

For cranes and kites, this assumption is quite misleading: a thousand years ago they would both have been far more widespread than they are today. Kites were the street-cleaners of medieval cities, snatching up any spilt food or unsavoury objects with alacrity, and earning a reputation as thieves and vagabonds. This explains Lear's angry insult to his deceitful daughter Goneril, whom he calls 'detested kite', and also the reference in *Coriolanus* to 'the city of kites and crows'. Although referring to Rome, this must surely have come about because Shakespeare had seen kites scavenging on the streets of London.*

As wetland specialists, cranes would have been less widespread than kites, but were still common enough to be caught and slaughtered by the dozen to supply vast medieval feasts. Indeed, until their watery habitats were destroyed in the late Middle Ages, these lanky waterbirds would have been found across much of eastern England. The evidence of their presence here can be seen from the many place names featuring the name, such as Cranfield, Cranbrook and

---

* The Bard's best-known line about kites is Autolycus's cautionary comment in *The Winter's Tale*: 'When the kite builds, look to lesser linen.' This refers to the kite's unusual custom of stealing items of underwear to decorate its nest, earning it a deserved reputation as a kleptomaniac.

Cranford, the last of which appears in the title of Elizabeth Gaskell's 1853 novel, which was televised in 2007.*

But over time, as the human population increased, persecution rose and wetlands were drained, both the kite and the crane began to decline in numbers. Red kites disappeared from the capital during the middle years of Queen Victoria's reign, eventually retreating to a few hidden valleys in central Wales, where they just managed to cling on, despite the attentions of egg collectors.

Cranes were not so fortunate: they vanished altogether as a British breeding bird during the Tudor period. Apart from the occasional wandering flock from the continent, they were absent for more than 400 years, until a small group returned to breed in Norfolk in the late 1970s. I can still remember my first, unforgettable sighting of cranes one chilly November afternoon in a remote corner of the Broads when, an hour or so before dusk, three huge birds flew past me uttering their haunting, honking calls. My first red kite is also sealed in my memory. Back in the mid-1970s, having spent three days combing the valleys of mid-Wales for these elusive birds, my mother and I finally struck lucky when a single kite drifted high overhead on a cloudless July day, its long wings glowing russet-orange against the deep blue sky.

Since then, both kites and cranes have made a dramatic comeback, and are far easier to see than they used to be. Cranes are still thriving in Norfolk, and have also been reintroduced onto the

* Incidentally, the widespread belief that the place names beginning with 'Cran-' actually refer to herons is given short shrift by Eilert Ekwall, author of the authoritative *Concise Oxford Dictionary of English Place-names* (Oxford, 1936; Fourth Edition 1959), who writes: 'There is no reason to assume any other meaning for the word than "crane", such as "heron". The two birds are always kept well apart in early records.' I agree with him.

Somerset Levels near my home. Red kites are now a regular sight in many parts of England and Scotland as well as Wales – one occasionally drifts over my garden on sunny spring days, while I have seen dozens of these aerobatic raptors hanging in the air over the M40 motorway in rural Oxfordshire, and even soaring over Lord's Cricket Ground in the centre of London.*

But not every bird name in everyday language is as obvious as the kite and the crane, as two tales – that of a young inventor and our best-known fictional spy – reveal. . .

6: Hobbies and Spies

The winter of 1946-7 was one of the coldest on record. Freezing temperatures persisted for days, weeks, then months, as the whole of Britain was blanketed with snow and ice. For a nation still reeling from the Second World War, and enduring the continuation of food rationing, it must have been a grim and miserable time.

But deep in the county of Kent, one young man was working hard to cheer the nation up, by promoting a way for the dads and lads of post-war Britain to have fun. A year earlier, Peter Adolph had come up with an idea he was sure would be a huge success: a kind of table football that involved each participant flicking the diminutive 'players' against the ball, to shoot, tackle, save or score a goal.

---

* By what seems to be pure coincidence – but is perhaps related to the recent comebacks made by both species – an indie rock band from Edinburgh formed in 2012 call themselves Kite and the Crane. Appropriately, perhaps, they specialise in telling stories, using rich harmonies and soaring vocals – just like their avian namesakes.

All he needed was a name: and one day, as he toiled to perfect the exact shape of his cardboard playing figures, he came up with one: 'Hobby'. But the officials at the Patent Office rejected his application outright. As one jobsworth pointed out to the crestfallen inventor, 'You might as well call a game "Game".'

Peter Adolph was back at square one. But then he had a clever idea. If he couldn't call his new game 'Hobby', surely he could use the scientific name of his favourite bird of prey, *Falco subbuteo* – the hobby?* And so, thanks to his ornithological expertise, the name of his product was born. A decade later, Subbuteo had become a fixture in homes up and down the country – and Peter Adolph was a millionaire.

So where does the bird's English name, hobby, come from? It first appears in the fifteenth century, spelt 'hoby', before it transmutes into the present-day spelling in 1642, at the height of the English Civil War. The name refers to the characteristic way this slender raptor hunts for its prey.

When hobbies return to Britain each spring, after a long and arduous flight from their African wintering grounds, they need a rapid boost of energy. They gather over large wetlands such as the Somerset Levels, Cotswold Water Park and the Stour Valley in East Kent, where they hunt dragonflies and other insects, providing a spectacular sight for watching birders.

After becoming more elusive for the rest of the breeding season, hobbies then reappear later in the summer, seeking out gatherings

---

* *Subbuteo* is Latin for 'small buzzard'. This is technically inaccurate as, despite their superficial similarity, falcons and buzzards are not related to one another. But it was nevertheless good enough for the founding father of the science of taxonomy, Linnaeus (see Chapter 3).

of swallows and house martins, and snatching their unwary young-sters out of the air with their razor-sharp talons.

Hunting both dragonflies and swallows requires a high level of agility, so the hobby sweeps back its wings and zigzags across the sky in hot pursuit of its victim. It is this jerky flight-action that gave the species its name – from the Old French verb 'hober', meaning 'to jump about'. However, unlike the connection between the scientific name of the species and the tabletop football game, the link with the word hobby – meaning pastime – is just a coincidence.

The influence of *Falco subbuteo* on the games industry is one of the more unusual examples of how bird names have been incorporated into popular culture. One often overlooked way that bird names enter society is as first or Christian names. The names of two falcons, Peregrine and Merlin (sometimes spelt Merlyn) are, mainly among the upper classes, given to boys, as in the veteran journalist and political commentator Peregrine Worsthorne and the former Home Secretary Merlyn Rees.*

Girls called Sylvia share their name with a genus of warblers, while Phoebe is the common name for three species of American flycatchers (in both cases the names have a classical origin, meaning 'of the woods' and 'bright as the moon' respectively). Robin, however, doesn't count – as the bird was called after the boy's name, not the other way around!

Bird names are also surprisingly common as nicknames for sporting teams: no fewer than five football or national league clubs

* The conservationist Sir Peter Scott, son of Scott of the Antarctic, named his son Falcon and one of his daughters Dafila (then the generic name for the pintail duck).

– Bristol City, Charlton Athletic, Cheltenham Town, Swindon Town and Wrexham – are known as the 'Robins' (because of the prominence of red in their playing strip), as is the rugby league team Hull Kingston Rovers. West Bromwich Albion (usually called the Baggies) are also known as the Throstles, a name that would presumably have pleased Max Nicholson; Norwich City, whose kit is yellow, are called the Canaries; while Newcastle United and Notts County, who both play in black-and-white, are known as the Magpies.*

Similarly, in Canada and the USA, a host of sporting teams are named after birds; most famously the major-league baseball teams the Baltimore Orioles, Toronto Blue Jays and St. Louis Cardinals. As with many British sports clubs, this is purely because of the colour of their strip, and not from any other affinity with the bird in question.

Sometimes the nickname has arisen as a result of the club's geographical setting. So Torquay United are known as the Gulls, and Brighton and Hove Albion the Seagulls, simply because they are based by the seaside.† But the origin of these bird-related nicknames isn't always obvious. Nowadays Crystal Palace's nickname is the Eagles, but until 1974 they were known as the Glazers. The name change happened when Malcolm Allison, one

* Cardiff City are nicknamed the Bluebirds (after the celebrated North American song-bird) because they play in blue. In 2012 their new owner, the Malaysian businessman Vincent Tan, controversially switched the colour of their strip to red – a lucky colour in the Far East. Less than three years later, after protests from fans, he was forced to change it back to blue, in line with the club's avian nickname.

† Sheffield Wednesday are known as the Owls, but this has no ornithological connection – it comes from the name of a local area of the city, Owlerton.

of the most flamboyant characters in football history, became their manager. Wishing to cultivate a more powerful image, he simply borrowed the nickname 'Eagles' from the Portuguese club Benfica.

No fewer than four amateur clubs in the English and Welsh leagues are known as the Linnets. This appears to be a curious choice, given that the linnet is not a very showy bird, and its only prominent colour is the pink patches that appear on the male's breast during spring and summer. When you discover that Burscough, King's Lynn, Runcorn Linnets and Barry Town don't play in pink, but in green, the name becomes even more baffling. The somewhat obscured reasoning behind this is that they are actually named after the species once known as the 'green linnet', a now long-forgotten folk name for the greenfinch, which is also commemorated in the title of a poem by William Wordsworth.

Birds also feature in the names of several music groups. In some cases, like the Eagles (and indeed the Byrds), there is no genuine ornithological link, but some bands were named deliberately after birds. Capercaillie is the name of a longstanding Scottish folk group, founded in the 1980s, and was chosen to celebrate that iconic highland grouse.

The band names Doves and Guillemots are no coincidence, either: founder members Jimi Goodwin (Doves) and Fyfe Dangerfield (Guillemots) are both keen birders – as are a surprising number of other members of rock bands, including Guy Garvey of Elbow and Martin Noble of British Sea Power, both of whom, however, chose non-ornithological names for their bands.

One of the most intriguing references to a bird name in popular culture is the goldeneye: a handsome species of diving duck that breeds in the Scottish Highlands and spends the winter on lakes and reservoirs in many parts of Britain.

Fans of James Bond will recognise Goldeneye as the name of author Ian Fleming's home in Jamaica – and, long after his death, the title of a 1995 film starring Pierce Brosnan as the eponymous hero. But sadly the villa was not named after this handsome duck, but rather Operation Goldeneye, a Second-World-War sabotage operation in which Fleming was involved (the operation, however, may well have been named after the bird).

There is, nevertheless, an avian connection with the Bond franchise. When Ian Fleming was looking for a name for his superspy hero, he wanted one that sounded 'as ordinary as possible . . . brief, unromantic, Anglo-Saxon and yet very masculine'. With the deadline fast approaching for the delivery of his first book *Casino Royale*, he happened to glance at his bookshelf, and noticed a slim volume entitled *Birds of the West Indies*. On the spine was the name of the author: the renowned American ornithologist, James Bond.*

That's not the end of the story. Several years later the real James Bond's wife wrote to Fleming complaining about the way her husband's name had become associated with the hard-drinking and womanising spy. Fleming sent a contrite reply:

Your husband has every reason to sue me . . . for practically

---

* In an interview in 1962 for the *New Yorker* magazine, Fleming claimed that when he wrote *Casino Royale*, 'I wanted Bond to be an extremely dull, uninteresting man . . . when I was casting around for a name for my protagonist I thought, by God, [James Bond] is the dullest name I ever heard.'

every kind of libel in the book. In return I can only offer your James Bond unlimited use of the name Ian Fleming for any purposes he may think fit. Perhaps one day he will discover some particularly horrible species of bird, which he would like to christen in an insulting fashion. . .*

Sadly, Bond never took Fleming up on his offer, so there is no Fleming's leaftosser skulking in the Amazonian rainforest, no Fleming's cisticola roaming the African plains, nor a Fleming's laughingthrush hiding halfway up a mountainside in Asia. But if there were it would hardly come as a surprise, even in these exotic locations. For there are an astonishing number of similarly bizarre official English names amongst what is, at the last count, the world's 10,700 or so species of birds. From Himalayan flameback to Indian pitta, malleefowl to magnificent frigatebird, sad flycatcher to joyful greenbul, and aberrant warbler to invisible rail, these birds and their wonderful names continue to inspire and delight us.

Now that we appear to have reached the point at which almost every species of bird in the world has been found and named, you might imagine that we are coming towards the end of our long and eventful story of the origins of English bird names.

---

* Ian Fleming did eventually make peace with the real-life Bond and his wife, giving them a first edition of his 1964 novel *You Only Live Twice*, with the inscription: 'To the real James Bond, from the thief of his identity'. A few months later, Fleming died, aged just fifty-six, from heart disease caused by his industrial consumption of cigarettes and alcohol. The cleaner-living James Bond survived another quarter of a century, dying in his home town of Philadelphia in 1989. Many years later, the signed copy of *You Only Live Twice* sold at auction for $84,000 (£56,000).

Yet that assumption might turn out to be a little premature. For thanks to exciting new advances in science, we have recently discovered – to our astonishment, delight and perhaps some apprehension – that the birds we already know about, and have given names to, may simply represent the tip of a much larger iceberg. And so we come to the final chapter of this story.

TOMORROW NEVER KNOWS

The Future of Bird Names

Names and attributes must be accommodated to the essence of things, and not the essence to the names, since things come first and names afterwards.

Galileo Galilei

1: Bird Names at a Crossroads

As dawn was about to break over Kibbutz Lotan, just outside the Red Sea resort of Eilat, we heard the strange, metronomic call of the scops owl – our first species of the day. Sixteen hours later, our 139th and last species was the night heron, as we watched a flock passing high overhead in the rapidly darkening sky.

By then, we were exhausted. We'd driven almost 250 miles through this arid, sun-drenched land, and seen a dozen species of warbler, ten birds of prey, half-a-dozen kinds of wheatear and more than a score of different waders. We'd found exotic birds, including wrynecks, bee-eaters and hoopoes, and more familiar ones, such as swallows, house martins and great tits.

But on this day, 1 April 2014, they all ranked equally. This was because we were taking part in that most curious of ornithological pastimes: a twenty-four-hour bird race, in which different teams try to see or hear as many species of bird as possible during the course of a single day. Our three-man team consisted of me, David Lindo (aka The Urban Birder) and Tim Appleton (founder of the British Birdwatching Fair).

As an international birding occasion, Champions of the Flyway takes some beating. A dozen teams from all over the world had converged on the Red Sea resort of Eilat to take part in this marathon event. That was the fun part; the serious purpose was to raise awareness of the plight of migrant birds, and funds to help save them from the many threats they face on their travels.*

And what travels these are. The vast majority of migrant birds in the world breed in the temperate or Arctic latitudes of the northern hemisphere, fly south in autumn to spend the winter below the Equator, and then head back north in spring to raise a family once again. They do so for one simple reason: light. In summer, the farther north you go, the more hours of daylight there are; and this – together with warmer temperatures – produces a glut of insects on which these birds can feed their hungry offspring.

These migratory birds follow three major global routes: known as the Africa-Eurasia, East Asia-Australasia and the Americas flyways, which between them witness the global travels of billions of birds each spring and autumn.

Israel is slap-bang in the middle of the Africa-Eurasia flyway. Each year tens of millions of birds, of more than 300 different species, pass through the narrow strip of land that divides the Middle East from Africa, flooding down towards their winter quarters south of the Sahara in autumn, and heading back north to breed in the temperate regions of Europe and northern Asia in spring.

We have known about this biannual spectacle since the dawn of civilisation. In the Old Testament Book of Jeremiah, written in the sixth century BC, the prophet clearly refers to the spring arrival of birds in the Holy Land: 'Yea, the stork in the heaven knoweth her appointed times; and the turtle [dove] and the crane and the swallow observe the time of their coming.'

* The money raised by sponsorship – more than $60,000 in the first year, and far more since – has gone to support conservation projects in Israel, Turkey and Georgia.

For decades, this migratory crossroads has attracted birders from all over the world, and this now-annual event has been no exception. At least a dozen nationalities were represented here: the Brits rubbing shoulders with Americans, Danes with Dutchmen, and, most tellingly of all, a joint Israeli-Palestinian team, who used their expert local knowledge to win the race, racking up an extraordinary tally of 169 species.

It was only afterwards that something struck me about the people taking part: not only did they all speak English, but throughout the contest they also used English bird names. This was even though their native languages included Hebrew, Arabic, Dutch, Finnish and German.

There were, it's true, a few concessions made by the Brits to our international colleagues: the use of 'northern wheatear' and 'barn swallow', for example, to distinguish our familiar species (known in the UK simply as the wheatear and swallow) from their more exotic relatives. But otherwise, the names corresponded to those you might hear back home in Britain, along with a handful of species whose English names reflect their limited Middle Eastern range, such as the Sinai rosefinch, Dead Sea sparrow and Palestine sunbird.*

The use of English bird names amongst birders of different nationalities is not confined to Israel. Wherever in the world I have travelled to watch birds, I hear these names spoken. Sometimes, as in India, Sri Lanka, Kenya and Botswana, this is because these countries were once part of the British Empire, and so English is

---

* At a brief stop for refreshments we also came across a flock of wolf-whistling Tristram's starlings, named after the Victorian bird collector Henry Baker Tristram (whom we met in Chapter 5) – a timely reminder of our previous colonial presence in the region.

still widely used in everyday speech. But I have also heard English bird names in Spain and Argentina, Morocco and Mexico, Poland and Sweden – and spoken by Spanish, French, Dutch, German, Swedish and Finnish birders all over the world.

In one respect, this simply reflects the fact that birding originated as a pastime in Britain, before spreading around the globe. But this growth in the popularity of birdwatching has also gone hand-in-hand with a far more important phenomenon: the inexorable rise of the English language.

English is the dominant language of the Internet, Hollywood movies and pop music. It is used by Interpol and the international airline industry, and dominates the worlds of television and information technology. English appears on billboards and in viral videos, in adverts and in scientific papers – wherever and whenever the writer wants to reach the widest possible audience. And the endless, twenty-four-hour buzz of social media – the new religion of the twenty-first century – is predominantly conducted in English.*

More than a third of a billion people now speak English as their first language: in Britain of course, but also in North America, South Africa, Australia and New Zealand. Yet this is dwarfed by the huge number of speakers who use English as their second (or even third or fourth) language – an estimated 600 million people around the world.† When we add the tens of millions of people who

---

* English is also gradually creeping into areas once dominated by other languages. In India's Bollywood film industry, for example, Hindi and Urdu are giving way to the use of English, along with a hybrid of Hindi and English known disparagingly as 'Hinglish'.
† More than the combined total of native speakers of Spanish, Arabic, Hindi and Russian, the next four languages in descending order of popularity.

have a working knowledge of English in their everyday lives, then English can justifiably claim to be the global *lingua franca* for the twenty-first century and beyond.*

It is ironic that, at a time when the days of the British Empire are long gone, and when Britain is rapidly withdrawing from the world stage, the English language is not only still so dominant, but increasingly so – although this is largely down to the continuing global power of the USA.

Looking back one-and-a-half millennia, to when those Anglo-Saxon invaders first crossed the North Sea and brought their strange Germanic tongue to our shores, the notion that English would have eventually risen to be the world's main language would have seemed unthinkable. But as the saying goes, 'a language is a dialect that has met with success', and English certainly fits that bill.

And so – with a little help from the Vikings and Normans, Chaucer and Shakespeare, and generations of explorers, empire-builders, moviemakers, songwriters and computer geeks – we have now reached that stage. English is well and truly here to stay.

As we have seen, English isn't just the global *lingua franca* – it is also the *lingua franca* of birding across the world. But despite the overwhelming dominance of English in this field, it certainly doesn't mean that bird names are universally accepted wherever you go. For a start, there's the perennial problem of what Oscar

* However, in terms of raw numbers English isn't actually the world's top language. Roughly 1.3 billion people – more than one in six of the entire world population – speak Mandarin Chinese. But we are entitled to take that figure with a large pinch of salt. For although 900 million native Mandarin speakers comfortably outrank those for whom English is their first language, when it comes to its status as a second language, English wins hands down.

Wilde (or George Bernard Shaw, opinion being divided as to who originated the phrase) called 'two nations separated by a common language': Britain and the USA.

Look through any North American field guide and you'll come across some strange and unfamiliar names: common loon, brant, parasitic jaeger, eared grebe, red phalarope, horned lark and Lapland longspur. For an unwary British birder visiting America for the first time, this can cause confusion; until, that is, you realise that these are actually very familiar species: great northern diver, brent goose, Arctic skua, black-necked grebe, grey phalarope, shore lark and Lapland bunting respectively. Despite decades of wrangling, the British and Americans simply won't agree on which names should take precedence.

From time to time, some authors have taken the plunge and attempted to sort out the situation. But this has only led to even greater confusion, as when the editors of the *Collins Bird Guide* (to the birds of Britain and Europe)[1] plumped for some rather strange, hybrid names, including 'great northern loon' and 'parasitic skua' (which by the time of the second edition had already reverted to Arctic skua).* The fact that they tried to make a compromise and failed simply highlighted the problem: Brits will continue to refer to divers and skuas, and Yanks to loons and jaegers, for many years to come.

A similar, but more colonially sensitive, situation has arisen in Africa. Here the legacy of empires – the Dutch as well as the British

---

* They also preferred the American horned lark and red phalarope (but helpfully added 'shore lark' and 'grey phalarope' in brackets), yet left Lapland bunting, black-necked grebe and brent goose unchanged.

– led to a schism between the English names used in East Africa and those, mainly derived from Afrikaans, used in South Africa.

Again, a quick comparative look through field guides for the two regions can be very confusing. Surely that strikingly blue, pheasant-like bird with the russet wings and yellow face is the same species as this one; yet in the East African guide it is called Ross's turaco, while in the South African book it appears as Ross's lourie. Of course they are the same species, as confirmed by both their shared eponym and their identical scientific name (*Musophaga rossae*).* The name 'lourie', from the Afrikaans, first surfaces in South Africa in the late eighteenth century, while in 1822 the visiting English ornithologist W. J. Burchell mentions the confusion already arising between the two alternative names, noting that 'In the aviary, I saw the Touracoo, called Loeri by the colonists.'

Likewise, in each guide we find plates featuring a series of plump, long-legged birds: one labelled as 'bustards' (East Africa), and the other as 'korhaans' (South Africa); while a group of strange waders resembling our own (misnamed) stone-curlew are shown as thick-knees in the East African guide and dikkops (meaning 'thick-head') in the South African one. Once again, they are the same family.

But gradually, as birding becomes more and more global, the Afrikaans-based South African names are beginning to give way to the more widely used (and English-based) East African ones. The latest edition of the main field guide to southern Africa lists turacos and thick-knees (with the South African names in brackets), but confusingly still keeps 'korhaan' for some of the smaller species of bustard.[2]

* Incidentally, this bird is named not after the Arctic explorer James Clark Ross (featured in Chapter 5), but for the wife of the governor of St Helena, Lady Eliza Ross.

Keeping up with these changes in bird names, with decisions made unilaterally by authors in each region, presents a perennial problem not just for travelling birders, but also for the international ornithological community, who need to avoid confusion in scientific papers and when communicating with colleagues in different countries. So when, in 2006, two US ornithologists produced a slim volume entitled *Birds of the World: Recommended English Names*,[3] many people heaved a sigh of relief.

Backed by the International Ornithological Congress – the United Nations of the bird world – Frank Gill and Minturn Wright (who in his day job is, appropriately, a lawyer) attempted to produce a consensus view on the world's bird names. The back-cover blurb summed up their aims and intentions: 'This book provides the first standardised English-language nomenclature for all living birds of the world . . . based on the rules and principles developed by leading ornithologists worldwide.'

It was a good and timely idea, and in the absence of something more definitive it is the best we have, at least in a volume conveniently small enough to be taken on your travels. But it still had to deal with minor issues (such as the US/UK difference between 'gray' and 'grey') as well as the thornier problems. These of course included the perennial issue of loons vs divers (they chose loons) and skuas vs jaegers, where they compromised, favouring skua for the two larger species (great and pomarine) and jaeger for the smaller duo (Arctic and long-tailed).

But the biggest problem faced by anyone who tries to standardise the English names of birds is that – just like the rest of our language – these are not fixed, but fluid. Most importantly, change doesn't happen because of top-down decrees, but through the normal processes of the evolution of the English language, from which, as we have seen, even some of our longest-established bird names are not immune.

The paradox of standardising the English names of birds is this: although in the short term it may make communication easier – especially between two different groups of English-speaking peoples, such as the Americans and British – it also runs the risk of losing the original reasons why the birds were named.

So although the eponymous bird names we celebrated in Chapter 5 may appear anachronistic, and although many other names we use are at best illogical and at worst downright misleading, if we change them, we lose the stories of their origin; we lose the complex connections between language, history and the real world; and we perhaps also lose a little of the contingency, contradiction and whimsy that make us human. And as we shall see, when the world's birdlife is facing greater threats than ever before, we cannot afford to forget these profound and ancient links between humanity and birds.

2: *Titmice and Ring-Doves*

The English language is constantly shifting, but slowly and gradually: it is only after a change in meaning has occurred and been widely accepted that we realise it has happened.*

Recent examples include 'decimated', which used to mean 'cut

---

* For example, some time during the early twentieth century the meaning of the word 'hopefully' changed from its original sense of 'in a hopeful manner', as in 'to travel hopefully is a better thing than to arrive' (a saying originally attributed to the Victorian author and explorer Robert Louis Stevenson) to the modern meaning, 'it is to be hoped'.

down by one-tenth', but is now widely used as a synonym for devastated; 'enormity', originally 'a great tragedy', but now simply 'a huge event'; and 'disinterested', now more or less synonymous with 'uninterested', rather than the original sense of unbiased. By adopting these new meanings, we effectively lose the original sense of each word. In many people's view, this risks diminishing the English language.

But as linguists have long pointed out, to try to resist such changes in spoken English is to fight against a tidal wave of actual usage. New words are being appropriated or invented all the time. Sometimes this is a deliberate act, as with the adoption of 'hygge' from Swedish, or the invention of 'Brexiteer' and 'chatbot'.* Others are coined accidentally, as when Sarah Palin used the word 'refudiate' (instead of 'refuse' or 'repudiate'), or George W. Bush said 'misunderestimate' (whose meaning is, as usual with the former President's sayings, wonderfully vague).[4]

But whether a completely new word has been coined, or an established word has changed in meaning, the pedants must simply grin and bear it. Otherwise, I suppose, we would all be speaking the language of Chaucer or Shakespeare.

Bird names change over time in much the same way. We have already seen how during the twentieth century 'redbreast' became robin, 'golden-crested wren' was simplified to goldcrest and, much further back in time, 'gowk' was displaced by cuckoo and 'ouzel' by blackbird.

Leafing through a list of bird names in a 1923 issue of the British Ornithologists' Union journal *Ibis*, we find almost a hundred names

* Just some of the Oxford Dictionaries' new words for 2016: https://en.oxforddictionaries.com/word-of-the-year/word-of-the-year-2016

that are no longer in general use. Many of these changes are the result of minor tweaks, such as the removal of hyphens in compound names such as 'sky-lark', 'sheld-duck', 'bean-goose', 'oyster-catcher', 'black-grouse' and 'marsh-harrier'.* Other changes, though, are more radical. A modern birder might struggle to work out the identity of 'Richardson's and Buffon's skuas' (now Arctic and long-tailed), while 'buff-backed heron' (cattle egret) has also long fallen out of fashion.

Some species have simply gained a descriptive epithet: thus at some point 'heron' became grey heron, and 'kite' turned into red kite, to distinguish them from their rarer relatives, the purple heron and black kite. Names that were in the process of changing are shown in the 1923 list as alternatives: such as 'wild duck or mallard', and 'ring-dove or wood-pigeon'.

One of the most striking changes in usage is the switch in the name of some of our most familiar garden birds, from 'titmouse' to 'tit'. The use of the older name – which dates back to the four-teenth century, and as we have seen simply means 'small creature' – lasted longer than we might imagine. So even though the shorter and more convenient term 'tit' has been in widespread use since the 1700s, a book published as recently as 1975 was still called *The Titmice of the British Isles*.[5]

However, just four years later a Collins New Naturalist volume, written by the Oxford scientist Christopher Perrins, rejoiced in the rather saucy title *British Tits*.[6] This was apparently confirmed only

---

* This reflects wider changes in the English language, in which hyphenated words have a tendency to be replaced by single words – as in 'bookshelf' and 'suitcase'; and the more recent trend towards 'portmanteau words', made from two abbreviated words yoked together, such as 'sitcom', 'Britpop' and the much-overused 'Brexit'.

after a lengthy correspondence between the author and the publishers, who were afraid the ambiguity might offend the delicate sensibilities of their readers.

With all these changes to bird names taking place gradually, over almost a hundred years, they have been accepted into general usage and, over time, become the norm. But in the final decade of the twentieth century, a radical proposal was made to change a significant minority of English bird names. Unlike previous changes, however, its proponents aimed to make it happen not gradually and organically, but virtually overnight. . .

It was as if Moses had come down from the mountain, breathing fire and fury, and carrying the stone tablets on which were carved the Ten Commandments. But this time the pronouncements did not deal with such minor transgressions as murder, adultery or coveting thy neighbour's ass. Instead, they condemned what to many was a far more pressing and significant subject: a proposed series of radical changes to the English names of birds.

The speaker was Ian Wallace, a man widely regarded as the godfather of modern birding. With his flowing white locks and beard, he certainly looked the part of an Old Testament prophet. More importantly, he commanded both affection and respect from his audience – as well he might, for through the sheer force of his personality, expressed through his lively writings and quirky illustrations, he has influenced successive generations of birders from the 1950s to the present.*

* One reviewer said of Wallace's captivating memoirs *Beguiled by Birds*: 'It makes you want to bring Ian home, feed him, open a bottle of something – preferably Scottish in

Never one to duck controversy, Wallace had seized an opportunity to speak in a debate before the great and the good of the bird world. This took place at a conference jointly organised by the British Trust for Ornithology and *Birding World* magazine, held at Swanwick in Derbyshire in March 1993, and aptly named 'Pride and Prejudice'.

Wallace's words, combined with his animated and energetic delivery, suggested an imminent apocalypse of Biblical proportions. Hands waving, voice rising in volume and pitch with every sentence, he railed against a new proposal that wholesale changes should be made to the names of the birds of the Western Palearctic – the zoogeographical region comprising Britain, Europe, North Africa and the Middle East.

Following Wallace's oration his opponent, the highly respected ornithologist Tim Inskipp, did his best. He put forward some excellent arguments, founded mostly in the urgent need to remove confusion amongst birders and ornithologists from different nations around the world. But in the face of Wallace's whirlwind, he simply had no chance. When a show of hands for or against the changes was taken at the conclusion of the debate, it was overwhelmingly in favour of respecting the status quo.

Ironically, given the result of the debate, few birders and ornithologists could deny that many of our bird names were indeed completely illogical. Why blackcap and whitethroat, and not 'black-capped warbler' and 'white-throated warbler', for example (as MacGillivray had attempted to rename them nearly two centuries

origin – wind him up and then sit back as he regales you with stories all night' (Gordon Hamlett, *Bird Watching* magazine).

earlier)? Why, as we have already seen, were British and American names for the same species or family sometimes different? And most of all, how, in this post-imperial world, could we possibly defend our continued use of single names for 'our' swallow, cuckoo, wheatear, kingfisher, jay and wren, when each is just one of dozens of species in their respective families found across the globe?

These were the driving forces behind the call for change. That was why a few months earlier, in the June 1992 edition of the influential monthly magazine *British Birds*, Tim Inskipp and Tim Sharrock had published a short but detailed paper setting out the reasons for the proposed changes, and a list of suggested new names.

These fell into three main categories. First, there were those birds for which the American and English names were significantly different. These had been discussed in detail three years earlier, at the 1990 International Ornithological Congress in New Zealand.

So while the names 'diver' and 'skua' remained, Inskipp and Sharrock's paper proposed that the descriptive English names should give way to the American versions. Thus white-billed diver (known in North America as the yellow-billed loon) became 'yellow-billed diver', while Arctic skua (known in North America as the parasitic jaeger) became 'parasitic skua'. Such messy compromises satisfied no one, and set the tone for the acrimonious opposition to the changes that would follow.*

The next category of proposed changes was for those instances where two similar species had names distinguished only by a

---

* One that really riled the purists was the proposed change from red grouse to the potentially confusing 'willow ptarmigan' (and consequently changing ptarmigan to 'rock ptarmigan', as it is known in North America).

qualifying adjective – such as ringed plover and its smaller, scarcer relative the little ringed plover; and black tern and its rarer cousin, the white-winged black tern. This was deemed to be illogical, and so the latter were to be changed to 'little plover' and 'white-winged tern'. Again, this was completely logical, and yet somehow felt 'wrong'.

Other suggested changes were more arbitrary. The small seabirds known for generations as Leach's and storm petrels were renamed 'Leach's storm-petrel' and 'European storm-petrel' respectively, on the grounds that this distinguished them from the larger petrel species. Further modifications included changing stock and rock doves to 'stock pigeon' and 'rock pigeon', turning dunnock into 'hedge accentor', and replacing bearded tit with the simple word 'reedling' (but not, however, adopting William MacGillivray's splendid suggestion 'furzeling' for the equally ill-named Dartford warbler).

At this stage, alarm bells were beginning to sound in the minds of most readers. It was hard to imagine any birder in the field ever using the proposed new names for any of these species. And if a name is never actually used, except in print, can it really be considered acceptable?

Then there was the addition of gaps between words, in order, so it was said, to avoid confusion and be consistent. So skylark and woodlark became 'sky lark' and 'wood lark' (presumably to match shore lark) and corncrake turned into 'corn crake'. Although this made logical sense, and even, it could be argued, reflected the older, hyphenated versions of these names, they still looked very odd when set down in print.

The third and final major proposal was the addition of a distinguishing epithet to almost a hundred one-word names: these were birds where only a single species in their family is commonly found in Britain, and so for centuries they have been known by a single-word name. Examples included pheasant, crane, cuckoo, kingfisher, bee-eater, roller, swift, nightjar, swallow, nuthatch, wren, wheatear and starling.*

These are, without doubt, classic examples of British insularity, arrogance and jingoism. Each is just one member of a much larger family, containing many more species found around the world. But because we named our own familiar species first, before we were aware of any of its relatives, most of us continue to call them by their original, abbreviated name, without any qualifying adjectives.

Thus 'our' nuthatch is just one of two dozen species, which include the Kashmir, Chinese, Corsican and Algerian nuthatches, the eastern and western rock nuthatches and, supreme amongst them all, the beautiful nuthatch, whose bright blue plumage lives up to its name. Likewise, what we call the 'swallow' is one of about fifty species, the 'wren' one of eighty, and the 'kingfisher' one of almost a hundred.

Hence the proposed new names, with added descriptors to bring them into line with the rest of the world. By far the largest category of proposed new descriptors was the fairly meaningless adjective 'common', to be applied to thirty-one species, closely followed by

---

* There are many other birds for which there is at least one other species bearing the same name: shelduck, teal, wigeon, pintail, shoveler, pochard, scaup, eider, golden-eye, fulmar, capercaillie, quail, gannet, shag, cormorant, bittern, osprey, buzzard, sparrowhawk, goshawk, kestrel, quail, coot, moorhen, lapwing, dotterel, turnstone, oystercatcher, curlew, whimbrel, redshank, greenshank, knot, snipe, woodcock, avocet, kittiwake, guillemot, puffin, wryneck, skylark, stonechat, redstart, nightingale, robin, blackbird, whitethroat, chiffchaff, goldcrest, treecreeper, jackdaw, raven, chough, jay, magpie, chaffinch, linnet, greenfinch, goldfinch, bullfinch, crossbill and serin.

the more helpful geographical distinctions 'Eurasian' (twenty-two species, such as wigeon and hobby) and 'European' (eleven species, including nightjar and bee-eater). 'Northern' was added to the names of eight species, but 'Western' to just one (the capercaillie).

Oddly, the committee in charge of these proposals then went off-piste. It was as though, bored with the addition of such dull and predictable words as 'common' and 'Eurasian', they rebelled. So amongst this rather mundane list there were a dozen marginally more imaginative labels: rock ptarmigan, pied avocet, red knot, black-legged kittiwake, Atlantic puffin, barn swallow, white-throated dipper, winter wren, wood nuthatch, black-billed magpie, spotted nutcracker and red-billed chough.

In some cases, this involved adopting a name widely used elsewhere in the world, particularly in places where two similar species occur. For instance, black-billed magpie was already in use in North America, to distinguish it from its close relative found there, the yellow-billed magpie. Similarly, the name black-legged kittiwake was already used to differentiate from its cousin, the red-legged kittiwake.

But ironically, what really riled some of the opponents to these changes was the inconsistency of the proposals. A hundred and fifty years earlier, William MacGillivray had at least had the courage to be truly radical: to sweep away the old and suggest an entirely new and systematic approach. Yet when it came to some of the least logical of our bird names, Inskipp and Sharrock held back. So they kept such oddities as fieldfare, redwing and black-cap, even though these do not provide any clue as to the family to which the birds belong.

The immediate reaction to Inskipp and Sharrock's proposals

was a potent blend of bemusement and hostility. One correspondent to *British Birds* called the whole debate 'a waste of time', and pointed out that – thanks to Linnaeus and his successors – we already had a perfectly good and universal way of telling species apart: 'Have Inskipp and Sharrock forgotten what the Latin system of scientific names is meant to be for?'[7] However, not everyone was against the changes: another reader praised the authors for 'producing such a well-thought-out and comprehensive review [of] this perennial problem'.[8]

But perhaps the most pertinent response to the proposals – Ian Wallace's verbal tour de force notwithstanding – came in the pages of a scruffy parody of *British Birds* (which is widely known as 'BB'). This was little more than a few cheaply printed pages held together by staples, which rejoiced in the title *Not BB*, and ran to five quirky and often hilarious editions.

In a short feature entitled 'Changes to the English Language', the anonymous authors produced their own version of the proposed name changes.[9] These included:

Black Vulture TO BECOME Afro-Caribbean Vulture
Garden Warbler TO BECOME Stately Home Warbler
House Sparrow TO BECOME Slum Weaver
Robin TO BECOME Northern Red-breasted Bush-Robin
Wren TO BECOME Jenny Wren

As the authors sardonically noted, in what would become the final nail in the coffin for the suggested changes:

The following names are so manifestly apt that they are TO REMAIN:

Barnacle Goose, Black-headed Gull, Dartford Warbler, Kentish Plover, Iceland Gull, Marsh Tit, Slavonian Grebe, Turtle Dove...

And yet, despite the widespread hostility towards the name-changes, a few of these new names – including barn swallow and northern wheatear – have gradually crept into use, especially when British birders travel abroad. They are also used in scientific papers, and in magazines such as *British Birds*, though I still can't get used to the clumsy 'sky lark' to describe that wondrous aerial songster – just try saying 'skylark' and 'sky lark' out loud, and you'll soon see what I mean. Shelley would surely be turning in his grave.

But the vast majority of the new names will never be spoken. And that, surely, is the key reason why they never really caught on.

My real objection to every proposal to impose a definitive list of English names on us – from MacGillivray's doomed attempt in the mid-nineteenth century to the *British Birds* affair – is not so much practical as philosophical. While I can understand the advantages of standardised names, and do occasionally use them myself when it will avoid confusion, the drive towards homogeneity goes against the very reason I am writing this book.

To me, the diversity of bird names is not an inconvenience but a wonder. The fact that we can choose to call *Prunella modularis* the hedge sparrow, hedge accentor or dunnock, or *Erithacus rubecula* the ruddock, redbreast or robin, or that there are more than thirty different folk names for the barn owl,* is for me not a cause of frustration, but something to celebrate. Like the rest of the English language – and especially the names we call ourselves and the places where we live – our bird names display a richness, complexity and downright quixotic quality that marks them out as part of our culture and heritage.

However, in a changing world, some bird names are now definitely considered unacceptable, as two stories from opposite sides of the Atlantic reveal.

3: Politics and Political Correctness

In the year 2000, the American Ornithologists' Union (AOU) made one of its official pronouncements on bird names. They had decided to change the traditional name for the duck *Clangula hyemalis* from 'oldsquaw' (a relatively late name, first appearing in print in 1834) to long-tailed duck – the name we have used in Britain since the naturalist George Edwards first coined it in the middle of the eighteenth century. Pamela Rasmussen, the distinguished US ornithologist based at Michigan State University, who was on the committee that made this decision, recalls that this proposal caused more controversy than any other name change, before or since.[10]

---

* Including church owl, white owl, screech owl (also, confusingly, the name of two dozen or more Neotropical species in the genus *Megascops*), screaming owl and hissing owl, respectively referring to the bird's home, pallid colour and strange, nocturnal call.

The AOU suggested that this was 'to concur with world-wide usage', even though it was abundantly clear that it was actually to avoid offending Native Americans, some of whom maintain that the word 'squaw' is unacceptable and demeaning. Ironically, though, this worthy intention may have been misplaced, as one anonymous contributor to a blog thread pointed out:

> Did anyone stop to think that possibly an original person from the Penobscot Nation may have named the bird, 'Oldsquaw', and removing that name may dishonor the origin of it? I heard that when an old Native American woman dies it is believed her spirit goes into a bird . . . hence 'Oldsquaw'.[11]

But the AOU's decision was small beer when compared with the wholesale changes carried out by the Swedish Ornithological Society in 2015. As they were compiling a list of more than 10,700 Swedish names for the world's birds, they came across some that they realised, to their horror, could easily be considered racist.

These included a small African duck named the *hottentott*, based on a derogatory term for the Khoikhoi people of south-western Africa;* *kafferseglaren*, which translates as 'kaffir-sailor', another deeply offensive South African insult, for the white-rumped swift; and *zigenarfågel* ('gypsy-bird') for the peculiar South American bird known as the hoatzin – the only bird, incidentally, whose youngsters have claws on their wings

---

* The official English name for this duck is still the 'hottentot teal'.

to enable them to clamber around the forest foliage. Four other names included the word *neger*, which translates as 'negro': these were changed to *svart*, a less offensive term translating simply as 'black'.*

Around the same time, the author Robert Macfarlane published his book *Landmarks*, full of rediscovered dialect words for features of the British landscape. As the journalist Patrick Barkham wryly observed in the *Guardian*, 'I wonder how many racist words he has discovered and quietly not added to his word-hoard?'

Barkham also touched on the question of whether any current English bird names can be considered offensive. Here we must tread carefully, as offence is very much in the eye – or ear – of the beholder. Surely even the most devout Roman Catholic is unlikely to take exception to the use of the name cardinal for the bright red North American finch, or a lawyer be offended by the name prothonotary warbler (the descriptor refers to a high ranking court official).†

But prudish people can still be offended by the apparently rude names of some common and familiar birds: tit, shag and booby are the first that come to mind (meaning 'small', 'crested' and 'stupid' respectively). Other dubious names, some of which must be said out loud to be properly appreciated, include hoopoe, hawfinch, chough, bonxie (the Shetland dialect name for the great skua, still in common use amongst birders), great bustard and nutcracker.

---

* Another potentially tricky name, 'negrofinch', has been quietly changed to 'nigrita', again to avoid giving offence.

† The prothonotary warbler itself has a bright yellow plumage, and is so named because papal officials in the Vatican wore uniforms of this colour. When US President Harry S. Truman was introduced to one such official, he is said to have asked, 'What the hell is a prothonotary?'

Across the pond, a similar list might contain dickcissel, tufted titmouse, horned puffin and that wondrous orange and black South American bird, the cock-of-the-rock. But apart from providing amusement for bored bloggers, in most cases there is no genuine linguistic linkage between the bird name and the apparently rude meaning.

This is not the case, however, when it comes to the ultimate taboo in rude bird names – one that puts tit, shag and booby in the shade: windfucker. The origins of this now obsolete folk name for the kestrel reveal the fascinating history of what must surely be the best known swear word in the English language today.

Anyone who has ever watched a hunting kestrel as it hovers in the air, holding its head virtually motionless while its wings beat rapidly to keep in position, has marvelled at the bird's skill and technique. The Victorian poet Gerard Manley Hopkins was suitably impressed, and celebrated the kestrel's extraordinary abilities in his 1877 poem 'The Windhover':

> I caught this morning morning's minion, kingdom
> > of daylight's dauphin, dapple-dawn-drawn Falcon, in his
> > > riding
> > Of the rolling level underneath him steady air, and striding
> High there, how he rung upon the rein of a wimpling wing
> In his ecstasy! Then off, off forth on swing,
> > As a skate's heel sweeps smooth on a bow-bend: the hurl and
> > > gliding
> > Rebuffed the big wind. My heart in hiding
> Stirred for a bird – the achieve of, the mastery of the thing!

But as a Jesuit priest, who dedicated this poem 'To Christ our Lord', Hopkins would surely have been deeply shocked by 'windfucker', an earlier name for our commonest falcon.

The first – and indeed only – reference to this folk name for the kestrel dates back to 1599, when the Elizabethan pamphleteer, playwright and poet Thomas Nashe wrote of 'the kistrilles or windfuckers that filling themselues with winde, fly against the winde euermore'. Soon afterwards, in the early seventeenth century, it was adopted as what the *OED* calls 'a term of opprobrium', in phrases such as Ben Jonson's 'did you euer heare such a wind-fucker, as this?'* Alternative versions included 'wind bibber' (Sussex), 'wind cuffer' (Orkney), 'wind fanner' (Surrey and Sussex) and the blunter 'fuckwind', which was still being used in the north of England as late as 1847.

On the surface, the origin of these names is clear: like 'windhover', they all refer to the way the kestrel's wings beat the air so that the hovering bird can stay in one place and keep its eyes fixed on its target below. But although we may be shocked at the use of the terms 'windfucker' and 'fuckwind', our ancestors might not have found them quite so offensive.

According to W. B. Lockwood, the word 'fuck' was originally a euphemism, meaning 'to beat'[12] – rather like the word 'bonk' is used as a euphemism for the word 'fuck' today. However, we have only his word for this, as the term 'windfucker' is the only recorded use of that word before it took on the offensive meaning it has nowadays. We can, though, assume that it won't be considered as an alternative name for the kestrel, at least in the foreseeable future.

* In his 1609 comedy *Epicene, or the Silent Woman*, to refer to Sir John Daw, a rather ridiculous character.

4: *Splitting Species*

In the aftermath of Inskipp and Sharrock's controversial proposals, while we in Britain were focusing on proposed changes to English bird names, on the other side of the Atlantic a more momentous revolution was occurring in the world of scientific ornithology. This would not simply shake up the names we give to different birds: it would change the way we look at the relationships between the species themselves.

In 1990 three US ornithologists and biologists, Charles G. Sibley, Burt L. Monroe Jr. and Jon E. Ahlquist, produced two blockbuster books that between them would put a metaphorical bomb under what had been, until then, the stable and predictable world of bird taxonomy. Their proposals would completely disrupt the longstanding way in which we classify the relationships between different species of birds into larger groups and families.[13]

Until Sibley, Monroe and Ahlquist came along, to determine which species belonged to the same family, and to differentiate one species as separate from another, ornithologists had mainly relied on the long-established principles of external and internal morphology. These involved looking at the physical form and structure of different birds, and using these characteristics to establish how they were related.

But this approach could put the cart before the horse, because it made no real attempt to reflect what scientists call 'phylogeny' – the history of the evolutionary descent of different organisms. Just because two species look similar, or have similar physical characteristics, doesn't necessarily mean they're related: they could have evolved to look alike because their lifestyles are similar.

The new approach put forward by these three scientists began with phylogeny: it was an ambitious attempt to recreate the 'Tree of Life', to accurately represent the way the various species of bird had evolved, and therefore to show the relationships between them. In two huge volumes, each weighing several kilos, which between them contained more than 2,000 pages of text, Sibley, Monroe and Ahlquist completely overturned our established knowledge and understanding of the way we classify birds.

For the phylogeny they employed was based on a controversial new biochemical technique known as DNA–DNA hybridisation. This involved heating strands of DNA taken from one species until they separated, and then recombining the individual strands with similarly isolated strands taken from another species. When this new 'hybrid DNA' was in turn heated, the higher the temperature needed for the DNA to separate, the more closely the two species being compared were related, and vice versa.

This revolutionary approach was – so the authors and their supporters claimed – 'the Holy Grail of avian systematics'. They believed it would finally provide a definitive answer to the thorny problem of how closely two species – or on a larger scale, two orders or families* – were actually related. Instead of looking at external

* All species of bird (and indeed any other organism) belong to a particular family, which may contain anything from several hundred species to just one. In turn, each family is combined with others to create an order. So, for example, the house sparrow *Passer domesticus* belongs to the family Passeridae, which in turn is part of the much larger order the Passeriformes.

features or internal structure, all you needed to do, they suggested, was to cook up samples of their DNA, and then do the maths.

The US team's suggested changes to classification were contentious, to say the least. They proposed wholesale changes in the family tree of the world's birds, involving some dramatic – and to some, frankly bizarre – new relationships. For example, they put those masters of the air, the albatrosses, into the same 'super-family' as the flightless penguins, and yoked together the apparently dissimilar families of grebes, shearwaters, waders, falcons and flamingos into another massive 'super-family' (Ciconiiformes).

Less controversially (at least at the time), they suggested that the bare faces and broad wings of storks and the New World vultures were not, as had previously been thought, the chance result of convergent evolution brought about by their scavenging habits, but had arisen because they were genetically close cousins.

Almost immediately, the backlash began. There was a widespread feeling amongst the wider ornithological community that although the overall aims might be laudable, the pioneering scientific methods being used were simply not accurate enough to support the conclusions. There was also a suggestion that Sibley was manipulating some of his experimental results to fit prior assumptions – either through carelessness or to get the answers he wanted – making it hard to know whether any particular set of results was valid or not.

During the quarter of a century since this bombshell first hit the world of ornithology, some of these radical conclusions have indeed been discredited.[14] These include, ironically, the one proposal with which most people had agreed – the placing of New World vultures in the same group as storks. This was later retracted as having arisen from erroneous data, and most authorities now place the vultures back with the Old World hawks and eagles in their original order, Accipitriformes.

Right up to his death in 1998 Charles Sibley passionately continued to defend the new approach, pointing to the fact that many of their findings had been accepted by the wider scientific community.[15] These included the once radical idea that Australasia's songbirds had – like that continent's marsupial mammals – evolved separately from those found elsewhere in the world, and so despite their superficial differences were in fact more closely related to one another than they were to their Old World counterparts (see Chapter 4). That one turned out to be spot-on.

Today, thanks to the pioneering work by the US evolutionary ornithologist Professor Richard O. Prum of Yale University, the big picture of avian phylogeny – at least at the level of orders and families – is becoming clearer, though there are still many gaps in our knowledge. In a 2015 paper in the journal *Nature*,[16] Prum and his colleagues produced a series of what one of their peers called 'robust conclusions, representing a decisive technical advance on Sibley and Ahlquist'.[17]

To the ordinary birder, their findings are actually quite comforting, as they appear to reflect the way we see and understand relationships between birds in the field. For example, one grouping consists of those aerial acrobats the nightjars, swifts and hummingbirds, while two huge groupings are broadly separated into waterbirds (including all diving, wading and shorebirds) and landbirds.

The authors believe that these splits occurred in the wake of the last mass extinction, the Cretaceous-Palaeogene, some 66 million years ago. This was almost certainly the result of a massive meteorite hitting the planet, creating catastrophic changes to the world's climate and atmosphere, and killing off three-quarters of the plant and animal species on Earth – including the non-avian dinosaurs. This left the playing field clear for new lineages to evolve, including modern birds (or as we should perhaps now call them, avian dinosaurs).[18]

These days, however, the argument about the potential relatedness at the higher level of orders and families has faded into the background. A second revolution has been taking place in the world of ornithology, putting a potentially far more iconoclastic issue under the spotlight: the whole way we decide what defines a species. It has had a profound effect on the names we give to birds, as the result has been a huge increase in the number of different kinds of bird found around the globe.

When I was growing up in the 1960s and 1970s, the number of different species of bird in the world was thought to be roughly 8,600. This figure had been arrived at many years earlier, in 1951, by the German/American evolutionary biologist Ernst Mayr and his colleague, the US ornithologist Dean Amadon. At the time it was generally assumed that this total would increase only very slowly, as a handful of new species (or re-discovered species hitherto thought to be extinct) might still be found in the remote rainforests of South America, Africa or south-east Asia.

For several decades, that's exactly what happened. Then things began to change, with the number of species suddenly rising dramatically, to more than 9,700.[19] As Charles Sibley later noted, only fifty or sixty of the thousand or so new species were previously unknown to science; the rest – around 95% – were the result of a new and radical way of classifying birds.

Before this time, the most widely accepted way of defining a species was Mayr's Biological Species Concept (BSC). This assumed, as we have seen earlier in the debate around the identification of the willow tit as a British breeding species, that if two different populations of birds overlap in range without interbreeding, they must be two separate species. But a problem arises when there are two populations that look or sound slightly different, but whose ranges do not overlap, which means that the hypothesis cannot be tested in the field.

Under the strict rules of the BSC, it had previously been assumed that these were *not* separate species, but merely races or subspecies. To get round this problem, Sibley and Monroe made one crucial change. They promoted the 'allospecies concept', which gives birds that look or sound significantly different from their relatives the benefit of the doubt, and regards them as separate species – whether or not this can be confirmed in the field.

This may all sound like an arcane and meaningless distinction: the academic equivalent of medieval scholars debating how many angels can fit on the head of a pin. But in fact it was a critical paradigm shift: not just scientifically, but from a practical viewpoint too. For birders all over the world, it has made a huge difference, as it revealed the hidden presence of an extraordinary number of new species – perhaps as many as 1,100.

At this stage it is worth reminding ourselves of the old joke, 'a species is whatever a competent taxonomist says is a species'.*

---

* In *Ever Since Darwin* (1977), the US biologist Stephen Jay Gould referred to 'the

Given the ambiguity, even the greatest experts in their field have been unable to agree on a working definition of when two discrete populations of birds can be defined as separate species, rather than just distinctive subspecies.

But whatever the arguments, the general move towards a looser definition of what makes a species has led to an epidemic of what ornithologists call 'splitting'. This is the process by which what were once considered distinctive races of a single species are 'promoted', thus creating two new species where only one had existed before.

This process has always been with us: when I started birding, back in the 1960s, pink-footed and bean geese were still considered conspecific – i.e. two different races of the same species. Soon afterwards, they were each elevated to specific status. Later on, the 'bean goose' was in turn split into two full species, known as tundra bean and taiga bean geese. Likewise rock and water pipits were lumped together as a single species until as recently as the late 1980s, despite their very obvious differences in appearance and ecology.

Today more and more species are being split: according to some authorities the familiar brent goose may comprise three different species: pale-bellied, dark-bellied and the North American version known as 'black brant'.

Further afield, there are now three different versions of the elegant raptor known as black-winged or black-shouldered kite (one in southern Europe and Africa, one in Australia and one, known as white-tailed kite, in the Americas); there are four different darters

---

fuzziness of all supposedly absolute taxonomic distinctions', while the Dutch author Kees van Deemter has gone even further: 'Species and subspecies are but a convenient fiction' (*In Praise of Vagueness*, 2010).

or 'snakebirds', where there were once two; and no fewer than six different versions of the giant cousin of our moorhen that used to be called 'purple swamphen', found from Spain and Portugal, through Africa and Asia, to New Zealand.

For keen 'world listers', desperate to see every species of bird on the planet, this unexpected development has been a mixed blessing. The good news is that there are suddenly all sorts of new birds to go out and see – or if they are lucky, to 'tick off' their list while sitting at home, as they have already seen them without hitherto realising that they were actually separate species. But for some, the new approach has proved deeply frustrating, because unless they have kept very detailed notes about the birds on their various travels, and exactly where they came across them, they have found it impossible to work out which of two or more new species they have actually seen.

The upshot of all this is that the current generally accepted total of different species in the world has now reached a figure of between 10,500 and 10,700, an increase of almost a quarter on Mayr and Amadon's original estimate. But is that the limit, apart from a handful of new discoveries to be made over the next few decades? Or might it be just the beginning of an explosion in the number of different species of bird in the world? I gained a fascinating insight into this issue in 2004, on a birding trip to Morocco.

The Dutch birder and ornithologist Arnoud van den Berg knows more about the birds of the Western Palearctic than virtually anyone. So when I accompanied him on a visit to Morocco I expected – and duly received – the benefit of his vast wealth of knowledge about that country's birds.

What I didn't expect was that, while we were watching one of the rarest birds in the world, a flock of northern bald ibises, Arnoud would casually point out a small, cormorant-like bird perching on the rocks below. I was even more surprised when he explained that this bird, the North African subspecies of the European shag, was potentially the most endangered bird we would see on the trip, with a global population of just a hundred pairs.

Another member of our group tactlessly pointed out that it was 'not a real species', which prompted a characteristically thoughtful response from Arnoud. He patiently explained that, given the difficulty in trying to define what is a species and what is not, we should perhaps take a different approach. In his view, we should simply focus on each distinctively different kind of bird – whether we consider it a subspecies or a full species – and do our best to conserve it. That way we would ensure that we retain avian biodiversity, and can leave future generations to argue whether or not a particular bird is indeed a different species from its cousin.[*]

Arnoud van den Berg is not the first naturalist to take this approach to classification and taxonomy. Back in the late nineteenth century, the Victorian ornithologist Richard Bowdler Sharpe, curator of the bird collection at the British Museum of Natural History, took a similarly pragmatic view. Indeed, he went even further: by ignoring the distinction between species and subspecies, he concluded that there were almost 19,000 species of bird in the world.[†]

[*] As Bret M. Whitney and Mario Cohn-Haft point out, in the Special Volume of *Handbook of the Birds of the World* (Barcelona, 2013), conservationists are now beginning to recognise subspecies and dubious species in their official plans, in order to preserve the building blocks of biodiversity before they disappear.

[†] In his journal *A hand-list of the genera and species of birds*, Vol. 5 (London, 1909).

Astonishingly, some ornithologists now believe that Bowdler Sharpe may have been right all along. In December 2016, a new study led by the highly respected American Museum of Natural History (AMNH) suggested that there could be as many as 18,000 different species of bird on the planet – close to Bowdler Sharpe's estimate, and not far off twice the current accepted total.[20] The authors based their conclusions on the concept of 'hidden avian diversity'; the idea that there are many birds out there that look so similar to one another that they have previously been either ignored, or thought to be subspecies.

Considering that birds are probably the most studied group of wild creatures in the world, this seems hard to believe. But perhaps we shouldn't be so surprised: after all, as recently as 1999 scientists discovered that the small bat known as the pipistrelle – one of Britain's most widespread mammals – was in fact two totally separate species, each echolocating using different sound frequencies.

In some ways this is also the logical consequence of the new way of looking at what makes a species. As Charles Sibley remarked, '"Splitting" and "lumping" will continue as we try to make nature fit our concepts. Of course, we like to think that we are making our concepts fit Nature.'

Fundamentally, this comes down to the mismatch between the way we try to classify the natural world and the way it actually arose – something that, of course, we can never truly know or understand.

So where does this leave English bird names? Well, for a start, it

Despite spending most of his life in the museum, Sharpe has several species named after him, including a rosefinch and a starling. He also had ten daughters.

would suggest that if there really are almost twice as many species out there, then we are going to need an awful lot more names. Perhaps fortunately, this is not quite true: in many cases the various subspecies already have a perfectly serviceable name, which can be adopted when the species is split.

Take the case of one of North America's most familiar and colourful birds, the Baltimore oriole. The Baltimore Orioles baseball team, based in Baltimore, Maryland, was named in the 1950s after the national bird of that state – a striking, orange-and-black songbird. But in 1973, to the horror of the team's many fans, the AOU decided to lump this species with its western counterpart, Bullock's oriole,* into a single species, which was given the deeply unimaginative name 'northern oriole'. The reason given for the change was that, in the zone where both forms encountered one another, ornithologists discovered that they were interbreeding and perhaps producing fertile offspring – a classic sign, at least according to the more traditional BSC, that they must be the same species.

Fortunately for devoted followers of the Baltimore Orioles, the story has a happy ending. Later research by a team of Canadian ornithologists showed that while there was some interbreeding between the two forms, it was nowhere near as frequent as had previously been thought, so in 1995 they were separated once again, and given back their old (and to my mind far more interesting) names.†

In other cases, when a species new to science is discovered, it is often named after the locality where it lives – especially when it

---

* Named after a Briton, William Bullock (see Chapter 5).

† A similar situation occurred with myrtle and Audubon's warblers, which are considered by some authorities to be two separate species, and by others to be one, known (rather unimaginatively) as the yellow-rumped warbler.

has a very limited territory, as many of them do. Leafing through the final 'Special Volume' in *Handbook of the Birds of the World*,[21] published as a supplement to the series in 2013, we find that of the eighty-four newly discovered species featured, the vast majority are named after the location where the bird was found.

These areas range from the geographically large, as with the New Zealand storm-petrel, to the tiny, such as the Rubeho forest-partridge, known only from a single, densely forested mountainside in northern Tanzania. Other species named after very localised place-names include the Delta Amacuro spinetail, from the Orinoco Delta in Venezuela, and the Acre antshrike, found only along a short section of Brazil's border with Peru. Another recently bestowed bird name, Jocotoco antpitta, sounds as though it comes from a location, but 'Jocotoco' is actually the name given by the local indigenous people to the bird – a useful reminder that although we often consider a species to be 'newly discovered', it may in fact have been known to its human neighbours all along.

This new way of looking at the relationships between birds does have other, more serious implications for the names we give to birds. On a broader scale, falcons have recently been found to be far more closely related to parrots (and adjacent in the classification system to songbirds) than they are to other diurnal birds of prey such as hawks, buzzards and eagles.

So can we still refer to falcons as 'raptors', or indeed 'birds of prey'? And if we do continue to do so, why do we not include owls

---

* The volume also includes the Rubeho warbler, previously considered to be an isolated population of Mrs Moreau's warbler, and found in an adjacent mountain range, but now regarded as a separate species. Ironically, this means that Mrs Moreau's warbler is under even greater threat.

under the same term?* After all, they are as closely – or distantly – related to the 'true' raptors as falcons are, and early ornithologists used to classify all three groups under the wonderfully evocative term 'rapacious birds'.

At a more detailed level, the latest DNA studies have revealed some surprising relationships – or perhaps that should be 'lack of relationships' – within one of our best-known bird families, the warblers.

We all know – or at least *think* we know – what a warbler looks like: in Britain at least, they are (mainly) migratory, insectivorous songbirds, often rather drab in plumage and hard to see, so that we tend to tell them apart by their songs. But as I look through the latest version of the BOUs' British List (updated December 2016), I see to my surprise that Cetti's warbler is now separated from the rest of its tribe by the long-tailed tit.[22] So does that mean that Cetti's warbler is not a warbler, or that the long-tailed tit is, or that neither species belongs to the warbler family?

Some authorities go much further, splitting Sylviidae, which used to include all the European warblers, into five separate families. These are the 'leaf warblers' (willow, chiffchaff etc.), 'bush warblers' (an African and Asian group, of which Cetti's is the only European member), 'grass warblers' (such as grasshopper and Savi's), 'marsh and tree warblers' (from the genera *Acrocephalus* and *Hippolais*, including reed, sedge and icterine) and finally the 'true warblers', of the genus *Sylvia*, whose members include our familiar whitethroat and blackcap. As if that wasn't confusing enough, this

---

* Although owls are often popularly referred to as raptors, the term is usually confined to day-flying birds of prey such as eagles, hawks, kites, harriers, buzzards and falcons.

last group may prove to not actually be warblers at all, but members of the babbler family.

If you are feeling a little baffled, then you had better get used to it, for this is the future of ornithology. In the meantime, we can either spend time arguing over whether 'warblers' actually exist, or take a more relaxed view, and continue to lump all these birds under that convenient (though perhaps scientifically inaccurate) linguistic term.

One result of all this change and upheaval, however, has been a very sensible proposal to standardise the sequence in field guides. When I was growing up the 'Wetmore Order' prevailed (established in 1930 by the US ornithologist Alexander Wetmore, and revised again in 1951 and 1960), with divers and grebes at the start and buntings and sparrows at the end. This had in turn displaced the sequence used in *The Handbook of British Birds*, published at the start of the Second World War, which was more or less in the opposite order, placing crows at the start and gamebirds at the end.

Modern guides have now changed yet again, and although they keep the old sequence for the majority of birds, they now usually start with wildfowl (ducks, geese and swans) and gamebirds (pheasants, partridges, grouse etc.). This can make it hard for those from an earlier generation to find these species rapidly in the book when out in the field.

If taxonomy continues to change every year or two, publishers will inevitably struggle to keep up, so we face potential chaos. No wonder that several authors, including the expat Briton Richard Crossley (who lives in New Jersey and has developed a series of pioneering and innovative books*), have called for a new, fixed and

---

* Such as Richard Crossley and Dominic Couzens, *The Crossley Guide: Britain and*

consistent sequence to be used in all field guides. This would be established independently of any further taxonomic changes, and instead would be based on simple categories such as 'seabirds', 'waterbirds' and 'land birds'. At a time when even the scientific names of some birds are changing,* anything that leads to greater stability and consistency is surely to be welcomed. And as we have seen, it broadly fits the latest conclusions regarding avian phylogeny.

Ironically this proposal is much the same as the system found in what is widely regarded as the very first portable bird book written in English, Thomas Bewick's *A History of British Birds*, published in two volumes (Land Birds and Water Birds) in 1797 and 1804.[23] This just shows that if we wait long enough, the way we look at birds really does turn full circle.

5: New Birds, New Names

From time to time, a pioneering ornithologist actually does discover a bird that is completely unknown to science. So it was that in 1991, the British ornithologist Paul Salaman found a new species of vireo – a small, olive-and-yellow, insectivorous Neotropical bird superficially similar to a warbler – in the Chocó department of western Colombia.[24]

Ireland (Princeton, 2014). The innovation lies in using a series of many different photos from different angles and perspectives, to create what he believes is a more realistic view of the bird.

* For example, as has already been noted, blue tit has gone from the genus Parus into a new genus, Cyanistes, while black-headed gull, formerly in the genus Larus (along with most British gulls), now has the scientific name *Chroicocephalus ridibundus*.

That it took so long for the bird to be discovered is hardly surprising, when you consider that the cloud-forest where it lives is not only remote, tricky to access and often blanketed in mist, but was also a hotspot in the long-running conflict between the Colombian government and the FARC guerrilla movement.

As we have noted, newly discovered (and newly split) species are often named after the region where they were found, and this species was indeed given the name Chocó vireo. Afterwards it might have sunk back into obscurity, were it not that its scientific name was then auctioned off to the highest bidder by Salaman, through the UK-based global conservation organisation BirdLife International. So it was that in 1996, for the surprisingly modest sum of $70,000, the Chocó vireo was granted the scientific name *Vireo masteri*.[25]

The name commemorated Dr Bernard Master, a retired doctor and lifelong birder from Ohio, who on New Year's Day 2010, after searching for three weeks, finally got to see the species that bears his name. As a dedicated 'world lister', whose aim is to see every single one of the world's bird species, Master was naturally delighted at having finally caught up with his eponymous bird.

When it was first announced that the species' Latin name was being sold to the highest bidder, the response ranged from outrage to laughter. *Birdwatch* magazine ran a competition to suggest other potential candidates for corporate sponsorship, which included such witty entries as 'Dulux roller' and 'Kellogg's corncrake', and the winner, the rather less wholesome 'Durex shag'.

Others were less amused at what they regarded as the thin end of the wedge. Would we eventually see birds being auctioned off to whichever multinational corporation could stump up the most money, allowing them to 'greenwash' their misdeeds by appearing to care about conservation? The influential World Wide Fund for Nature (WWF) was especially vocal in its opposition, but has since been proved wrong: many species names have been 'sold' in the past two decades, including a new species of barbet in Peru, which reportedly raised over $300,000 for conservation.

And the good news is that the Chocó vireo has also been discovered at several other locations, including across the border in north-west Ecuador – as predicted by Paul Salaman.[26]

But let us push the moral of this tale further: despite what purists may think, should we not perhaps be following this idea to its logical conclusion, and naming more and more of the world's endangered species after anyone – individual or company – prepared to donate enough hard cash to save them?*

Why shouldn't the global corporations who claim to want a sustainable future actually put their hands in their pockets and donate proper amounts of money to bird and wildlife conservation – and in exchange have a species named after them? Or should that be *re*-named? For example, the Hood (or Española) mockingbird, found only on a single island in the Galápagos, already boasts the scientific name *Mimus macdonaldi*. However, this is not after the ubiquitous burger-retailer, but to commemorate the confederate soldier and naturalist Colonel Marshall McDonald [sic] who, oddly, specialised not in birds, but fish. Maybe we should approach his

---

* This is already starting to happen: the World Land Trust has recently launched its 'Name an Orchid' campaign, supported by Sir David Attenborough, in which people are invited to give the name of themselves or a loved-one to newly-discovered orchid species from Ecuador: http://www.worldlandtrust.org/name-an-orchid.

multinational near-namesake and ask them to make a suitable offer.

As we noted in Chapter 5, some of the people after whom birds were named were not necessarily the most deserving: Lady Amherst may, for example, have been a remarkable woman, but her ornithological credentials were pretty much non-existent. Likewise, Thekla Brehm, whose only claim to fame is that, when she died in 1857 at the tender age of twenty-four, her grieving father gave her name to a newly discovered species of lark, which had been shot in Spain by her elder brothers.

And then of course there are the deserving, among whom I would count the woman after whom one of the world's most obscure and elusive birds was named: Winifred Moreau. In an era when the couple's extensive ornithological research was automatically attributed for the most part to Reg Moreau, it is rather wonderful that her name lives on in her eponymous warbler, a testament to her contribution to the world of ornithology – and also to the strength of Reg and Winnie Moreau's marriage.

Fifty years after I first came across this bird in the pages of *Birds of the World*, the search for Mrs Moreau's legacy led me to travel five thousand miles to the Uluguru Mountains in the heart of East Africa, and trek several thousand feet up a forest track, where I hoped to finally come upon the bird whose name provides the title of this book.

EPILOGUE

Winifred's Warbler

If the names are lost, the knowledge also disappears.
Johann Christian Fabricius, *Philosophia Entomologica* (1778)

Dawn breaks over the Uluguru Mountains in eastern Tanzania, as we rise and prepare for the day ahead. I am about to embark on the final leg of my quest to see a very special bird. Our local guides, Elia and James, are quietly confident; I only wish I could share their optimism.

The journey here has been a long and eventful one. A few days ago, I flew almost five thousand miles, with my companions Kevin and Graeme, from the UK to Dar-es-Salaam. There we met our leader Roy, who drove us in his battered Land Cruiser from the hot, fetid lowlands around the Tanzanian capital into the Eastern Arc Mountains, where we pitched camp by a fast-flowing stream.

Known as 'Africa's Galápagos', because millions of years of ecological isolation have led to a huge diversity of endemic plants and animals, this is the only place on the planet where the species we are searching for can be found. Now we are about to set off on a trek to one of the highest mountains in this remarkable range, a peak the locals call Kilangala. Here I hope to finally catch up with the bird in question: Mrs Moreau's warbler – now also known, rather less formally, as Winifred's warbler.

We make slow progress: not least because, as we are visiting this region for the first time, we keep coming across new and exciting birds, each with its own bizarre and delightful name. We see stripe-cheeked greenbul and white-chested alethe, African hill-babbler and yellow-bellied waxbill, white-tailed crested flycatcher and scarlet-chested sunbird – the last hovering momentarily by a flower, showing off its dazzling red breast as it sups the nectar.

As we trek higher up the hillside, the mist begins to clear and the temperature rises with the morning sun. A flock of swallows swoop around us, hawking for tiny insects in the sky. At first we ignore them, until Elia points out that these are not our familiar British swallows, as we had assumed, but the rare Angola swallow – another new bird for all of us. We pause to watch them, and take in their subtle differences in plumage and flight action.

But every time we delay, I feel increasingly anxious: will we be too late to find the bird we are searching for? And, as with any hill-climb, whenever I think we have got to the top, yet another rise in the land appears before us, until I despair of ever reaching our destination.

Eventually, after two long and exhausting hours, we arrive on the forested ridge just below the summit. Drenched in sweat, we take long gulps from our water bottles, whose contents are now unpleasantly lukewarm. But we can't afford to rest. With forest birds, the first few hours after sunrise are the key; later in the day they often fall silent, making them almost impossible to find amidst the dense foliage. As we enter the forest, it is indeed much quieter than the terraced farmland below, though we know it holds many birds found nowhere else on Earth: Loveridge's sunbird, Uluguru mountain greenbul and, of course, our target bird.

Fortunately, we have a secret weapon. Elia has brought sound equipment and a speaker, so that he can play the song of Mrs Moreau's warbler. Hopefully this will entice the bird to appear, and perhaps even sing back to what it will assume is a rival male intruding on its territory. So as we hike along the tree-lined ridge, every hundred metres or so we stop, play the call, and listen. Yet every time we do so . . . nothing.

Time and again we repeat this ritual: stop, play, listen . . . and move on. I am beginning to get nervous: what if we don't see the bird? Would it be worse if I hear it but don't manage to see it? And how will I feel if I do glimpse it, but get what birders call 'untickable views', frustratingly too brief to appreciate its key identification features? Even that would be better than nothing, I think grimly as we trudge towards the summit.

Then, just as I have almost given up hope, Elia pauses, and gestures urgently down below us and to the left. He thinks he has heard the warbler's call. We step off the path into the forest, and make our way gingerly through dense foliage, treading carefully on the uneven and treacherous ground. I look up momentarily as a bright blue butterfly floats past, and notice that we seem to be heading towards a small patch where two saplings have grown across one another, to form a distinctive, X-shaped cross.

And then I hear it for myself. The unmistakable notes of not just one, but two birds – a breeding pair, performing together in a synchronised duet. Elia plays the sound again, and the birds immediately respond. Then he excitedly grabs my arm: 'There . . . *there*!'

Fumbling with my binoculars, I lift them to my eyes and look towards where he is pointing. The sound is really loud now – a series of flute-like notes, so perfectly integrated I can't tell which are being sung by the male and which by the female. But still I see no movement.

Behind me, I can hear Graeme, Kevin and Roy, each exclaiming in turn as they manage to get a sighting of the bird. Cries of delight and relief as they congratulate one another make me even more frantic. My heavy breathing has made my lenses fog up, and I now face the very real prospect that everyone else will see the bird I have travelled so far to find – but that I shall miss out.

I take a deep breath and try to stop panicking. Then I hear Graeme's calm, reassuring, Scottish brogue: 'Look Stephen, *there* – X marks the spot!'

I look again, at exactly the point where the two branches cross. And sitting right out in the open, so obvious I can't believe I have taken so long to see it, is a small, slender bird. Brownish buff, with a long, thin bill, and an orange chest, throat, head and neck, it looks rather like a robin whose red breast has extended upwards to cover its whole face and crown. As if to acknowledge me, it utters one more burst of song, and then melts back into the forest.

It has been a long time coming, but Mrs Moreau's warbler is finally, as birders say, 'in the bag'.

I think back to what Reg Moreau must have thought when he first laid eyes on this bird. How did he feel when he realised that it was a species unknown to science? When did it occur to him that he could name it after his beloved wife Winnie? And how did she react when he told her of his intention to do so?

Sadly, I have not been able to find any account of this momentous discovery in his writings. Maybe it was just too personal to put down on paper. Then again, that allows me to let my imagination run free: to visualise the moment when they returned home to Amani, and he revealed to Winnie his plans to name the bird after her. Did they have a celebratory gin and tonic on the verandah, as the sun went down over the Usambaras? I like to think so. . .

My reverie is broken, as the male warbler hops into view once again. This time, to my delight, his mate joins him. Once again, they begin to duet: a wonderfully tuneful performance – short, but very, very sweet. Then, after a few moments, they disappear back into the dense, dark-green foliage. The show is finally over.

We turn, and begin the long hike down the mountain and back to camp. I need some space and time to reflect on my encounter with the birds so, as my companions head along the path, I lag a little way behind.

How do I feel? Relieved, certainly. Happy, and fulfilled, after almost fifty years of waiting, that my long quest is finally over. The final piece in the jigsaw of the Moreaus' story has fallen into place for me. And what a bird! It was far more exciting than I could have imagined: its perky stance, subtle but attractive plumage, and delightful song, all made the experience quite unforgettable.

But I also feel a deep sense of sadness. As we climbed up the mountain earlier this morning, and the mist parted to reveal the whole landscape, it soon became clear just how much of the forest has already been cut down for farming. From the lower slopes, almost to the summit, the land has been cleared and planted with crops, to feed a rapidly growing local population.

I can hardly blame them for wanting to produce food for their families. But every tree that is felled marks another setback for the endemic birds of this region; birds like Mrs Moreau's warbler, which are found here, and nowhere else in the world. As I walk away from the duetting couple, with the last notes finally fading away into the forest, it strikes me as highly likely that this species will go extinct during my lifetime. For, as the latest report from BirdLife International reveals, the global population may now be as low as 500 individual birds.[1]

Today, we face a huge and disturbing paradox. Even as we are discovering more and more new species – either by finding them for the very first time, or by 'splitting' them because of differences in their DNA – many of the world's birds are heading towards the edge of extinction. What chance does Mrs Moreau's warbler – and its recently split cousin the Rubeho warbler, found in an adjacent mountain range – have of surviving in the modern world, where billions of human beings demand so much land and space?

It dawns on me that this is where my passion for bird names has finally reached the end of its long journey. It began when, as a ten-year-old boy, I first came across the name Mrs Moreau's warbler in *Birds of the World*. It developed through my lifelong passion for birds, and my growing love of the English language, both of which come together in the names we have given to birds down through the ages. And it ends with the realisation that my fascination with the history and origin of bird names – whether of common and familiar, or rare and unusual species – is ultimately because these names hold within them the incredible variety of birds around the globe, and the rich stories of their interactions over time with us.

From the familiar robin, chaffinch and blackbird (whose names turned out to be far less straightforward than we might have imagined) to the Uluguru violet-backed sunbird, Udzungwa forest partridge and Mrs Moreau's warbler, bird names are far more than just words. Every single one of them tells a story – a story that runs parallel with our own human narrative, expressed through our history, language and culture.

The naming of birds is, of course, a purely human pursuit; as we have seen, it helps us make sense of a complex and eternally diverse avian world. The birds themselves are entirely oblivious to what we decide to call them. And yet we insist on doing so, and indeed we go further, in celebrating our own world by the names we choose to bestow. In his own small way, that's what Reg Moreau was doing when he decided to immortalise his wife – and their love and devotion towards one another – in the name of this obscure little bird.

So what happens if Mrs Moreau's warbler disappears from the face of the earth? The extinction of any species is a tragedy, not just for the creature in question, but for us too; in John Donne's words, like any man's death, it diminishes us. But when we lose a species its name is also diminished, for who can hear of the most famous extinct bird without thinking of the proverbial phrase 'as dead as a dodo'? What was once a living, breathing creature is now simply a symbol of extinction and loss; no longer part of the wondrous diversity and complexity of the natural world.

To me, this shift in meaning is almost as important as the loss of the living bird. For, as this story has revealed, the names of birds are central to our own identity – a crucial part of what makes us human.

As John Clare aptly lamented, 'O words are poor receipts for what time hath stole away'.[2]

The names we have given to birds down the ages reflect every aspect of our own lives: primitive superstitions, myths and legends, invasions and conquests, shifts in language, rigorous scientific observation, our love of sound, colour and pattern, and a sense of place. And, last, but certainly not least, some commemorate the extraordinary achievements of the men and women after whom they are named: including, of course, Reg and Winnie Moreau.

May their warbler continue to sing forever.

NOTES

INTRODUCTION

1 Michel Desfayes, *A Thesaurus of Bird Names*, Musée cantonal d'histoire naturelle (Paris, 1998).

2 John Wright, *The Naming of the Shrew* (London, 2014).

3 http://aishwaryashivapareek.com/post/104398138332/does-a-cat-know-he-is-a-cat-does-a-dog-know-he-is

4 Joanne Harris, *Runemarks* (London, 2007).

5 Matthew Woodring Stover, *Caine's Law* (London, 2012).

6 John Fowles, *The Tree*. This has recently been republished by Little Toller Books (Dorset, 2016), with a perceptive introduction by the author William Fiennes.

7 W. B. Lockwood, *The Oxford Book of British Bird Names* (London, 1984).

8 ibid.

9 BBC 4 (2009) and (London, 2011).

10 A. F. Harrold, 'Among The Ornithologists', in Of Birds & Bees (Reading, 2008).

PROLOGUE

1 David Moreau, *More Wrestling than Dancing* (London, 1990).

2 Nancy J. Jacobs, 'The Intimate Politics of Ornithology in Colonial Africa', *Journal of the Society for Comparative Study of Society and History*, 2006.

3 W. L. Sclater and Reginald Moreau, *Taxonomic and Field Notes on Some Birds of North-Eastern Tanganyikan Territory*, Ibis 2: 487–522 (1932).

CHAPTER 1

1 From *The Exeter Book, an Anthology of Anglo-Saxon Poetry*, Israel Gollancz (ed.) (London, 1893).

2 From translation by Kevin Crossley-Holland (Enitharmon Press, 2008).

3 From W. S. Mackie (ed.), *The Exeter Book, Part II: Poems IX-XXXII* (London, 1934).

4 James Fisher, *The Shell Bird Book* (London, 1966).

5 See David Crystal, 'English as a Classical Language, https://archive.org/stream/Omnibus42/09%20Crystal%20English%20as%20a%20Classical%20Language_djvu.txt

6 David Anthony, *The Horse, the Wheel and Language* (Princeton, 2007)

7 A. F. Harrold, *Of Birds & Bees* (Reading, 2008).

CHAPTER 2

1 Allan Massie, *Daily Telegraph*, 12 October 2012. http://www.telegraph.co.uk/history/9606163/In-everything-we-say-there-is-an-echo-of-1066.html

2 Lockwood, *op. cit.*

3 Thomas Fuller, *The Historie of the Worthies of England* (London, 1662).

4 Charles Hindley (ed.), *The Works of John Taylor: The Water-Poet* (London, 1872).

5 Charles Johnson (ed. and trans.), *Dialogus de Scaccario* (1177) (London, 1950).

6 Simon Horobin, *How English became English* (Oxford, 2016).

7 John Brereton, *Briefe and True Relation of the Discoverie of the North Part of Virginia in 1602* (1602), Wisconsin Historical Society Digital Library and Archives.

8 Jeremy Mynott, *Birdscapes* (Princeton, 2009).

CHAPTER 3

1 The rather grandly titled *Inventory of all garments, jewels, silks, etc., in the queen's Garderobe of robes in the charge of Sir Thomas Gorges as surveyed by Sir Thomas, Lord Buckhurste, Lord Treasurer and others appointed by a commission under the great seal 4 July.*

2 Lockwood, *op. cit.*

3 Roy Porter, *The Enlightenment* (Basingstoke, 1990).

4 Keith Thomas, *Man and the Natural World: Changing Attitudes in England 1500–1800* (London, 1983).

5 For a more detailed analysis of this, see my earlier book *A Bird in the Bush: A Social History of Birdwatching* (London, 2004).

6 In A. H. Evans (ed.), *Turner on Birds* (Cambridge, 1903).

7 Thomas Moffett, *Health's improvement or, Rules comprizing and discovering the nature, method and manner of preparing all sorts of foods used in this nation* (London, c. 1595).

8 James A. Jobling, *Helm Dictionary of Scientific Bird Names* (London, 2010).

9 William Dampier, *A voyage to New Holland, etc., in the year 1699* (London, 1703).

10 Ray Reedman, *Lapwings, Loons and Lousy Jacks* (Exeter, 2016).

11 Anna Pavord, *The Naming of Names* (London, 2005).

12 John Wright, op. cit..

13 Tim Birkhead, *The Wisdom of Birds* (London, 2008).

14 Anna Pavord, op. cit.

15 John Wright, op. cit.

16 W. H. Mullens, 'Some Early British Ornithologists and Their Works', in *British Birds* (1908–9).

17 Gilbert White, *The Natural History and Antiquities of Selborne* (London, 1789).

18 In James Fisher, op. cit. See also my book *A Bird in the Bush* (London, 2004).

19 T. C. Eyton, *A History of the Rarer British Birds* (London, 1836).

20 ibid.

CHAPTER 4

1 John Latham, *A General History of Birds* (Winchester, 1821–8). This built on his earlier work, *A General Synopsis of Birds* (London 1781–1801), and its later summary, *Index Ornithologicus* (London, 1790–1801).

2 Charles Swainson, *The Folk-Lore and Provincial Names of British Birds* (London, 1885).

3 Charles Swainson quoted in W. H. Mullens and H. Kirke Swann, *A Bibliography of British Ornithology from the earliest times to the end of 1912* (London, 1917).

4 Quoted in *A Bibliography of British Ornithology*.

5 Robert Hughes, *The Fatal Shore* (London, 1996).

6 ibid.

7 ibid.

8 Ian Fraser and Jeannie Gray, *Australian Bird Names: A Complete Guide* (Collingwood, 2013).

9 See Robin Jackson, *A Guide to Scots Bird Names* (revised edition, Aboyne 2013), and also Francesca Greenoak, *British Birds: their Folklore, Names and Literature* (London, 1997).

10 Stephen Moss, 'The Bird Poetry of John Clare' (unpublished dissertation, Cambridge, 1981).

11 Quoted in the Introduction to Robinson's 1982 anthology *John Clare's Birds*, co-authored with the ornithologist Richard Fitter (Oxford, 1982).

12 James Fisher, op. cit.

CHAPTER 5

1 Barbara and Richard Mearns, *Biographies for Birdwatchers: The Lives of Those Commemorated in Western Palearctic Bird Names* (London, 1988).

2 For more about these men and women, see Bo Beolens and Michael Watkins, *The Eponym Dictionary of Birds* (London, 2014).

3 Barbara and Richard Mearns, *Audubon to Xantus: The Lives of Those Com-

memorated in North American Bird Names (London, 1992).

4 Thomas Pennant, *Arctic Zoology* (London, 1784).

5 In Christopher Lever, *The Naturalized Animals of Britain and Ireland* (London, 2009).

6 In James Fisher and Ronald Lockley, *Seabirds* (London, 1954).

7 In *British Birds* magazine, vol. LXXIX (1975).

8 William Parry, *Journal of a second voyage for the discovery of a North-West Passage* (London, 1824); quoted from Michael Densley, *In Search of Ross's Gull* (Leeds, 1999).

9 Elliot Coues, quoted in *A Bibliography of British Ornithology*, op. cit.

10 ibid.

11 Apsley Cherry-Garrard, *The Worst Journey in the World* (London, 1922).

12 In *The Handbook of British Birds*, edited by Witherby et al (London, 1938–41).

13 Fridtjof Nansen, *Farthest North* (London, 1897).

14 For more information on this mysterious seabird, I highly recommend Michael Densley, *In Search of Ross's Gull* (Leeds, 1999).

15 From Robert Ralph, *William MacGillivray* (London, 1993).

16 *A Bibliography of British Ornithology*, op. cit.

17 Alfred Newton, quoted in *William MacGillivray*, op. cit.

CHAPTER 6

1 Edmund Selous, *Bird Watching* (London, 1901).

2 W. H. Hudson, *British Birds* (London, 1895).

3 Phyllis Barclay-Smith, *Garden Birds* (London & New York, 1945). Incidentally, this is the first mention I can find of the phrase 'garden birds' – which strikes me as surprisingly late in the day

4 E. M. Nicholson, *Birds and Men* (London, 1951).

5 *British Birds*, vol. I (1907).

6 ibid.

7 William Yarrell, *Supplement to the History of British Birds* (London, 1845).

8 Mark Cocker and Richard Mabey, *Birds Britannica* (London, 2005).

9 For more information on the corncrake's decline, and the status of other birds during the late nineteenth century, see Simon Holloway, *The Historical Atlas of Breeding Birds of Britain and Ireland 1875–1900* (London, 1996).

10 K. H. Voous, *Atlas of European Birds* (London, 1960).

11 BirdLife International estimate: http://datazone.birdlife.org/species/factsheet/22694443.

12 Quoted on the BBC News website, 25 December 2015, http://www.bbc.co.uk/news/magazine-34848546.

CHAPTER 7

1 Lars Svensson, Killian Mullarney and Dan Zetterstrom, *Collins Bird Guide* (2nd edition, London, 2009).

2 Ian Sinclair, Phil Hockey and Warwick Tarboton, *SASOL Birds of Southern Africa* (3rd edition, Cape Town, 2002).

3 Frank Gill and Minturn Wright, *Birds of the World: Recommended English Names* (London, 2006).

4 For more examples, see Simon Horobin, *How English Became English* (Oxford, 2016).

5 John A. G. Barnes, *The Titmice of the British Isles* (London, 1975).

6 Christopher Perrins, *British Tits* (London, 1979).

7 Simon Dowell, *British Birds* vol. 85 (1992) p. 620.

8 I. M. Lewis, *British Birds* vol. 85 (1992) p. 620.

9 Dr Martin Williams, Simon Stirrup, Dave Hatton and Dan Duff. *Not BB* is still available online at: http://www.drmartinwilliams.com/not-bb/not-bb-iii.html.

10 Author in conversation with Pamela Rasmussen.

11 http://robins-chaos.blogspot.co.uk/2010/01/politically-incorrect-duck-or-long.html (2010).

12 In *The Oxford Book of British Bird Names*, op. cit.

13 Charles G. Sibley and Burt L. Monroe, *Distribution and Taxonomy of Birds*

of the World (New Haven, 1990), and Charles G. Sibley and Jon E. Ahlquist, *Phylogeny and Classification of Birds: A Study in Molecular Evolution* (New Haven, 1990).

14 For a very helpful discussion, see G. W. H. Davidson, 'Scientific Controversy over Avian Taxonomic Changes, based on DNA Hybridisation', *The Raffles Bulletin of Zoology* 46 (2), 1998.

15 See, for example, his article 'On the Phylogeny and Classification of Living Birds', reproduced here: http://digilander.libero.it/avifauna/classificazione/sequence5.htm. Burt Monroe died in 1994, aged sixty-three; Jon Ahlquist (born 1944) is still alive.

16 'A comprehensive phylogeny of birds (Aves) using targeted next-generation DNA sequencing', by Prum et al. http://www.nature.com/nature/journal/v526/n7574/full/nature15697.html.

17 Professor Daniel Osorio, University of Sussex, *in litt.*

18 For a really clear pictorial and diagrammatic guide to the relationships between birds on a species and family level, check out OneZoom http://www.onezoom.org/. More detailed findings can be seen at http://birdtree.org/ (A Global Phylogeny of Birds). Alternatively, see the paper by Erich D. Jarvis *et al*: 'Whole-genome analyses resolve early branches in the tree of life of modern bird', in *Science* 346, 1320 (2014).

19 See http://www.ornitaxa.com/SM/SMOrg/sibley3.html.

20 See http://journals.plos.org/plosone/article?id=10.1371/journal.pone.0166307.

21 *Handbook of the Birds of the World: Special Volume – New Species* (Barcelona, 2013).

22 https://www.bou.org.uk/wp-content/uploads/2016/12/British-List-12-Dec-2016.pdf.

23 Thomas Bewick, *A History of British Birds* (Newcastle, 1797 and 1804).

24 See *Threatened Birds of the World* by BirdLife International (Barcelona and Cambridge, 2000).

25 For an entertaining account of its discovery and naming, see David Turner, *Was Beethoven a Birdwatcher?* (Chichester, 2011).

26 D. M. Brinkhuizen and A. Solano-Ugalde, 'Range extension of Chocó Vireo *Vireo masteri* in Ecuador, with a description of the species' song', *Cotinga* 34: 73–77 (2012).

EPILOGUE

1 http://www.birdlife.org/globally-threatened-bird-forums/2016/11/mrs-moreaus-warbler-bathmocercus-winifredae-request-for-information/
2 From 'Remembrances'.

ACKNOWLEDGEMENTS

This book arose from a lifelong fascination with birds and language, which began when my mother took me as an infant to feed the ducks near my home, and developed through her dedicated encouragement of my love of reading, books and language.

Many years later, these came together when I met Laura Hassan of Faber, who immediately saw the potential of the complex and fascinating story of how birds got their names. Laura has been fantastically supportive throughout the writing of the book, as has editor Katherine Ailes, whose perceptive comments and ability to see how the narrative should develop have been incredibly helpful. My dear friend Graham Coster copy-edited the book, making many helpful last-minute suggestions, while my agent Broo Doherty has, as ever, provided wise advice and great support. I would also like to thank the team at Faber, Fred Baty in editorial, Eleanor Crow in design, Kate Burton in publicity and John Grindrod in marketing.

Several experts have kindly taken time to read through excerpts and make corrections and suggestions. They are the linguists David Crystal and Simon Horobin, and ornithologists Jonathan Meyrav, Richard Prum, Paul Salaman, Arnoud van den Berg and Ian Wallace, along with the team behind the satirical magazine *Not BB*. Any errors that remain are of course my own.

The Appendices – lists of bird names under various categories, included for my more obsessive readers (you know who you are!) – were a perennial topic of conversation on boat trips along Peru's Manu River in May 2017. I would like to thank my companions Neil Glenn, Jo Wimpenny, Kyle Carlsen and Brian Egan for their very helpful suggestions (and some really silly ones). Nigel Redman also used his vast knowledge of the world's birds to add a number of names to this section. The expedition to Tanzania, featured in the Prologue and Epilogue, was organised by Zoe and Roy Hinde of Wild Things Safaris, and led by Roy and our excellent guide Ezra. I should also like to thank Colin Watkins and Nigel Simpson, both of whom provided very helpful and detailed advice to help us plan our trip; thanks also to Nigel for his generous gift of Martin Woodcock's evocative portrait of Mrs Moreau's Warbler.

I have also been inspired by a number of other people who have found the origin of bird names compelling. The late W. B. Lockwood, philologist and author of the slim but indispensable volume *The Oxford Book of Bird Names*, has been a constant inspiration. Barbara and Richard Mearns, authors of two fine books on the origin of eponymous names, *Biographies for Birdwatchers* and *Audubon to Xantus*, have provided much useful biographical information on the people in Chapters 4 & 5. I also referred to the extraordinary two-volume work by Michel Desfayes, *A Thesaurus of Bird Names*.

Three of my greatest friends kindly read the whole book from cover to cover, providing really helpful comments throughout. They are my childhood birding companion Daniel Osorio, Graeme Mitchell, with whom I now regularly go birding in

Somerset, and Kevin Cox. Kevin and his wife Donna also kindly offered me the use of the cottage in the grounds of their Devon home as a writing retreat.

Graeme and Kevin joined me on our fabulous trip in search of the elusive Mrs Moreau's warbler, the eponymous title of this book. I could not have wished for better companions on this, the journey of a lifetime.

STEPHEN MOSS

APPENDIX

Positive and Negative Bird Names

POSITIVE AND UPBEAT

beautiful nuthatch, jay, firetail, rosefinch etc.

elegant parrot, tern, honeyeater, tit, sunbird, trogon, pitta etc.

exclamatory paradise whydah

festive coquette

foxy cisticola

gorgeous bushshrike

joyful greenbul

handsome flycatcher, francolin

immaculate antbird

laughing dove, gull, kookaburra etc.

laughingthrushes

lovely cotinga, fairywren, sunbird

magnificent frigatebird, sunbird, riflebird, bird-of-paradise etc.

many-coloured rush-tyrant

marvellous spatuletail

paradise jacamar, kingfisher, drongo etc.

rainbow pitta

resplendent quetzal

royal sunangel, parrotfinch, penguin, albatross, flycatcher

sacred ibis, kingfisher

sociable lapwing

splendid fairywren, astrapia, starling, sunbird
superb fruit dove, lyrebird, pitta, parrot, starling, sunbird, bird-of-paradise etc.

NEGATIVE OR UNDERWHELMING

bentbills
drab water-tyrant
dull-blue flycatcher
dull-coloured grassquit
fearful owl
go-away-birds
inaccessible rail
intermediate egret
invisible rail
lachrymose mountain tanager
lazy cisticola
least tern, bittern etc.
medium ground finch, tree finch
middle-spotted woodpecker
modest tiger parrot
mourning dove, wheatear, warbler etc.
one-colored becard
plain antvireo, pigeon, flowerpecker etc.
sad flycatcher
screamers
shy albatross, heathwren
simple greenbul
snoring rail
sombre tit
solitary sandpiper, snipe, eagle, cacique etc.
spotless starling, crake
stout cisticola

tiny greenbul, tyrant-manakin, hawk, cisticola, sunbird etc.

unadorned flycatcher

unicolored antwren, tapaculo, jay, thrush, blackbird

uniform swiftlet, crake, finch

weebill

widowbirds

Long and short names

LONG (MORE THAN TWENTY-FIVE LETTERS — HYPHENS AND SPACES NOT COUNTED)

26 LETTERS: chestnut-backed jewel-babbler, cinnamon-breasted tody-tyrant, Eastern wattled cuckooshrike, grey-headed canary-flycatcher, King of Saxony bird-of-paradise, Northern rough-winged swallow, plumbeous-crowned tyrannulet, purple-tailed imperial pigeon, Rüppell's long-tailed starling, Southern rough-winged swallow, Western wattled cuckooshrike

27 LETTERS: American three-toed woodpecker, amethyst-throated moun-taingem, black-and-white tody-flycatcher, black-casqued wattled hornbill, chestnut-fronted helmet-shrike, Eurasian three-toed woodpecker, Northern beardless tyrannulet, Northern brown-throated weaver, Southern beardless tyrannulet, Southern brown-throated weaver

28 LETTERS: black-and-white casqued hornbill, chestnut-breasted chlorophonia, chestnut-crowned sparrow-weaver, cinnamon-bellied flowerpiercer, cinna-mon-rumped foliage-gleaner, Donaldson Smith's sparrow-weaver, ochra-ceous-breasted flycatcher, red-bellied paradise flycatcher, slaty-backed night-ingale-thrush, slender-billed scimitar babbler, yellow-casqued wattled hornbill

29 LETTERS: black-and-white shrike-flycatcher, black-and-yellow silky-flycatcher, lesser necklaced laughingthrush, white-bellied crested flycatcher, yellow-throated woodland warbler

30 LETTERS: buff-breasted paradise kingfisher, greater necklaced laugh-

ingthrush, Middendorff's grasshopper warbler, rufous-vented paradise
flycatcher, Ruwenzori double-collared sunbird
31 LETTERS: Prigogine's double-collared sunbird

SHORT (FEWER THAN 6 LETTERS)

5 LETTERS: besra, cutia, galah, ifrit, kamao, kikau, kioea, maleo, malia, twite, veery
4 LETTERS: dodo, huia, liwi, kagu, kaka, nene, omao, ruff, rook, smew, sora, weka
3 LETTERS: emu, kea, moa, tui
2 LETTERS: ou

NB: only standalone names acceptable: coot, shag, wren etc. are always quali-
fied (e.g. Eurasian wren)

Parts of the Body in Bird Names

backed, banded, beaked, bearded, bellied, belted, billed, breasted, bridled, browed,
capped, cheeked, chested, chinned, crested, collared, crowned, eared, eyed, faced,
flanked, footed, fronted, headed, helmeted, hooded, horned, legged, lored, man-
dibled, mantled, masked, moustached, naped, necked, necklaced, plumed, ruffed,
rumped, scarfed, shouldered, sided, spectacled, superciliaried, tailed, thighed,
throated, tipped, toed, toothed, tufted, vented, webbed, whiskered, winged

Birds Named after States in the US

Arizona woodpecker
California condor, gnatcatcher, gull, quail, scrub jay, thrasher, towhee
Carolina chickadee, wren, parakeet
Connecticut warbler
Florida scrub jay

Hawaiian akepa, amakihi, coot, creeper, crow, duck, elepaio, hawk, petrel
Kentucky warbler
Louisiana waterthrush
Mississippi kite
Tennessee warbler
Virginia rail

Birds Named after Man-Made Objects

barn swallow, owl etc.
boat-billed heron
booted racket-tail
buttonquails
canvasback
fantails
gartered trogon
Gould's jewelfront
helmeted woodpecker, hornbill, myna etc.
helmet-shrikes
house martin, finch, wren etc.
ladder-tailed nightjar
lancebills
lyre-tailed nightjar
mitred parakeet
needletails
ovenbird
pennant-winged nightjar
pin-tailed snipe, pintail
razorbill, razor-billed curassow
riflebirds
saddlebacks

saddle-billed stork
saw-wings
scimitarbills
scissor-tailed flycatcher, nightjar
scythebills
sheathbills
shoebill
shovel-billed kookaburra
sickle-winged guan
spadebills
spoonbills
spoon-billed sandpiper
standardwing
sword-billed hummingbird
tambourine dove
trainbearers
trumpeter swan, finch, hornbill etc.
umbrellabirds
whipbirds
wire-tailed swallow
yellow-scarfed tanager
yellowhammer

Birds Named after Elements, Compounds and Minerals

bronzed drongo
bronze mannikin
bronze-tailed peacock-pheasant
bronzewings
cobalt-winged parakeet
copper sunbird, seedeater, pheasant etc.

copper-rumped hummingbird

goldfinch

goldeneye

golden eagle, pheasant, weaver, sparrow, bush robin etc.

lead-coloured flycatcher

leaden antwren, honeyeater, flycatcher

metallic starling

metaltails

silver oriole, pheasant, teal

silver-beaked tanager

silverbills

silverbird

silvereye

silvery grebe, pigeon, kingfisher

steel-blue whydah, flycatcher

steely-vented hummingbird

Birds Named after Gems and Precious Stones

amethyst sunbird, starling, brown dove, woodstar

beryl-spangled tanager

berylline hummingbird

Brazilian ruby

crimson topaz

diamond firetail, dove

emeralds

emerald cuckoo, dove, starling, tanager

emerald-spotted wood dove

fiery topaz

garnet pitta, robin

garnet-throated hummingbird
opal-crowned tanager, manakin
pearl kite
pearl-breasted swallow, conebill
pearly-eyed thrasher
ruby-cheeked sunbird
ruby-crowned kinglet, tanager
ruby-throated hummingbird, myzomela, bulbul
ruby-topaz hummingbird
sapphire-throated hummingbird
sapphire quail-dove, flycatcher
sapphires
Siberian rubythroat

Politically Incorrect Names

dwarf bittern, tinamou, sparrowhawk, koel etc.
hottentot teal
kaffir rail
midget flowerpecker
negrito
negrofinch
oldsquaw
pygmy antwren, falcon, eagle etc.

Birds Named after Professions, Callings and Religious Orders

adjutants
apostlebird

bearded mountaineer
bishops
blacksmith plover
capuchinbird
cardinals
coppersmith barbet
friarbirds
lanceolated monklet
millerbird
miners
monk parakeet
nunbirds, nunlets
prothonotary warbler
purple grenadier
secretarybird
tailorbirds
tinkerbirds
tyrants
weavers

Bird Names derived from Mythology, Ancient Civilisations etc.

Aztec rail, thrush
Calliope hummingbird
Cinderella waxbill
eastern, Say's and black Phoebe
Griffon vulture
Inca tern, flycatcher, dove, jay, wren
collared Inca
Lucifer hummingbird

Mayan antthrush
Mesopotamian crow
Montezuma quail, oropendola
Persian shearwater
Pharaoh eagle owl
Satanic nightjar
Stygian owl

Birds' Names Including Other Animals' Names
(not including other birds)

antbirds, antpeckers, antpittas, antpipits, antshrikes, ant-tanagers, antthrushes,
    antvireos, antwrens
bat hawk, falcon
bee-eaters
buffalo weavers
bullfinches
catbirds
cattle egret
cicadabirds
cowbirds
fish crow, fish eagles, fish owls
flycatchers
frogmouths
fox sparrow, kestrel
lizard cuckoos
mousebirds
oxpeckers
rhinoceros auklet
snail kite

snake eagles

spiderhunters

squirrel cuckoo

tiger herons

Birds Named after Royalty and Nobility (in order of rank)

emperor penguin

imperial eagle, shag, snipe, pigeon, woodpecker, Amazon

monarchs

king vulture, eider, quail

kingbirds

kingfishers

Queen Carola's parotia

Prince Ruspoli's turaco

princess parrot

Princess Stephanie's astrapia

duchess lorikeet

Lord Derby's parakeet

Lord Howe woodhen, parakeet, gerygone

Lady Amherst's pheasant

Thirty-three Amazing Names

bananaquit

bearded mountaineer

bokikokiko

bokmakierie

brownish twistwing
chuck-will's-widow
crinkle-collared manucode
fasciated tiger-heron
firewood-gatherer
forty-spotted pardalote
giant cowbird
glowing puffleg
hardhead
horned screamer
kinglet calyptura
lachrymose mountain tanager
leaf-love
Luzon bleeding-heart
marvellous spatuletail
oleaginous hemispingus
pink-legged graveteiro
Rock-loving cisticola
scaly-throated leaftosser
screaming piha
sharp-tailed streamcreeper
shining sunbeam
strange-tailed tyrant
teardrop white-eye
Upper Magdalena tapaculo
vermiculated screech owl
whip-poor-will
zigzag heron
zitting cisticola

INDEX